W9-BWG-680

RACHMANINOFF

RACHMANINOFF

by Victor I. Seroff

Biography Index Reprint Series

 BOOKS FOR LIBRARIES PRESS
FREEPORT, NEW YORK

INTERNATIONAL STANDARD BOOK NUMBER:

0-8369-8034-4

LIBRARY OF CONGRESS CATALOG CARD NUMBER:

70-126328

PRINTED IN THE UNITED STATES OF AMERICA

To my dear Eva

TABLE OF CONTENTS

FOREWORD BY
VIRGIL THOMSON

WHETHER *success in the world was a deep desire of Sergei Rachmaninoff I do not know, but success was his in a way that musicians seldom experience it. It came to him in his own lifetime, moreover, and through the practice of three separate musical branches. As a composer, as a conductor, and as a touring virtuoso of the pianoforte he received world-wide acclaim. His domestic life, too, seems to have been remarkably satisfactory. A more optimistic temperament than his would probably have glowed with happiness.*

Actually, his letters and recorded conversations are gloomy. Like Tchaikovsky, whom he adored, and who usually wept a little on almost any day, he seemed to find his best working condition a dispirited state. Indeed, even more than in the case of Tchaikovsky, his depressive mentality has come to represent to the Western world a musical expression both specifically Russian and specifically attractive. Whether this opulence of discontent is found equally pleasing in the Soviet Union I do not know; but Rachmaninoff, in spite of his conservative political opinions, has been adopted since his death as a Russian classic master in Russia. This success is another that would have pleased him profoundly, I am sure, though he would no doubt have acknowledged it with a mask of woe.

There is probably some resemblance between contemporary Russia and the United States underlying Rachmaninoff's great glory in both countries. The official mood of cheerfulness is in both cases a thin topsoil through which rich wells of blackness gush forth constantly, relieving the emotional poverty of sustained optimism and providing for accepted states of mind both a holiday and a corrective. Rachmaninoff's music is no toner-up of depressed nations. It is a pillow, not a sword. It is most heartily enjoyed in those countries where the national energies are strong enough to need a sedative.

The professional career of Sergei Rachmaninoff was that of a major talent. His natural gifts of ear and hand were impeccable; his training was nowhere short of completeness; recognition in professional life came early. The only kind of success he never achieved was that of intellectual distinction. He would have liked being a popular musician, a conservative musician, and an advanced one all at the same time. But as a young modernist he suffered defeat at the hands of his contemporary Alexander Scriabin, and there is reason to believe that later he entertained some bitterness about the impregnable position occupied in the intellectual world of music by his junior compatriot Igor Stravinsky.

There is no question, however, about Rachmaninoff's mastery. He composed, as he played the piano, in complete fullness and control. The nature of his expression—his passionless melancholy, his almost too easy flow of melody, his conventional but highly personal harmony, the loose but thoroughly coherent structure of his musical discourse—is often distasteful to musicians. They tend to find it a retreat from battle, an avoidance of the contemporary problem. But it is not possible, I think, to withhold admiration for the sincerity of the sentiments expressed or for the solid honesty of the workmanship. Rachmaninoff was a musician and an artist, and his expression through the divers musical techniques of which he was master seems to have been complete.

Following his life through Mr. Seroff's revealing narrative, one is impressed with how easily most of this came about. There were few major crises—only three, as I read the story. In the earliest of these he fought for two years and won. That victory marked his return, aided by a good nerve doctor, from intense neurotic despair. In the other two emergencies he refused to take a stand. One of these was provoked by the revolutionary troubles of 1905 and '06, which came when he was having a brilliant success as conductor in a state-supported opera house. A radical position would not have jeopardized his career; and neither, I think, would a reactionary one. Rachmaninoff merely made himself distasteful to both sides by a lukewarm attitude, lost his job, left the country. By moving to Germany at this time he laid the foundations for his later international career, but he also alienated himself from the Russian scene that meant so much to him in terms of sentiment.

A few years later, working again in Russia as a conductor, he found himself rather unexpectedly involved in a combat between the rising conductor Serge Koussevitzky and the composer Scriabin. Again Rachmaninoff tried to avoid the issue, which this time was that of modernism as a cause. When the smoke cleared away our hero had lost to Koussevitzky the position of chief introducer of the young Russian composers and to Scriabin that of Russia's most advanced composer. So again he left the land.

Otherwise his life was calm. He had few quarrels with press or managements. He made money. His fame grew. After his definitive expatriation in 1917 he became a genuinely popular figure in the United States both as pianist and as composer. He retained that popularity till his death in 1943 at the age of seventy. His music seems not to have lost favor, moreover, since that time. It is part of our century's history, a creation, a contribution, a personal monument.

Its author was a family man, a warm friend to half a dozen compatriots, a public figure, but one whose preoccupation was entirely with "the poetry of intimate moods." The life of this successful but retiring figure has not previously been told in America. Mr. Seroff, who has a gift for bringing Russia's musical ways to life, has told it so vividly, so convincingly, that I, for one, who have long indulged in myself a hostile indifference to Rachmaninoff, have found him through these pages a touching figure. Not a pitiful one, mind you, merely a being of strength and weakness, timidity and courage, surrender and persistence, in other words, an artist and a man. I could not be more grateful.

NEW YORK, 1949

Illustration
Section

Madame Boutakova, the composer's maternal grandmother, to whom he was devoted as a child, for she thoroughly spoiled him. She often took him to church with her, and the tolling of cathedral bells was one of the strongest musical influences of his early life. (See pages 10-11)

Vasily Rachmaninoff, the composer's father, who had a reputation as a great man for both ladies and babies. He used to feed, bathe, and spoil little Sergei when he was at home. He deserted the family before the children grew up, though not before running through most of the family fortune. (See pages 5, 7)

Lubov Rachmaninoff, the composer's mother, who was much sterner than his father, who punished Sergei frequently, but who planned diligently to make a musician of her talented child. Rachmaninoff seldom spoke or wrote about either of his parents. (See pages 5, 35)

Nicolai Sverev, the piano teacher with whom Rachmaninoff lived from the ages of twelve to sixteen. Sverev exerted a great influence on young Rachmaninoff, and there is a striking facial resemblance between them. Eventually their friendship broke up stormily. (See pages 12-36)

Serge Koussevitzky from a photograph
taken while he was still a double-bassist
at the Bolshoi Theater, in 1903. Two
years after this photograph was taken he
left the theater and, first, became a
double-bass virtuoso giving recitals on his
instrument and later on led concerts in
Moscow, where Rachmaninoff, at the
time, was the leading conductor. (See
page 82)

Feodor Chaliapin, the basso, and Rachmaninoff from a photograph taken in
1900. At this time, Chaliapin still
dressed like a young dandy but was already acknowledged one of the greatest
singers Russia ever produced. He was a
member of the Mamontov opera company, where Rachmaninoff was beginning to gain a reputation as conductor.
(See page 68)

Mr. and Mrs. Rachmaninoff, from a photograph taken during their stay at Dresden in 1907, at which time they had been married five years. Finding the German society of the city not much to their taste, the Rachmaninoffs stayed pretty much to themselves, and the composer concentrated here on operas and other large works. (See pages 109-119)

Alexander Scriabin from a photograph taken about 1912 at the time that Serge Koussevitzky was promoting him as one of Russia's greatest composers. This musical partnership created considerable turmoil in Moscow and, indirectly, affected the career of Rachmaninoff as conductor and composer. (See pages 160-178)

Studio portrait of Rachmaninoff taken in New York in 1909 on his first visit to the United States. It was a visit taken with great trepidation, though eventually the United States became Rachmaninoff's permanent home and he became an American citizen. (See pages 126-128)

Portrait of Marietta Shaginian painted by Tatiana Hyppius in 1911. The following year this brilliant young bluestocking wrote Rachmaninoff her first fan letter and thus began a long and odd relationship between them. (See pages 129-135)

Mr. and Mrs. Sergei Rachmaninoff before their home. The family resemblance is quite clear in this photograph of the two cousins who knew each other from childhood and who were very seldom parted from the day of their marriage in 1902 till the death of Rachmaninoff. (See page 188)

Sergei Rachmaninoff and his daughter Tatiana in the days when the family spent a part of each year in Europe though their home was in the United States. Tatiana married Boris Conus and became the mother of Sasha. (See page 192)

During the last years of his life, Rachmaninoff's greatest interest and happiness lay in his grandchildren. Here he is shown with Sophinka (Sophia Volkonsky) and Sasha (Alexander Conus). (See pages 208-210)

An informal portrait of Rachmaninoff painted at Huntington, Long Island, in 1940 by Boris Chaliapin, one of the sons of Feodor, the great basso. The Chaliapins were lifelong friends of Rachmaninoff's, and the pianist used to play Russian dances for the younger generation to dance to. "That is not the way it should go at all," Boris used to insist.... When Rachmaninoff lay dying in California, Feodor, brother of Boris, was one of the few intimates admitted to the sickroom. (See pages 225, 231)

Rachmaninoff in evening regalia, during his last years in the United States, ready for a concert. He customarily carried an electric heating pad for his hands, which he further protected with heavy gloves. (See pages 225-232)

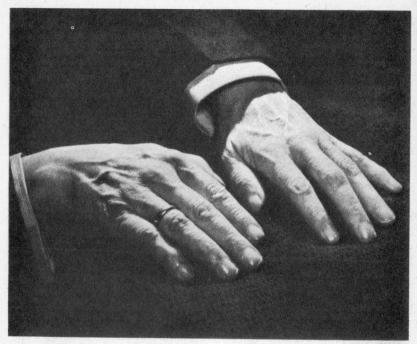

(Left) Rachmaninoff's hands.

(Below) A series of photographs taken by Eric Schaal during a rehearsal at Carnegie Hall, for Rachmaninoff's last appearance with orchestra. He was preparing his own Paganini Variations (see page 210) to be played with the New York Philharmonic-Symphony under Dimitri Mitropoulos. The pianist's anxiety to play with the orchestra rather than have it follow him is evident in this series.

Rachmaninoff always hated having his picture taken and repeatedly turned down the requests of Eric Schaal, photographer for *Life* Magazine, for a session before the camera. In December, 1942, the great pianist finally consented, and this was the impressively tragic likeness Schaal found on his film. Four months later—and four days before his seventieth birthday—Rachmaninoff died.

Rachmaninoff

.I.

Childhood

Y OUNG MAN, I see a brilliant future written on your face."
These were the first words that the Russian writer Anton
Chekhov spoke to Sergei Rachmaninoff. It happened after a
recital in Yalta given by Feodor Chaliapin, whom Rachmaninoff, then in his twenties, was accompanying.

"This was the greatest compliment I have ever been paid,"
Rachmaninoff said to me in New York almost half a century
later, in February, 1943, a few hours before he started on his
last tour of the United States. As he said this he turned to me
with a smile that brought out all his warm, human quality.

What Chekhov foresaw came to pass, but he must also have
seen in that face the stern repression that made Rachmaninoff
a lonely man all his life. For even as a young man he had
developed that integrity of spirit and that attitude of a man
apart which discouraged familiarity. Only those who knew
Rachmaninoff intimately ever saw him smile or heard him
laugh. For the others, and for his public, his face remained
a somber mask. It was not a typically Russian face. Indeed,
the high cheekbones, the shape of his gray eyes, which looked

1

at one coldly rather than severely, and the contour of his head, accentuated by the short-cropped hair—these formed the basis for the not uncommon assumption of Rachmaninoff's Mongolian origin. Actually, however, the Mongolian element in his heritage was rather remote, as may be seen from a glance at his ancestry.

According to the book *Historical Information About the Family of Rachmaninoff*,[1] the family traced its ancestry back to the Hospodars Dragosh, founders of Moldavia, a country under Mongolian domination for a century during the Middle Ages. In 1483, one of the Hospodars, Stefan IV, "the Great," married his daughter Helen to the eldest son of Ivan III, Grand Duke of Moscow. Soon afterward Helen's younger brother followed her to Moscow, and it was with his son, Vasily, nicknamed Rachmanin, that the family of Rachmaninoffs started.

This nickname can be attributed to any of several origins, since the word *rachmany*, from the same root, has varying meanings in different districts of Russia; but in the Moscow and Tver districts it means "hospitable," "generous," or "spendthrift." Of all Sergei Rachmaninoff's ancestors, it was his father, Vasily, who most thoroughly lived up to all three of these epithets, thus affecting radically the fate of his whole family.

Their wealth they inherited from the composer's great-great-grandfather, Gerasim Yevlevich Rachmaninoff, who took part in the enthroning of Empress Elizabeth, Peter the Great's daughter, and who in 1751 received an estate in the Tambov district as his reward "for faith and ardor." When he retired he bought the neighboring estate, Znamenskoe, which remained in the possession of Rachmaninoff's family.

[1] Compiled by Feodor Rachmaninoff; Kiev, 1895.

The first musician in the long Rachmaninoff genealogy was the composer's great-grandfather, Alexander Gerasimovich. According to *Historical Information* he was an excellent violinist. At the age of twenty-three he married Maria Bakhmetyev, whose family was well known for its musical talent. Maria herself was particularly fond of singing. After the birth of their two children, Alexander, following his wife's wishes, retired from the service and settled down in Znamenskoe, where he organized an orchestra and chorus in which both he and his wife took an active part.

His son Arkady (Sergei's grandfather), a pupil of John Field's, was a piano virtuoso and often took part in benefit concerts. The famous musicians who came to perform in Tambov frequently asked him to join them, and in St. Petersburg he was invited to the musicales at the homes of Count Vielgorsky (a friend of Pushkin and Glinka) and Lvov (the composer of the Russian Imperial anthem). Some of his compositions were published, and the manuscripts of a few songs and two polkas dedicated to his daughters Varvara and Maria were found in the archives.

Apparently, before the birth of Sergei, the Rachmaninoff family never distinguished itself by any particular achievements, and there is no mention of the name in Russian history or literature except for a reference to Arkady Rachmaninoff in the memoirs of Elena Chvoschinskaya, born Princess Golizin.[2] She tells of the frequent visits she paid as a young girl to the Rachmaninoffs at Znamenskoe, which lay within twelve miles of her father's estate.

The Rachmaninoffs, who were among the most respected and beloved families in the district, were particularly known for their hospitality. They were well off and kept stables. Their

[2] *Russkaya Starima*, 1897.

large mansion, built on a hill against the background of the forest with a river running below in the fields, was usually filled with visiting young friends of the nine Rachmaninoff children.

"We used to wake up to the accompaniment of the beautiful sounds of Chopin, Field, and Mendelssohn music," wrote Elena Chvoschinskaya, "for Arkady Rachmaninoff went straight to the piano as soon as he got up. Usually in the morning we all met in the sitting room, each one with her needlework, while our hostess or her sister read aloud to us. But after tea in the afternoon Arkady Rachmaninoff took his place at the piano and, striking a few chords from the song he wanted me to sing, would ask me to join him. These musicales usually began with an aria from *Russlan and Ludmilla*."[3]

Sergei's only recollection of his grandfather coincided with the beginning of his piano studies, when one day old Arkady Rachmaninoff paid the family a visit. The boy remembered how, in preparation for this event, his mother carefully cut his nails, which made him think that this was a prerequisite to good piano-playing. While he performed his simple little pieces, his grandfather sat next to him and improvised what seemed to Sergei a very elaborate accompaniment. This was the only time Sergei ever saw him, for the old man died soon afterward.

One of Arkady's sons, Vasily, the composer's father, volunteered in the Russian army at the age of sixteen and fought during the conquest of the Caucasus (1857-59) against Shamyl, the leader of the mountaineers in the hills of Dagestan. After retiring from the army he married Lubov Boutakova, only daughter of General Peter Boutakov, and made his home on one of the estates of his parents-in-law, the Oneg, in

---

[3] Mikhail Glinka's opera.

the Novgorod district. Six children were born to Lubov Rachmaninoff. Of these the third, Sergei, was born at Oneg on April 2, 1873.

There is little information available on the composer's parents. In a book of recollections,[4] Sergei Rachmaninoff did not say much about them, nor is there any reference to them in his letters or in any articles relating to him. I am therefore quoting here the few lines about his father from a paper on Sergei Rachmaninoff, written by the composer's sister-in-law, Sophia Satin, and now in the Moscow Museum:

"It is very difficult to describe the character of Vasily Rachmaninoff, for it was a composite of contradictions. He had the reputation of being a featherbrained fellow always pursuing women. 'He spent hours playing the piano, not the well-known pieces, but something—God knows what . . . but I would listen to him to the end,' wrote one of Vasily's sisters." He was extremely kind, could not bear seeing tears and would do anything to calm a crying child. He took care of the children as though he were their mother, bathing and feeding them and—when they were growing up—spoiling them. They in turn were drawn closer to him than to their mother, who was strict and who tried to organize their lives.

Information about Sergei's mother is similarly scanty. She lived to a ripe old age, dying in Novgorod in 1929; yet, except for one or two remarks in Sergei's letters written during his early twenties, there is no reference to her in his entire correspondence. Rachmaninoff told me that he remembered his mother's motto, "There is a time for everything," and that later, as a mature man, he planned his day carefully. I have heard from those who knew him well (and I have also read in an article by the younger Feodor Chaliapin) that in the latter

[4] *Rachmaninoff's Recollections Told to Oskar von Riesemann,* 1933.

part of his life he arranged his afternoon naps in such a way as to make one day feel like two: going to bed for two hours, he started a new day after his afternoon sleep.

In his childhood Sergei preferred his good-humored, easygoing father, who gave his offspring freedom for their childish pranks. But, unfortunately, the elder Rachmaninoff was away a great deal of the time, and then little Sergei was often punished. One of his early recollections connected with music was that for his punishment he was told to go and sit under the piano.

In many respects, Rachmaninoff's childhood resembled that of Modest Moussorgsky. As with Moussorgsky, Sergei's mother was his first piano teacher, and his general education, like Moussorgsky's, was in the hands of private tutors and governesses, including German and French, as soon as he had outgrown the care of his old nurse.

The boy must have shown some promise in his piano studies because it was presently decided to engage a regular teacher for him; and for the next three years Miss Anna Ornazkaya, a recent graduate of the St. Petersburg Conservatory, took charge of his music lessons. But all the Rachmaninoff traditions—of family and of social class—militated against any consideration of a professional musical career. Again we find a parallel in Moussorgsky's life; in his family, as in those of César Cui and Nicolay Rimsky-Korsakov, the only profession that was even considered was the army or the navy. "Music," Rimsky's father announced, "should be regarded merely as a pleasant pastime, preferable to cards or drinking." And however strongly Sergei's mother, supported by Anna Ornazkaya, hoped for a musician's career for him, Vasily was determined to make Sergei an army officer. The boy was to enter the military college for officers of the Guard, the "Corps of Pages" in St. Petersburg to which only the elite were admitted but to which Sergei, as the grandson of a general (on his mother's side), was eligible.

However, by the time the boy was nine years old and ready to have the decision made for him, the problem resolved itself very simply. The consequences of Vasily's improvidence and extravagance had at last caught up with him, and there could now be no question of an elegant and expensive military career for his sons. Rachmaninoff's family was financially ruined. Out of the five estates which Sergei's mother had brought with her as her dowry, Vasily, who had retired from the army "in order to manage them better," had lost four through various risky enterprises. Oneg—the estate on which they lived—had to be sold at public auction, and the family moved to St. Petersburg, where Sergei's brother Vladimir entered an ordinary military school while Anna Ornazkaya managed to secure a Conservatory scholarship for Sergei under her old teacher, Professor Cross. This marked the beginning of a new life for the Rachmaninoffs, not only because of the change from country to city but also because of the incompatibility of Sergei's parents. Although there was no official divorce (such matters being very complicated by the laws of the Russian Orthodox Church), Vasily Rachmaninoff left his family to their fate and never returned. That they were able to get along at all was due to the fact that most of their expenses were met by Grandmother Boutakova, with whom they lived.

Sergei's mother never did recover from Vasily's desertion. The result was an unhappy atmosphere in the home—and no one to supervise Sergei's home work. He naturally wandered into the streets of the big city with all its alluring pleasures for a youngster. He was often to be found either at the skating rink, where his proficiency was developing into the virtuosity he should have been attaining at his piano, or stealing rides on the horse-drawn trolley cars, trying to compete with the newsboys in jumping on and off the fast-moving cars running on ice-covered streets (a rather dangerous game for the safety of the future virtuoso's hands), or just aimlessly wandering about the city.

At home no one was the wiser. Every day his grandmother gave him ten kopecks for carfare to the Conservatory which he spent at the skating rink. When he was periodically obliged to show the hateful book that recorded his Conservatory marks, he used to lock himself into the bathroom and, by adding a right angle to every figure 1, thus turning it into a 4,[5] emerged with the grades of a really good student. Only once was his trick detected—when one of his Conservatory teachers called on the family and innocently commiserated with the boy on failing in all his major subjects.

These were undoubtedly the happiest years of Sergei's childhood. He particularly loved the summers he spent at Borisovo, the country place that his grandmother bought after Vasily had lost all the others. Here he could live the unrestricted and unsupervised life of a country boy, swimming, boating, or roaming through the woods with his friends in the village. Here he had no fear of punishment, whatever he did, since his adoring grandmother could find no fault with her favorite.

Three years of this irresponsible existence passed with no apparent progress in either his general or his musical education, their sole effect being a marked increase in the boy's laziness and complete lack of discipline.

Yet two events which left a deep impression on the twelve-year-old Sergei belong to this period of his life.

"I have to thank my sister Elena," he said much later,[6] "for

---

[5] In Russian schools the marks run upward from 1 to 5.
[6] *Rachmaninoff's Recollections.*

the most beautiful and profound musical impressions I received at that time and even during my whole childhood. She was five years my senior and fourteen years old when we moved to St. Petersburg. She was an unusual girl: beautiful, clever, original, and, in spite of her slight figure, of Herculean physical strength. The fact that she could bend a silver ruble with the fingers of one hand impressed us boys tremendously.

"At that time she was gifted with a glorious voice, which even now seems to me the most beautiful I have ever heard. Although she took no lessons, she could sing everything, for nature herself had seen to the training of her wonderful contralto voice. My enjoyment in hearing her sing can hardly be described.

"It happened that just at that time, Tchaikovsky, who later played such a significant part in my musical development, became known and popular in Russia. It was through my sister Elena that I was first introduced to his music, which touched me to the heart. She used to sing 'None But the Lonely Heart,' and this—as well as some other songs which she rendered magnificently in spite or perhaps because of her youth—pleased me beyond words. She usually accompanied herself, but sometimes I had to take my place at the piano, and the result was not very satisfactory, for I was too self-willed to consider the feelings of the singer; I simply played as it pleased me and left the singer to follow as best she could. These attempts to perform together often ended in my sister's exclaiming, 'Oh, get out!' and boxing my ears."

Two and a half years later, Elena began to study with Ippolyt P. Pryanishnikov, a well-known voice teacher in St. Petersburg. After an audition at the Imperial Maryinsky Theater she was engaged as one of the members of the company —"an honor which previously can hardly have been bestowed

9

upon so youthful a singer. But she died of pernicious anemia before she had an opportunity to appear before the footlights."[7]

For his other musical impression Sergei was indebted to his grandmother. A very devout woman, she regularly attended the services at the various churches and cathedrals all over the city, taking Sergei along with her. The tolling of the bells, the unrivaled beauty of the singing, often by the best choirs in St. Petersburg, proved to be a source of inspiration from which Sergei was to draw for the rest of his life.

It was also at this time that Sergei made his first attempts at improvising. Proud of her grandson, Madame Boutakova made Sergei perform for her guests; but he soon tired of playing Kuhlau's or Diabelli's sonatinas and Cramer's studies over and over again and, instead, improvised pieces of his own which he announced as the work of Chopin or Mendelssohn, gambling on the ignorance of his audience.

At the Conservatory his progress was not remarkable, and though he played at the pupils' concerts no one among the faculty members saw anything noteworthy in his playing. In fact, Karl Y. Davidov, the director of the Conservatory, thought Master Rachmaninoff a lazy and mischievous boy, while as for his talent, it was not above the average. And he said as much to Siloti, who came to inquire about his cousin Sergei.

The twenty-two-year-old Alexander Siloti was then a rising star among pianists, and it was to him that Lubov Rachmaninoff appealed for advice as to what to do with her son. After Davidov's remark Siloti almost left the city without hearing Sergei, but finally—perhaps because Lubov was his aunt—he listened to him for an hour before taking the train to Moscow.

[7] *Rachmaninoff's Recollections.*

"There is only one man who can do anything with him—Zverev, my former teacher in Moscow." This was Siloti's verdict, and to Zverev it was accordingly decided that Sergei must go—to Zverev and to his first encounter with hard work and discipline.

The boy had one last carefree summer at Borisovo. When the day came for him to leave for Moscow, his grandmother took him to church for the last time, counted out the money he would need for his journey, bought his ticket, sewed into his gray jacket another hundred rubles with a *ladanka* (a small bag containing sacred objects and worn as an amulet), and, giving him her blessing, bade him farewell. Sergei had said good-by to the only person who, during his childhood, had offered him nothing but love and tenderness. As the train pulled out of the station, he sat in his seat and cried. Thus he greeted with tears the beginning of his own independent life, a life which offered him little happiness and gave him much pain.

. II .

Adolescence
and Nicolay Zverev

In moscow's musical world the name of Nicolay Zverev commanded unusual respect and authority. Yet he did not even have the title of professor at the Conservatory, and was merely a piano teacher in a "lower division"—that is, the first five grades. His reputation was that of being a severe teacher who terrorized his pupils, and stories were told of the "loose wrist" which in fits of rage he used freely to slap them. Few of his contemporaries knew the exact year of his birth, and people who remember him have spoken to me of him as an extremely old man. Perhaps it was his face that produced this impression; yet the records show that when he died in 1893 he was only sixty-one, and when Sergei Rachmaninoff became his pupil he was but a year or two over fifty.

Tall and imposing, Zverev spoke with remarkable self-assurance, looking calmly at the world through kind (and probably once beautiful) eyes surmounted by heavy black eyebrows. Apparently nobody ever dared to ask him questions, so that it was hardly known how good a musician he was. Did he play the piano at all? And if he did, how well? According to his pupils Sergei Remezov, Anatoly Galli, and Alexander

Siloti, he was "a very elegant and musical pianist with an unusually beautiful tone"; and they commented particularly on his extraordinary interpretation of Beethoven's Opus 27, the so-called "Moonlight" Sonata. But this is all that was remembered of him as a pianist.

The most valuable characteristic of Zverev's teaching was his knowledge of how to place the pupil's hand correctly on the piano so that the further development of technical ability would not be hampered by stiffness of wrist or arm. And he must have been successful in the fundamentals, for the professors of the upper grades—Safonoff, Taneyev, and Pabst, who had their own methods and to whom Zverev eventually turned over his pupils for further instruction—were always happy to work with them because there was no need to correct or start again from the beginning.

Zverev was ruthless with a pupil who played with tense wrists and arms and whose touch was rough and ugly. To avoid all unnecessary movements of the elbows and to achieve complete relaxation in order to develop varied technical skills, he insisted that his pupils practice a great many exercises and études. He did not allow them to play unrhythmically—"illiterately without punctuation," as he said—maintaining that in a clearly defined rhythmical approach lay the foundation of every musical structure. Those who heard Rachmaninoff later as a concert pianist could easily recognize this Zverev training in his playing. Furthermore, Zverev knew how to interest his students in the work they were doing by varying their programs and by teaching them the necessary regularity in work and patience in striving for perfection.

"My dear sir," he would remark to a pupil as he majestically tossed his head against the back of his armchair next to the grand piano, "you are playing like a cobbler!"

The "dear sir" might have been eight years old, frightened out of his wits, and completely unable to take in *why* he was "playing like a cobbler." Never mind—Zverev did not believe in explaining or demonstrating. Indeed, he may not have known how to explain, and, as for "showing" the pupil, this he may not have been able to manage, by this time, with his big, bony hands and crooked, clumsy fingers. Yet he undoubtedly possessed some kind of intuitive talent, the power to awaken in his pupils such a love of music and such an interest in solving the problems they met that his teaching could not be considered anything but successful. Perhaps Zverev's was a nature whose musicianship was entirely inside him, incapable of being expressed in any direct, outward form.

From the way he carried himself and from the gracious fashion in which he acknowledged respectful greetings in restaurants and night clubs, one might have thought Zverev something more than merely a piano teacher in the lower division. And it was true that he once had been, at any rate. In his youth he had resembled Sergei's father: he, too, squandered more than one fortune on a gay life, but he differed from Vasily Rachmaninoff in regard to his music: no mere amateur, he had studied with the outstanding piano teachers of his generation.

Zverev was born on March 13, 1832, in the district of Volokalamsk of a rather poor family of the Russian gentry, and was sent as a boy to the Moscow gymnasium with a military career as his intended future. Lev A. Mey, a poet well known in Russia, who at this time was one of the directors of the school, took such an interest in Zverev that he persuaded the boy's parents to give up their plans for his military future and let him enter the Moscow University instead. However, Zverev was never graduated because at this point he suddenly inherited a big fortune consisting of several estates in different districts of Russia, whereupon he left the University so as to "put his affairs in order" (as he said), then went to St. Petersburg and there took a position in the civil service.

From infancy Zverev had loved music, and while living in Moscow he had studied piano with Alexander Dubuque. Now that he was in St. Petersburg he became far more interested in his music than in his civil service duties, and undertook piano study with Adolf von Henselt, a pupil of Hummel's.

Zverev's style of living was on a large scale; he hated to dine or sup alone and believed in living sumptuously and having as many guests as he had friends. But the consequence of this luxurious life was that he woke up one morning to the stark reality that his last estate had been sold and that not a penny was left of his fortune. Since he had not proved himself a particularly zealous civil servant, he resigned his office and moved to Moscow, where Alexander Dubuque had promised him enough piano students to provide him with a better income.

Alexander Dubuque was the patriarch of Moscow pianists of the John Field school, having taught Alexander Villoing, who in turn was the teacher of the two Rubinstein brothers. He was now to prove useful to Zverev, not only because of the large circle of friends and acquaintances from whom he could recruit pupils for the younger man, but also because he was an important personage in the Moscow musical world. He had considerable influence in the Moscow Conservatory, where he had become a professor when it was founded in 1866. By 1872, however, when he was regarded as both old and old-fashioned, he retired from public life to his apartment—an ill-ventilated place smelling of dust, mold, and snuff. Here Dubuque, looking more like an old woman than a man, shuffled round in worn-out slippers, unkempt and greasy-looking, with traces of snuff under his nose and on his ancient, spotted bathrobe. But he was still sought out by musicians. They had not forgotten that Mili Balakirev (whose virtuosity was compared to Liszt's and Anton Rubinstein's) had said in one of his rare moments of modesty: "If I can play the piano at all, it is entirely due to the ten lessons I had with Dubuque." Furthermore, he was regarded with almost religious reverence because he had known Beethoven, to whom he had been presented in 1823 as a promising young pianist.

It was at Dubuque's that Zverev, meeting Tchaikovsky, asked him for lessons in musical theory. The composer consented, even though at the time he was not giving private lessons. The association between Zverev and Tchaikovsky grew into a close friendship.[1]

In a short time Zverev became the favorite teacher in houses of the rich merchants, and later he accepted the Moscow Conservatory post that he still held at the time of this story. Idle gossip insisted that he owed the appointment to his close friendship with Nicolas Rubinstein—a friendship based on his sharing in Rubinstein's legendary drinking orgies. But to attribute his standing as a musician to this circumstance was a base slander: too many great and remarkable pianists such as Rachmaninoff, Scriabin, Maksimov, Pressman, Keneman, Koreschenko, Igumnoff, Bekman-Scherbina, Kashperova, Samuelsohn, and others who came out of his school were living proof of his teaching ability.

The stories of Zverev's severity (which sent cold shivers down Sergei's spine whenever he thought of the man with whom he was going to study) were a part of the famous Rubinstein tradition. Since Zverev was older and more despotic

---

[1] *The Diaries of Tchaikovsky,* translated by Vladimir Lakond.

than Nicolas Rubinstein, it is probable that it was not Rubinstein but Zverev who originated the tradition of severity. Perhaps the tradition bore Rubinstein's name because of the glamour of his life. Rubinstein, coming to a morning class directly from a night club or a brothel, terrified his pupils— especially the girls, who sometimes hid in panic under the piano. It was part of the Rubinstein tradition for great teachers to be terrors; fantastic tales were told of their behavior.

Zverev occupied a large apartment with his sister on Roujeini Pereulok; neither of them ever married. Here he maintained a sort of *pensionnat* for a few Conservatory pupils, never more than three at a time, whom he chose from the most talented. He accepted money for his teaching only from the rich and from the Conservatory, never taking a penny from those who were talented and poor.

Those who entered his *pensionnat* received not only their tuition free of charge but their board and clothing as well. Though they were simply dressed in gray tunics with gray trousers to match, similar to the uniform in the Russian high schools, their clothes were made by the same elegant tailor who dressed Zverev. He was very kind and thoughtful toward his protégés, but in turn he expected absolute obedience to himself and to the principles which ruled his house: he insisted on full control of their occupations, their morals, even their daily habits. They were forbidden to go boating, skating, or horseback riding: Zverev feared for their hands. And a cardinal rule was that as long as they remained in his *pensionnat* they must have as little as possible to do with their parents and relatives, not even going home during their vacations. Of certain other aspects of this original arrangement I shall speak at a later stage in my story when Sergei Rachmaninoff learned more about them.

Zverev himself worked very hard. His day began with his private lessons at eight in the morning—an hour before his lessons at the Conservatory, where he taught until two o'clock. From then until ten at night he rode all over the city giving private lessons, and at ten he returned home to dine.

This was the regime into which the twelve-year-old Sergei was initiated—severe, relentless, its every hour strictly regulated. His program, like the programs of the other *pensionnaires*, was carefully supervised by Zverev's sister, the master himself being out of the house so much of the time. Sergei shared a bedroom and two grand pianos with two other boys, Mikhail Pressman and Leonid Maksimov, both extremely gifted. Each of them was required to practice for three hours daily by the clock, except on Sundays, when they were allowed to rest. Since the two pianos were in the same room, the schedule of their working hours was so arranged that twice a week each of the boys had to start his practicing at six in the morning. It was particularly hard on them to get up so early in winter. Two powerful lamps were lit in the room—one for light and the other for warmth—and no allowance was made if they had returned home late the night before from theater, concert, or after-theater supper. The one whose turn it was the next morning had to take his place at the piano at the scheduled hour. Often he was so sleepy that he did not play well, stumbled, and hit wrong notes. This would wake up Zverev and, attired only in his nightshirt, he would storm into the room and, by beating the offender and swearing at him, would make him forget his lost sleep.[2] Besides supervising their piano studies, he kept a watchful eye on their work in

[2] M. L. Pressman: *A Little Corner in the Musical Moscow of the Eighties*; ms. in Moscow, GZMMK.

other subjects at the Conservatory, and woe to the one who got a bad report.

Sunday evenings were reserved for dinner parties, which, as an important part of his social activities, were almost as dear to Zverev as his music. It was not unusual for the dinner table to be set for twenty people, and among the guests one frequently saw Taneyev, Siloti, Anton and Nicolas Rubinstein, Modest and Peter Tchaikovsky, the singers Tartakov and Jakovlev, and, of course, old Dubuque. The three protégés were included, and after a sumptuous repast they provided entertainment, each playing the piece he knew best—a Cramer study or a Mozart sonata—for an audience of select intellectuals whom Zverev wanted to impress with his teaching ability.

Sergei Rachmaninoff recalled later that this exhibition of Zverev's pupils' skill was not limited to these after-dinner performances on Sunday. Very often during the week Zverev would call for one of them to come to the house where he was teaching at the moment; and, after the boy had played, he would proudly announce, "See, that is the way to play the piano!" Nor did he seem perturbed by the fact that on this same morning, after hearing the same boy play the same piece at home, he had shouted, "Is that the way to play the piano? Get out!" The motives for such "guest performances" may conceivably have been quite commercial, since they constituted one way of recruiting pupils from the rich merchant houses.

Zverev, however, was solicitous that his *pensionnaires* should see and hear the best at the theaters, the opera, and concerts. Sitting with him in the most expensive box (for Zverev would not be seen anywhere else in the house), the boys saw and heard all the great Russian artists as well as those who came from abroad—Eleanora Duse, Salvini, Rossi, and a score of others. Of them all, Anton Rubinstein left the deepest impression on the growing Sergei.

In order to understand the importance of Rubinstein's influence, one must remember that in the recent history of music no one except Franz Liszt had enjoyed such popularity and absolute authority. Anton Rubinstein, coming to Moscow to conduct the hundredth performance of his opera *The Demon*, consented to visit the Conservatory and listen to a few pupils.

"A young man and a girl student sang," Rachmaninoff related later,[3] "and Josef Lhévinne and I, who were the same age—either twelve or thirteen—played the piano. My piece was Bach's *English Suite* in A minor."

That night at Zverev's, Rubinstein was feted and Sergei was given the honor of leading the great Anton to his place at the table. During the dinner nothing interested Sergei except what Rubinstein said.

"I remember one of his remarks which made me very thoughtful. A pianist of growing reputation—I believe it must have been young Eugen D'Albert—had recently given concerts in Moscow and St. Petersburg and was being hailed by the overenthusiastic press as the one and only worthy successor to Rubinstein. Someone asked Rubinstein whether he had heard him. 'Yes,' was the laconic answer. But the questioner persisted, inquiring how he liked the playing of this young pianist. Rubinstein leaned back and, eyeing him sharply from beneath his bushy brows, said (as it seemed to me) with a touch of bitterness and irony: 'Oh well, everyone can play the piano nowadays. . . .'"

Fifty-eight years later Sergei Rachmaninoff repeated Rubinstein's remark almost word for word. We were talking about

[3] *Rachmaninoff's Recollections.*

the remarkable teaching given to the instrumentalists in the United States, and Rachmaninoff, impressed by the high technical level of the young performers, leaned back in his chair and, raising his forefinger, said to me: "Just look at who plays how!"

Sergei was not only drinking in the isolated remarks of men of power and authority. He also watched them move, talk, and breathe, as it were, digesting everything and making it his own. Years later he spoke of an incident that took place during a performance of *The Demon*, with Rubinstein conducting.[4]

"The house was sold out, and the most brilliant audience that Moscow could command filled the boxes and stalls and crowded right up to the galleries. As the curtain rose on the second scene and the orchestra played the well-known passage in C minor, to which the audience listened with critical attention, one noticed that the stage was not too well lighted. A few short, dry taps of the conductor's baton plunged the orchestra into immediate silence, and through the sudden stillness that hung over the whole theater one heard Rubinstein's disagreeably grating voice: 'I have already asked for better stage lighting at the rehearsal!' There was some more hurried movement behind the scenes, and suddenly the stage was flooded with brightness almost as strong as daylight. Rubinstein calmly picked up his baton, which he had placed on the score, and began conducting the scene all over again. This autocratic attitude in front of an audience numbering two thousand people made an indelible impression on me."

Indeed it did. Sergei was learning that in order to be master of the situation you have to behave and speak like a master. His character was rapidly changing. No longer the spoiled and mischievous grandmother's pet, he was becoming a thought-

[4] *Rachmaninoff's Recollections.*

ful, proud, unusually self-controlled youngster, thanks to the tight rein which Zverev held on his boys and the principles he inculcated in accordance with the Zverev-Rubinstein tradition. All those who were worthily trained in this tradition had to be absolutely honest and straightforward and maintain a completely unmercenary attitude toward their art. No compromise with artistic conscience was tolerated, and the coveted title of "Free Artist" was upheld as sacrosanct.

Zverev respected his pupils' individualities and refused to let them be subjected to humiliation (except, of course, at his own hands). He relentlessly suppressed any manifestation of bragging on their part, any sign that they were seeking publicity, any destructive criticism of classmate or friend. And into the framework of such principles the malleable Sergei Rachmaninoff fitted perfectly.

When the summer came, Zverev took his nurslings with him to the Crimea, where he usually lived on the luxurious estate of one of his Moscow merchant friends. Now he rented a villa near by instead, so that the boys might live with Ladoukhin, a Conservatory teacher of harmony, whose strenuous task it was to take them through the two- or three-year Conservatory course in harmony within the three summer months.

It was during either the first or the second summer in the Crimea[5] that (according to Mikhail Pressman) Rachmaninoff wrote his first composition. Suddenly he became very pensive, even somber, and he sought seclusion. The other boys saw him walking with head bent, or looking off into the distance and whistling something hardly audible, or waving his hands as though he were conducting an orchestra. He remained in this state for several days.

Then, very mysteriously, when he and Pressman were alone

[5] There is some conflict in the dates as reported.

he called him to the piano and began to play. "Do you know what this is?" he asked.

"No," replied Pressman, "I don't."

"And do you like this organ point in the bass, with this chromatic progression in the upper register?"

Pressman nodded.

"I composed it myself," Sergei said proudly, "and I am dedicating it to you!"[6]

With the coming of winter, the boys returned to Moscow, where life at Zverev's went on with the regularity of the seasons. New courses were undertaken, such as reading musical literature on two pianos; and lessons in theoretical subjects were added to the curriculum as the students mounted the *Gradus ad Parnassum*. At Zverev's request a competent pianist, Madame Belopolskaya, came once a week to the house to play with them all the classical and new symphonic works in two-piano arrangement for eight hands—an experience that the boys enjoyed. They played through many Haydn, Mozart, and Beethoven symphonies as well as the overtures of Mozart, Beethoven, and Mendelssohn. Their favorites were the Beethoven symphonies, and in these they achieved such virtuosity that Zverev suggested to the Conservatory's examining committee that it should hear them play eight-hands. For this occasion Semeon Samuelsohn, another Zverev pupil, joined the boys.

It would have been interesting to see the expression on the face of Taneyev, who was chairman of the committee, when

[6] This piece was never published, and there is no record of Rachmaninoff's ever having mentioned it again. Found among his manuscripts after he left Russia, it is now in the Central Museum of Musical Culture in Moscow. Rachmaninoff marked as "Opus 1" four pieces: Song, Prelude, Melody, and Gavotte. (The published Opus 1 is his piano concerto written in 1890-91.) Professor Alexander B. Goldenweiser, who was a classmate of Rachmaninoff and Pressman, dated this early manuscript "1887" in pencil.

the four boys marched to the pianos to play a Beethoven symphony, for they had brought no notes with them. He almost jumped from his chair. "Where is the music?"

"They play by heart," replied Zverev calmly, looking over the heads of Taneyev and the others on the committee.

The boys played Beethoven's Fifth, and then, while Taneyev was muttering, "But how is it possible? . . . To play by heart . . . ," Zverev ordered them to play the Scherzo from Beethoven's Sixth.[7]

But there was one more subject which, curiously enough, was regarded by Zverev as an integral part of his educational system. The boys were to be taught the "art of living"—and by no one less than himself. This peculiar course, which started with lessons on how to hold a knife and fork correctly at table, embraced all the aspects of masculine behavior. The aim was to prepare the boys "for any eventuality." They were given dancing lessons, being taken every Sunday to a house where four girls, likewise pupils of Zverev's, were their partners. But they did not like these lessons and complained that the dancing positively poisoned their day of rest.

When they reached the age of fifteen—which Zverev considered the crucial point on the way to maturity—he began to take them out to elegant restaurants,[8] where they were to learn the rituals of eating and drinking. From there it was only one step to the "mysteries of life," and when, in Zverev's opinion, they were ready for it, he led them to the night clubs, to the Gypsies, to women.

It is very curious how akin the whole mold of the Zverev-Rubinstein tradition was to the old Hussars' regimental moral code. It encouraged the same bravado in early sexual relation-

[7] M. L. Pressman: op. cit.
[8] The Diaries of Tchaikovsky.

ships as in the devil-may-care attitude of their drinking bouts and their gambling at cards. The close comradeship of the members of this clan, their conception of honor (which above all meant punctiliousness in paying one's card and restaurant debts), freedom in one's convictions and behavior (less concerned with political theories than the choice of sexual companions)—all this sounds like a code of morals and behavior concocted by military-college boys on the eve of graduation.

Gypsies and Gypsyism form a special chapter in Russian life and particularly in the life of Russian intellectuals in both Moscow and St. Petersburg. Some found inspiration in Gypsyism; others found their ruin. Pushkin and Apukhtin, Lev Tolstoy and Alexander Block, Tchaikovsky, Varlamov, Davidov, the two Rubinstein brothers, and a score of others admired the singing of the Gypsies and spent many a night in their company. Though some of the restaurants had Gypsies on their programs, many preferred more intimate contact and often went directly to the Gypsies' homes on the city outskirts.

The qualities of every Gypsy singer were carefully scrutinized, some critics being experts in this matter. The good Gypsy singer had to have "a tear," or "a sob," in his or her voice. The listeners usually wept, as was expected. And it was not always for purely artistic enjoyment that the men visited them; the young Gypsy women were notably successful with the drunken crowd, and many even managed to marry aristocrats and rich industrialists.

Zverev adored "Gypsying," and his pupils found his enthusiasm contagious. For it is undeniable that the tastes of all Russians—regardless of what social stratum they come from, regardless of their professions—meet at this focal point. Vodka, champagne, and Gypsies—these form one harmonious Russian chord.

Sergei Rachmaninoff was then very young, and his character and tastes were just beginning to be formed. The Hussarlike Rubinstein-Zverev bravado and the Gypsies left a definite imprint on the whole Rachmaninoff literature, just as had the sound of church bells, which had already taken deep root in his being.

. III .

The Moscow Conservatory
and Taneyev

After two years of preparatory tutelage with Zverev, the fifteen-year-old Sergei was graduated from the lower division of the Conservatory and became a piano pupil of Alexander Siloti, who had just joined the faculty of the upper division. There were two other teachers in the upper division, Paul Pabst and Vasily Safonoff, but Siloti was Zverev's former pupil, and it had been on his advice that Sergei came to Moscow to study with Zverev. Furthermore, he was Sergei's first cousin and a pupil of Rubinstein and Liszt. Thus it was natural that Sergei should choose Siloti's class for his advanced piano studies.

As for the theoretical studies, they were divided between two teachers, the composers Arensky and Taneyev. Anton Arensky had the class in free composition and fugue, and Sergei Taneyev taught counterpoint. Both men left a definite mark on Rachmaninoff—one on his music, the other on his character.

According to the stories told, Arensky hardly ever drew a sober breath and did not like teaching, but fortunately he took great interest in Sergei right from the start. Arensky's influence was twofold: on the positive side his influence showed in Rachmaninoff's songs and particularly in the full melodic piano accompaniment, while on the negative side it was due to Arensky that Rachmaninoff's music had much of a "salon" character.

As for Taneyev, it was the personality of this remarkable man that impressed Rachmaninoff, who looked up to him as a model of high principles and ideals. When Sergei Taneyev died in 1915, Rachmaninoff, then forty-two years old, wrote an obituary—his only writing for publication—in which he said: ". . . Through his personal example Taneyev taught us how to live, to work, and even to speak, because he had his own 'Taneyev way' of speaking—concise, clear, and to the point. He only said what was necessary. This man never uttered superfluous words. He seemed to me to be the personification of 'Truth on Earth' which Pushkin's Salieri rejected."

Taneyev, whose name is known to comparatively few outside of Russia and whose compositions and theoretical treatises have not yet come into their own even inside Russia, was a highly significant figure in the history of Russian music. A pupil of Tchaikovsky, he so far surpassed him in his theoretical knowledge that it was Tchaikovsky who sought his advice and criticism rather than vice versa. While Taneyev belonged to the Moscow group of musicians opposed to "The Mighty Five" (the nationalists) and the theories they advocated, the goal of his musical credo for Russian music was basically the same as theirs. Some ten years before Sergei Rachmaninoff became his pupil in counterpoint, Taneyev wrote (in February, 1879)[1] what he thought the Russian composer should do in order to write "Russian" music—a problem that has stirred and trou-

[1] Taneyev: *Personality, Works and Documents;* Moscow, 1925.

bled Russian musicians from the time of Glinka, protagonist of Russian National music, down to the present day of Prokofiev and Shostakovich.

Taneyev expresses his own musical credo thus:

The forms of Western European music (sonatas, symphonies, etc.) emerged gradually. They developed from the fugue, which in its turn evolved from the contrapuntal forms of folk and church melodies. No form developed accidentally; all forms of necessity evolved from preceding ones. It can therefore be said that folk songs and church melodies lie at the basis of all European music. For several centuries people worked over their forms, and the result of their labors is to be seen in modern forms of Western European music. Thus folk melodies contained *in potentia* all of modern European music. Only human intelligence was needed to convert them into rich forms of music.

When Russian musicians study Western European music, they encounter musical forms complete and ready-made. Either they compose in the European style or they try to make the Russian song fit into European forms, forgetting that the Russian song is something external and alien to European music. The form of every composition is closely bound up with the material of which it is made. . . .

A Russian musician is like an architect who, on seeing a log house, would begin to build something similar out of stone, trying to lay the stones in such a way as to achieve the same curves. It is clear that before long the architect would realize that nothing could come of his attempt. . . .

Russian musicians realize this instinctively. . . . Nor can it be otherwise. European forms are alien to us, but we have none of our own. We have no national music. Tchaikovsky (the finest Russian) wrote a textbook on harmony, but what harmony? European! We have no harmonic system of our own. . . . The task of every Russian musician is to promote the creation of a national music. The history of Western European music offers us the answer to the question, what must be done to achieve this? The same mental effort that was applied to the song of Western European peoples must be applied to the Russian song; only then will we have a national music. . . .

Suppose we learn all there is to be learned from the old contrapuntalists and undertake this difficult but very glorious task. Who knows, perhaps we shall bequeath to the next generation new forms, new music. Who knows, perhaps, in some scores of years, perhaps at the beginning of the next century, Russian forms will appear. It does not matter when they appear; what matters is that they must appear. . . .

Though the last phrase sounds as though it might have been written by Moussorgsky—banner-bearer of "The Mighty Five"—Taneyev differed with the St. Petersburg group in advocating just what they were denying: the necessity for a thorough study not only of contemporary European musical forms but of their whole genesis as well. It is indeed curious that so clear and logical a presentation of this idea should come from a musician of the Moscow group, composed as it was of men who had little to boast of in their intellectual or cultural achievements. These men were men of feeling, not of intellect; it was hardly to be expected that abstract ideas would interest such people as Nicolas Rubinstein and Zverev, whose free time was spent in continual debauchery, or even Tchaikovsky.

Taneyev was considered such an extraordinary man (which he indeed was)—a scientist, even a higher mathematician—that rumors circulated about his incredible knowledge of the mysterious, of the mathematical calculations with which he was to conquer the theory of sound; and this reputation in turn created almost a superstitious fear of him, as though he were a medieval alchemist or a sage. Because he did not drink, he was regarded as an ascetic who sacrificed every happiness in life for the sake of music. He led an isolated life, at first in a little house on Sivzev Vrashka and later on the Mertvy

Pereulok, the "Street of the Dead," an address which only added a peculiar ghostly touch to his personality. The houses he occupied were small, provincial in character, and lacking such modern comforts as bath, electricity, and running water; and most of them were situated on the outskirts of Moscow —not the Moscow of the twentieth century, but that of the nineteenth, the "large village" whose unpopulated streets, often deep in snow, were lighted at night by oil lamps.

Even as a very young man, when the road to recognition, fame, and wealth lay open before him, Taneyev retired to one of these out-of-the-way houses to live alone with only his old nurse for company; he never married. He gave up his career of concert pianist (though he was a brilliant pupil of Nicolas Rubinstein's) as easily as he gave up his share in the wealth he had inherited from his rich family, out of which he was swindled by his brothers. He resigned from the position of director of the Moscow Conservatory at the age of thirty-two to devote his entire life to music as he understood it. Contrary to the rumors and even legends about him, which attributed all sorts of qualities and characteristics to his person, Taneyev was an extremely kind and simple man. Abhorring mysticism in all its forms, he had an aesthetic conception of religion as something nationally, historically, scientifically valuable which it was imperative to study. He was a man of liberal political convictions which he did not feel called upon to express in public. That his position was misinterpreted was due to his difficulty in achieving a coherent expression of his mathematical and philosophical ideas; he was not sufficiently familiar with the idiom of those fields. Yet his logic was nearer to that of a philosopher or mathematician than to that of a musician. From what I have read of his works and heard from Leonid

31

Sabaneyeff,[2] I gather that Taneyev believed that the beauty of combinations of sound depends on definite laws which can be discovered and established with mathematical precision, and that he devoted his whole creative talent to the effort to discover those formulas. In his personal life, according to those who knew him, he was the epitome of a priest of pure art.

It was not at once, however, that young Rachmaninoff appreciated the quality of the man who tried to teach him counterpoint. He was—it must be remembered—hardly more than fifteen years old, only just beginning to understand what self-discipline implies, and counterpoint bored him. "I could not," he said later, "take the faintest interest in counterpoint in the strict style, in all these imitations and inversions, these augmentations and diminutions and other embellishments of an ugly cantus. I found it all dreadfully dull, and none of the rapturous praises and eloquent sermons of the highly esteemed Taneyev could convince me to the contrary."[3] Rachmaninoff was shirking his assignments in somewhat the same way he had dodged work a few years before in St. Petersburg.

As years went by, Rachmaninoff changed his attitude both toward Taneyev's teaching and Taneyev himself. It was only natural that Rachmaninoff, surrounded by all those will-less and morally weak musicians, should subconsciously look up to Taneyev. He considered him as the supreme judge of the musical and literary "insignificant," as well as the "Masters" who sought his advice. I am sure that in those early years of his youth when Rachmaninoff was only beginning to make his own decisions, Taneyev "the man" stood in his mind as his guide. And I say "the man" advisedly, for there is little discernible effect of Taneyev's rationalistic theories in the

[2] A Russian musician and critic who was a pupil of Taneyev's.
[3] Rachmaninoff's Recollections.

music of Rachmaninoff, while the effect of the man's character is clearly seen in Rachmaninoff's own as it developed from this version.

Though Sergei was no longer Zverev's pupil, he still lived in his house and was still supervised by him. During the four years he lived with Zverev their friendly relations were marred only by Zverev's occasional outbursts of temper. The beatings —"these chastisements," as Rachmaninoff called them—that usually followed Zverev's rages were less resented while Sergei was younger than after he reached sixteen. It was at this period (October, 1889) that the final break came. According to Rachmaninoff's own account,[4] he asked Zverev one evening for a room to himself and for help in renting a piano, explaining that if he was to do his work well—his theory and composition—he must have greater privacy and freedom.

"Our talk began calmly and proceeded in a perfectly peaceful manner," Rachmaninoff relates, "until I must have said something that infuriated him. He flared up in an instant, screamed, and flung at me every article he could lay hands on. I remained quite calm, but added fuel to the fire by remarking that, as I was no longer a child, the tone he adopted toward me did not seem very suitable. The whole scene ended disgracefully."

Usually such quarrels had been followed by a reconciliation, but this time a whole month passed without their exchanging a word. Then Zverev ordered Sergei to meet him after his lessons in town, when he took his ex-pupil to the house of the Satins'—Sergei's relatives, whom he had been permitted (by Zverev's rules) to visit only twice during the past four years.

"It looked," Rachmaninoff continues, "as if they expected us, for a regular family council had assembled there and the

4 *Rachmaninoff's Recollections.*

sitting room was pervaded by an atmosphere of solemnity. When we had seated ourselves, Zverev made a little speech, which he delivered in a dignified and almost businesslike manner, and which amounted to this: He had found that our respective temperaments were not compatible and that, at the moment, it was impossible for him and myself to live together. But he naturally did not wish to leave me alone and unsupported, and had, therefore, brought me here in the hope that someone present might be ready to take me in and look after me. He begged my relations to make up their minds as soon as possible. For the rest, I could naturally do as I liked. After this we rose, and, without even mentioning the details of the matter or arriving at any decision, we walked home as silently as we had come."

Thus when Sergei Rachmaninoff walked out of Zverev's house next morning, he put an end to a relationship which had played an important role in the forming of his character as a young man and as a musician. The four years he spent with Zverev had transformed him from a spoiled and mischievous child to an "old" boy of sixteen.

It is indisputable, according to Leonid Sabaneyeff and others who knew Rachmaninoff at that time, that certain of his most salient traits were due to his association with Zverev. The shyness and awkwardness which he developed then never left him even after he became a famous musician. That he succeeded in hiding these—or at least disguising them—under an air of self-command and aloofness was facilitated by the peculiar cast of his features. Even in youth his face had not been that of a young man; it was old-looking, with deep creases that lent an expression of disappointment and even disapproval. Those who knew him during his adolescence noted, interestingly, a certain resemblance to Zverev himself, starting with features and ending with manner—the way they carried themselves, and their marked ability to keep people at a distance despite their very warm and kind natures.

This crisis in Rachmaninoff's life was further complicated by his mother who, when she heard what had happened, sent word that he should join her in St. Petersburg. He had good grounds for refusing. It would have meant leaving Moscow and the Conservatory, whose tradition had taken a strong hold on him. In addition, he already felt antagonism toward the St. Petersburg group of musicians, including Rimsky-Korsakov, even though he really knew little about them. According to his own *Recollections*, he regretted later that he had refused, since accepting would have given him the chance to study under Anton Rubinstein, who had resumed his teaching at the St. Petersburg Conservatory. Instead, Sergei stayed in Moscow, going to live with his aunt, Madame Satin, his father's sister, and at her house everything was done to help him to continue his studies in peace.

There is, however, another version of this crisis that has been passed down from one musician to another without ever reaching either confirmation or print. Leonid Sabaneyeff, a pupil of Taneyev and Zverev and a well-known and respected music critic and author, recently both told and wrote me the following.

It seems that Yury Sakhnovsky,[5] a prominent figure in Moscow's artistic world, music critic on the *Russkoe Slovo* (the most distinguished newspaper in Moscow), and close friend of Rachmaninoff's, told Sabaneyeff that it was not Zverev who broke with Rachmaninoff, but Rachmaninoff who left Zverev, and that it was not on account of "a room with a piano" but

[5] Music critic of the *Curier* (1901-1903), *Russkaya Pravda* (1904), and *Russkoe Slovo* (1909-1917).

on account of Zverev's homosexuality. There is no documentary evidence for the Sakhnovsky version,[6] and it will always remain a question whether Rachmaninoff was or was not aware of the reputation that Zverev's *pensionnat* certainly had. It was sometimes referred to as "The Monastery," sometimes as a "Zoo" (the root of Zverev's name means "beast"), and sometimes as "Zverev's Harem" (Zverev never took girl students into his *pensionnat*, though many of them were talented).

Sakhnovsky categorically stated that, regardless of any specific incident or of the time when it may have occurred, the issue remained the same, and that—despite Rachmaninoff's character, which was modeled on Zverev specifications—he refused to go along with Zverev all the way on this particular nuance of "freedom of conscience." Finally, Sakhnovsky said that it was Zverev and not Rachmaninoff who felt guilty over the break and who sought an opportunity for a reconciliation, while Rachmaninoff sacredly guarded his teacher's "secret."

Whichever is the correct version, the episode undoubtedly constitutes Sergei Rachmaninoff's first step toward independence, his earliest manifestation of a will hitherto unawakened.

[6] Homosexuality was punishable by Russian law with maximum of 10-12 years of hard labor in Siberia. (Laws, August 15, 1845; April 17, 1863; June 11, 1885.)

. IV .

Tchaikovsky and Rachmaninoff

THERE WAS FRICTION among the faculty members of the Moscow Conservatory and Alexander Siloti refused to return for another year. This fact made Rachmaninoff get down to serious work: in order to avoid being transferred to another teacher shortly before graduation he decided to speed up his work and be ready for the final examinations a whole year early. It was doubtless the stamina developed through Zverev's teachings and Taneyev's example that made such an undertaking appear possible. Had it not been for this decision, Rachmaninoff would probably have become a pupil of Vasily Safonoff, who, though an excellent musician, was not in favor with the Zverev-Rubinstein group.

Safonoff was loved and hated, admired and feared, because of his contradictory nature, which combined keen intelligence, a broad culture, and a kind heart with an iron will and idiosyncrasies that bordered on foolhardiness. But no one could deny his exceptional musical gifts as a pianist, a teacher, and later as a conductor and an administrator when he succeeded Taneyev as the director of the Moscow Conservatory in 1889.

When on Tchaikovsky's recommendation he had come to the
Conservatory in 1885 to become a professor in piano, he was
greeted (by nearly everyone except Taneyev, who knew and
admired his qualities) with a hostility which was in accordance
with the traditional Muscovite feeling toward anybody from
the St. Petersburg school.

During the four years since then, however, Safonoff had
proved himself worthy of Tchaikovsky's and Taneyev's respect, having built up his piano class to a standard that made
the Muscovites take notice. So wholeheartedly devoted was he
to the work he was doing at the Conservatory (he did not give
private lessons) that he did not spare his time or strength in
sharing his wealth of knowledge, often working with a pupil
for two or three hours instead of the customary half hour, and
continuing the lesson at his home either at night or very early
in the morning. As in Zverev's class, Safonoff's pupils developed a phenomenal musical memory, for he insisted that
they play everything by heart even when they brought him a
new piece for their first lesson. He had the gift of recognizing
the individual potentialities of each pupil, and he knew how
to make them "think and feel" in their own way. A whole
pleiad of brilliant musicians, several now famous, were graduated from his class: Scriabin, Josef Lhévinne, Nicolay Medtner,
Leonid Nikolaev, and many others; and indeed, half the Moscow musicians were eventually indebted to him. Scores of
private music schools were founded by Safonoff's former
pupils (some are still in existence), all continuing the Safonoff
tradition.

He organized and trained the Conservatory orchestra so well
that Arthur Nikisch found it up to his standards when he conducted it on one of his rare visits to the city. And finally Moscow owed to Safonoff's ingenuity the new building of the Con-

servatory. He alone had been able to lure the needed two hundred thousand rubles from the rich merchant Solodovnik, who ordinarily would not part with ten kopecks. Yet, despite all this, the Zverev-Rubinstein party regarded him as an outsider and an intruder and had as little as possible to do with him. And this was one more reason why Rachmaninoff did not wish to study under him.

Safonoff came from a Cossack family from the Tver district, but contrary to the family tradition he became a musician. At one time he took private lessons with Leschetizky and Villoing and later was graduated from the St. Petersburg Conservatory. The Muscovites resented his close tie with the St. Petersburg musicians. They attributed his occasional rough manners to the example of his father, a tall Cossack general who dressed in Cossack uniform with cartridges in his chest pockets and a belt from which on three sides of his body hung revolver, dagger, and saber, and who, without taking off his huge fur cap, used to stroll into the Conservatory to visit his son. This sight—six feet and two hundred pounds of living symbol of the monarchy's unshakable power—irritated the Muscovites, who considered themselves liberals and freethinkers, while Safonoff was an outspoken monarchist. And finally, he was both envied and feared in Moscow because his marriage to a daughter of one of the Government's cabinet ministers put him in a very strong position.

I mention these apparent irrelevancies because later on they became a deciding factor in the relations of Rachmaninoff with the Moscow Conservatory as long as Safonoff remained its director. But at this time Safonoff gave his consent to Rachmaninoff's desire to jump one school year and to undergo his final examinations a year early.

Rachmaninoff's native musical endowment made it possible

to achieve the task he so bravely set himself. Many stories illustrate his exceptional ear and memory, the one told by Professor Alexander B. Goldenweiser belonging to this period:[1]

"Rachmaninoff's musical gifts, even aside from his creative ability, surpassed any others I have ever met, bordering on the marvelous, like those of Mozart in his youth. The speed with which he memorized new compositions was remarkable. I remember how Siloti, with whom we were both studying at the time, told Rachmaninoff to learn the well-known Brahms *Variations on a Theme of Handel*. This was on a Wednesday, and it was but three days later that Rachmaninoff played them like a master. It was his practice to memorize everything he heard, no matter how complicated it was.

"One of our classmates in composition, G. A. Alchevsky, and I once stopped for a visit with Rachmaninoff after school. (Rachmaninoff was then living with the Satins.) During the conversation Alchevsky mentioned the symphony he was composing, and Rachmaninoff asked him to play it. Alchevsky played the first movement. Three years later the two men happened to be at one of my musicales, and Rachmaninoff asked Alchevsky about his symphony.

" 'I wrote the first movement and then gave up,' replied Alchevsky.

" 'Too bad,' commented Rachmaninoff. 'I liked the symphony and remember it well.'

"He thereupon went to the piano and played almost the entire first movement."

One of the most notable changes effected in Rachmaninoff's character since he had been subjected to Zverev's discipline was the emergence of ambition. Having lost his laziness, he was now developing what the Germans call *Sitzfleisch*—that

[1] Zitovich: *Rachmaninoff*—Collection of articles and material; Moscow, 1947.

capacity to sit and concentrate which became even more valuable to him in his later years. Meanwhile, his immediate ambition was to be graduated with the Great Gold Medal, hitherto awarded only twice since the founding of the Conservatory—to Taneyev and to Arseny Koreschenko, a talented pianist.[2] In order to win this honor, he must first of all pass his examinations in piano and fugue *cum laude*, and it was this goal that he now worked hard to reach.

Suddenly, however, his progress was checked by an unfortunate setback. While spending the summer vacation on his grandmother's estate, he developed a severe case of malaria, from which he had not fully recovered on his return to Moscow. At the time, he was sharing rooms with his friend from the Conservatory, Mikhail A. Slonov, a singer and pianist, with whom Rachmaninoff always discussed his plans, his thoughts, and the progress of his work. He was then writing his first piano concerto, several songs, and a quartet.

All this was interrupted when the persistent fever finally struck, confining him to his bed. Fortunately he had a friend in Yury Sakhnovsky, mentioned earlier, a wealthy young man some eight years older than Rachmaninoff; and Sakhnovsky came to the rescue, moving Sergei to his apartment in the mansion belonging to his father, a rich merchant and landowner. At the same time Siloti called in an eminent physician, Professor Alexander Mitropolsky. The diagnosis was "brain fever," and the patient was ordered to take a complete rest.

After several months of careful treatment Rachmaninoff recovered—but only to find that (in his own words) he had lost half of the facility with which he used to compose. This did not, however, deter him from repeating his request that

---

[2] A. N. Koreschenko (1870-1918), a pupil of Taneyev and Arensky, composed three operas, a ballet, and a large number of instrumental works in a style based on Tchaikovsky's and Arensky's.

Arensky allow him to take his final examinations that year rather than the next.

To do this he was required to compose a symphony, several vocal pieces, and an opera. Despite his determination to be graduated that year, his work on the symphony progressed slowly and, as it seems, with no satisfaction to either Arensky, Taneyev, or the youthful composer himself. But with his usual self-confidence he refused to listen to the criticisms of his teachers and did not change a single bar in his composition.

The subject of the opera *Aleko*, with the libretto written by Nemirovich-Danchenko of the Moscow Theater, was chosen by the members of the committee who were to examine the three candidates—Rachmaninoff, Nikita Morozov, and Lev Conus.

Sergei was again living with Slonov and with Vasily Rachmaninoff, his father, for whom, through Sakhnovsky's help, he had found a job in Moscow, and who came to stay with them. When the subject of the opera was handed to Sergei, he could hardly get home to his writing desk quickly enough to start writing the score. He was practically composing the opera as he ran home on his long legs. But to his despair his father had a business appointment and was using the room with the grand piano for the whole afternoon. After pacing up and down the apartment for several hours, Sergei finally flung himself on his bed and cried like a baby. However, he made up for lost time and with the help of Slonov, who copied the sheets of the written manuscript, he finished the opera in the extraordinary time of seventeen days.

With no desire to minimize such a feat, but rather to add to the credibility of his achievement, I must mention here that apparently Rachmaninoff was well acquainted with this form of composition for, according to a paper read in October,

1945, by the musicologist B. V. Dobrohotov at a scientific session in Moscow devoted to Rachmaninoff's work, *Aleko* was not Rachmaninoff's first attempt at composing in this form. Since the age of fifteen he had repeatedly considered dramatic subjects—such as *Esmeralda*, after Victor Hugo's novel, or separate scenes from Pushkin's *Boris Godunov*. Manuscripts have been found of monologues from *Boris Godunov* and of a vocal quartet from Pushkin's *Mazeppa*.

Rachmaninoff's one-act opera *Aleko* showed the definite influence of *The Queen of Spades* by Tchaikovsky, which had just been produced with great success. It unanimously pleased the examining committee; Rachmaninoff was awarded the highest mark for opera, and was thus graduated in 1892 with the Great Gold Medal.

Among the members of the committee was Zverev. Touched to tears by the success of his former pupil, he took Sergei aside, congratulated him, kissed him, and presented him with his own gold watch, a gift with which Rachmaninoff never parted. Although this marked their reconciliation and Rachmaninoff kept on seeing Zverev until the latter died in September, 1893, Zverev was the only close friend to whom Rachmaninoff never dedicated a single piece of music.

The fact that Rachmaninoff was graduated with the Great Gold Medal, the addition of his name on the marble plaque along with Taneyev's and Koreschenko's, and the tale of the speed with which the opera had been written—with minute details, arguments over whether it was accomplished in fourteen days or seventeen, and the remarks of every member of the committee—all these soon reached far beyond the walls of the Conservatory. Rachmaninoff discovered that he had many more friends, admirers, and even relatives than he had dreamed of. But there were two other sequels that proved to be of much greater importance.

Karl Gutheil, a Moscow music publisher who, having made a fortune in popular music, now decided to branch out into serious, had for some time been seeking a young composer whose name would add prestige to his list. When the reports of this new talent reached his ears he approached Zverev—for Gutheil had his own way of doing business. Zverev in turn told Sergei about it, but suggested that he had better talk to Tchaikovsky and get advice first; and he made an appointment for Sergei to play his opera for Tchaikovsky as soon as the latter should return to Moscow.

"Sergei, you are lucky," it seems Tchaikovsky said to him. "What did I not do before I found a publisher, even when I was a good deal older than you! I did not receive a penny for my first composition, and I consider myself fortunate that I did not have to pay in order to see myself published. I consider it almost a miracle that Gutheil not only offers you fees but even asks you to state your own terms!" And in his shrewd and experienced way he advised Sergei to let Gutheil fix the conditions, which would leave Sergei free to accept or reject.

When it came to the point, however, Gutheil also proved to be noncommittal: he was interested in the opera, in the songs, and in the two pieces for cello and piano, but made no firm offer. This cat-and-mouse game went on for some time, neither party specifying terms. Then, at last, Gutheil mentioned the sum of five hundred rubles as his idea of a fair price for all three opuses. Had Rachmaninoff not been well coached for this moment, he would probably have fainted, his earnings so far having amounted to just fifteen rubles a month from the single pupil he had![3]

[3] It may be added that until his death Gutheil remained Rachmaninoff's publisher and friend.

The second rewarding by-product of Sergei's success was a visit to the capital. One of his relatives who was connected with the Imperial Court urged him to come to St. Petersburg so that he might launch a career there with the help of the powers. "This was the only time," according to Rachmaninoff, that he "used other than purely artistic means to reach an artistic goal."

On Sergei's arrival, therefore, he was duly introduced into "society" and was taken to meet Eduard Nápravník, conductor at the Imperial Opera. But the fate of *Aleko* was really decided at the birthday party of an influential lady, wife of the director of the Seal. As her guests were applauding Sergei's playing of two dances from the opera, she suggested to the manager of the Chancellery office that *Aleko* should be produced, and promised to come herself to the opening night. And a performance was thereupon scheduled for April 23, 1893, at the Bolshoi Theater.

As *Aleko*'s final chords were drowned in tumultuous applause and calls for the composer, the twenty-year-old Sergei came out on the stage, an accepted member of the family of Russian composers. Although the influential lady did not, after all, attend the performance, three other persons did who meant considerably more to Sergei: his father, his grandmother (Arkady Rachmaninoff's widow), and Peter Tchaikovsky, who leaned out of his box and applauded so vigorously that Sergei attributed the success of the opera almost entirely to him and his influence.

But not even this big night could so encourage Rachmaninoff, to swell his pride as a musician, as did Tchaikovsky's few remarks and the way in which they had been made while the two were sitting in a far corner of the hall during a rehearsal.

"Do you like this tempo?" asked Tchaikovsky.

45

"No," said Rachmaninoff.

"Why don't you tell them?"

"I am afraid."

During the interval Tchaikovsky said to the orchestra men: "Mr. Rachmaninoff and I think that the tempo here might be taken a little quicker."

And later he turned to Rachmaninoff, and said: "I have just finished an opera in two acts, *Yolanthe*, which is not long enough to fill an evening. Would you object if it were performed together with yours?"

"He actually said these words," Rachmaninoff recalled later. " 'Would I object?' He was fifty-three years old, a famous musician—and I was only a beginner of twenty!"

But Rachmaninoff's *Aleko* never reached the European stage; even in Russia it was not included in the regular operatic repertoire, though given occasionally. The critics by and large regarded Rachmaninoff as a talented young man with knowledge and good taste, and agreed that he might become a good opera composer because he had feeling for the stage, an understanding of how to write for voice, and was endowed with a melodic gift. Nevertheless, he seemed to be an admirer of the gentle, the elegant, and the pretty, and was more successful in lyricism than in the realistic expression of drama. Therefore: as the work of a twenty-year-old boy, still a student, *Aleko* was beyond praise; but as an opera worthy of the Bolshoi Theater it left a great deal to be desired. This, at least, was the opinion of the critics of the day.

The chief weakness of the opera seems to me to lie in the triviality to which Pushkin's *The Gypsies* was reduced by Nemirovich-Danchenko's libretto, which ignored the psychological basis of the poem. It may be that Pushkin's treatment of the abstract idea of freedom was a little risky for the eighteen-nineties, edged too near subversion; but to omit it altogether, when it constituted the real nucleus of the story, was to make of the drama merely an episode of personal jealousy. However this may have been, Rachmaninoff himself found Danchenko's treatment very congenial to his own ideas, and hence his enthusiasm for the task and the facility with which he wrote the score.

In later years Feodor Chaliapin (in Rachmaninoff's opinion "several heads above any other who interpreted the role of Aleko") made himself up to resemble Pushkin—whether because of Pushkin's autobiographical reference in the text, or because Chaliapin thought it one way to improve the opera, I do not know; but the effect was merely ludicrous since Pushkin's fundamental idea was still missing, and the innovation, by turning Aleko into Pushkin, made of the poet the jealous murderer of his sweetheart and his rival.

That Rachmaninoff apparently perceived only the poem's external qualities—its color, its atmosphere, the possibilities it presented for translation into music, chorus, and dance—was natural. He could hardly guess Pushkin's reason for choosing to write about the Gypsies, that sole anarchic social group that is not to be invaded by our moral code, our ideas of freedom. Sergei was no Moussorgsky. He belonged to the group of Moscow musicians who (as I have said) "felt" rather than reasoned, pleasant fellows with no general culture and little general education. The Conservatory supplied them with an understanding of their professional field, but their academic education was, on the average, only that supplied by four years in Russian high schools.

It was in Tchaikovsky's compositions that these men found the ideal music they were looking for: simple and melodious, richly emotional. Not for them the new, the original, the extraordinary; what they liked was music expressing the familiar, commonplace emotions. And, accepting the Western European forms, they clothed these simple, primitive emotions in a sort of literary musical language.

But the success of *Aleko* with the examining board had immediately spurred Sergei to plan another opera. Modest Tchaikovsky, the composer's brother, sent him a scenario for an opera after Zhukovsky's *Undine*. The idea had probably originated with Peter Tchaikovsky, who was very much concerned over Sergei's future and who himself had once been attracted by Modest's scenario. The possibilities in *Undine* apparently interested Rachmaninoff too, for after consulting Arensky (who also had at one time been considering the scenario for a score of his own) Sergei wrote to Modest Tchaikovsky that he "personally liked everything" in Modest's plan and "would begin with pleasure to work on the opera." "There is, however," he continued in the same letter, "one factor that causes me misgivings—that even if I do compose it, the chances are that it will never be produced. A production would be too expensive for a provincial town; and it would not be produced at the St. Petersburg theaters because the subject can hardly please their director—as he has already confessed to me. So my work, and big work at that, would be wasted."

Sergei therefore suggested that Modest Tchaikovsky talk first to Ivan A. Vsevologsky, the director who had heard *Aleko*. But five months later he wrote again to Modest asking him not to work further on the libretto since he himself had not come to any decision. "I am still very uncertain about what I am going to do; besides, I have to travel and therefore could not devote much time to the work."

With this letter of October 14, 1893, ends all the available information about the projected opera *Undine*. It was not until years later that Rachmaninoff turned again to the dramatic form. Meanwhile he was preoccupied not only with the problem of where and how he was going to live but also with the question of what particular branch of musical activity he would choose for his profession.

. V .

Prelude in C-sharp Minor

AFTER HIS GRADUATION from the Conservatory, Sergei for the first time in his life was on his own. The second-rate Hotel America at which he lived was situated on one of the wide and noisy boulevards and was used by traveling salesmen, students, and persons of no clearly defined occupation. There, in the spring of 1893, he composed his Prelude in C-sharp minor—a piece that was to equal Paderewski's *Menuet* in its wide popularity and was to become so intimately associated with Rachmaninoff's person that he was sometimes called "Mr. C-sharp Minor."

When I asked Sergei Rachmaninoff what inspired him to write his Prelude, he said simply: "Forty rubles. My publisher offered me two hundred rubles for five short pieces for piano, and that Prelude was one of them."

Innumerable are the stories that have been concocted about this Prelude—about the dramatic background that "inspired" it and the circumstances in which it was written. Some, for instance, connect the piece with the composer's vision of Napoleon's invasion of Russia: Kremlin bells, the French army, the cruel fate that befell Russians condemned by the Tsars to walk all the way to Siberia.

Nothing of the kind was in the composer's mind. Indeed, as Rachmaninoff himself repeatedly stated, the composition has no "program" as its background and should not be twisted into a tone poem or a piece of musical impressionism. On the contrary, the Prelude was conceived as absolute or pure music. Here are the composer's comments on it years later[1] and his advice on how to play and interpret it.

Absolute music (to which this Prelude belongs) can suggest or induce a mood in the listener; but its primal function is to give intellectual pleasure by the beauty and variety of its form. This was the end sought by Bach in his wonderful series of Preludes, which are a source of unending delight to the educated musical listener. Their salient beauty will be missed if we try to discover in them the mood of the composer. If we must have the psychology of the Prelude, let it be understood that its function is not to express a mood, but to induce it.

The prelude, as I conceive it, is a form of absolute music, intended, as its name signifies, to be played before a more important piece of music or as an introduction to some function. The form has grown to be used for music of an independent value. But so long as the name is given to a piece of music, the work should in some measure carry out the significance of the title.

For example, in the work under consideration, I endeavor to arrest attention by the opening theme. These three notes, proclaimed in unison in treble and bass, should boom solemnly and portentously. After this introduction the three-note melody runs through the first section of twelve bars, and counter to it, in both clefs, runs a contrasted melody in chords. Here we have two distinct melodic movements working against each other, and the effect is to arrest the attention of the listener.

The nature of the principal theme is that of a massive foundation against which the melody in the chords furnishes a contrast

[1] *Delineator*, v. 75. February, 1910.

to lighten up the gloom. If worked out too long the effect would be one of monotony, so a middle movement intervenes quickly. The change of mood is abrupt, and for twenty-nine bars the music sweeps along like a rising storm, gaining in intensity as the melody mounts upward. The movement is carried out in single notes instead of chords, and at the climax the original movement re-enters with everything doubled both in right and left hands. After this outburst has spent itself, the music grows gradually more quiet and a coda of seven bars brings the work to a close.

The listener has been aroused, stimulated, and then quieted. His mind is alert and open for what follows. The Prelude has filled its office.

If the pupil must have his mental status fixed, let him keep in mind what I have just said. Then let him study carefully the anatomy of the composition. The divisions of the work are simple.

The first technical caution is to strike just the right pace in the proclamation of the opening theme and then maintain that pace strictly throughout the first section. One common mistake is to play this opening theme too loudly. I admit there is great temptation to pound it; but the climax does not come at the outset. I have marked these three notes ff. You will find several fff marks later on. So save your strength. The chords of the intervening melody should be pressed out lightly and caressingly, and the player should be careful to make the top note in the right-hand chords sing. The mistakes to avoid are the tendency to strike these chords unevenly or with an arpeggio effect and to lose the evenness of pace. The difficulty in the first section will be to maintain this evenness through the third and fourth beat in each bar.

The three notes of the first theme are not to be struck too loudly but with sufficient force to make the tones carry through.

In the agitated section the melody in the right is carried by the first note in each group. But for this I might have marked the passage *allegro con fuoco*. The player must accommodate his pace to his technical ability. He must not hurry the passage beyond his capacity to make the melody stand out.

The repetition of the first movement in doubled octaves calls for all the force the player is capable of. The pupil must be cautioned against mistaking fury for breadth and majesty. It will be safer to take this passage even a trifle more slowly than at the opening, and above all have regard for the evenness of the decrescendo. I begin to let this effect become apparent after the sixth bar of this movement.

Notice particularly that the melody in the coda is carried by the middle notes of the chords in both the right and left hands. These notes must be accentuated slightly. Beware of the temptation to arpeggiate the final chords.

As for any dramatic episode which "inspired" Sergei to compose this Prelude, as I have said, there was none. The five hundred rubles that Gutheil paid him for his opera and two other opuses had long ago been spent, so when Gutheil offered another two hundred rubles for five short pieces for the piano, Sergei wrote them—at forty rubles each, the equivalent of twenty dollars. He did not even bother to have any of them copyrighted in his own name. Later, when he became a world-famous pianist, he could not decide whether this oversight had or had not worked to his disadvantage. On going to England in 1908 he learned that all the pianists there were playing his Prelude; so were American pianists.

"Under the circumstances," he speculated, "I should be thankful, I suppose, that I wrote the composition. But I am undecided whether my oversight in neglecting to secure international copyright for it was altogether fortunate for me. Had I copyrighted it, I might have had wealth as well as fame from it. And again, I might have achieved neither. For when I learned of the wide success of this little work I wrote a series of ten preludes, my Opus 23, and took the precaution to have them copyrighted by a German publisher. I think them far better music than my first preludes, but the public has shown no disposition to share my belief. I cannot tell whether my judgment is at fault or whether the existence of the copyright has acted as a blight on their popularity. Consequently it will always be an open question with me whether intrinsic merit or absence of copyright was responsible for the success of my earlier work."

Though in Russia he eventually lived down this piece as a composition that belonged to his youth, outside of his native country no Rachmaninoff recital was considered complete unless he played it. And when, tiring of it, he began to alter its original version, the critics in England remarked that Rachmaninoff did not know how to play his own piece!

Sergei Rachmaninoff played the Prelude in C-sharp minor for the first time in public at a concert in Moscow on September 26, 1892. "Fifty years ago last September I made my debut as a concert pianist," Rachmaninoff said to me as he was reminiscing over the long span of his musical life. "It was at a concert in Moscow. At the Electric Exposition." He nodded, smiling. "Yes, there was such a thing. I played the first movement of Rubinstein's D minor concerto with the orchestra under the direction of Hlaváč."[2]

Though he took part as a pianist in many student concerts at the Conservatory, played several of his piano compositions during the season of 1891-92 in Vostryakov's Hall, and performed his First Piano Concerto on March 17, 1892, with Safonoff accompanying, it was this concert at the Exposition that he considered as officially dating the beginning of his career as a concert pianist.

When he spoke to me, he had already for some time been referred to by musicians as "The General," and in the great army of pianists all over the world there was only one "General." (In later life his fee per concert ranged from three

[2] Vojtĕch Hlaváč, Czech conductor.

thousand dollars up, in contrast to the fifty rubles he had received for playing at the Exposition.) But he did not become famous overnight. "Not the way Chaliapin did," he said, and holding up his long forefinger he repeated twice: "In one season! In one season!"

The Moscow music critics wrote that Mr. Rachmaninoff (some people did not yet know how to pronounce his name and made the mistake of accenting the third instead of the second syllable) performed the concerto well, technically and musically, and that "the three solo pieces: Chopin's *Berceuse*, the Waltz from Gounod's *Faust* in Liszt's arrangement, and his own C-sharp minor Prelude gave as much pleasure."

Sergei was invited to give two concerts in the provinces. But at the time he did not think of his piano-playing as a money-making proposition or even as a means of support. In a letter to his friend Slonov he spoke primarily of his compositions, for he thought of himself only as a composer.

". . . My arrival in Kharkov[3] depends on Orel, where I was invited to play. The sooner I give my concert in Orel, the sooner I will come to Kharkov. . . . Generally speaking, I have the blues. . . . Since you left only one thing has pleased me. Here is what happened. One of the Petersburg reporters came for an interview to see Tchaikovsky after the performance of his *Yolanthe*. Tchaikovsky told him that the time had come for him to stop composing and clear the road for younger men. 'Are there any?' asked the reporter. 'Yes,' said Tchaikovsky, and named Glazunov in Petersburg and Arensky and me in Moscow.

"This really pleased me. Thanks to the old man for not forgetting me! When I read this, I went to the piano and composed the fifth piece. Thus I am going to publish all the

[3] Slonov was in Kharkov.

five pieces together." And when six days later Sergei gave his recital in Kharkov, he played his Opus 3—Élégie, Prelude, Mélodie, Polichinelle, and Serenade.

However, the main reason that his first concerts did not lead to the great pianistic career that he later achieved lay in the fact that though his pianism was good, there was nothing outstanding about it. And Sergei admitted in his letters written during the summer previous to his concertizing that he did not practice very much because he was too preoccupied with his compositions. Among the important works of this time were *The Rock*, after Lermontov's poem, and *Fantasia* in four parts for two pianos, which he dedicated to Tchaikovsky.

The Rock was Sergei's first experiment in program music. Because Lermontov's poem by the same name has been used as the epigraph on the title page of Rachmaninoff's composition, and because it also appears on Chekhov's short story "On the Way," it has been suggested that Sergei was inspired by Chekhov's story. But, though somber in its mood, Sergei's composition hardly reflects Chekhov's story. This tale deals with a middle-aged man meeting a young woman in a deserted spot on the road; the spark of mutual attraction which might have changed the course of both their lives dies away because of their departure in different directions.

Rachmaninoff's rather naïve composition is much closer to a short poem of Lermontov's which is far from posing any psychological problems. It speaks of a mountain on which a little cloud rested through the night and tells how it floated away at dawn, leaving its mark on the mountain's gullies; the mountain remained alone in the desert, "thinking its deep thoughts and weeping."

As for *Fantasia* for two pianos, it was again program music written after four poems by Lermontov, Byron, Tyoutchev, and Khomiakov. This work, which has become very popular among duo pianists, is particularly well known for the last movement, which is a sort of carillon, a brilliant display of the sound of bells so nostalgic and dear to the Russian ear.

But the sudden death of Tchaikovsky in November of 1893 dashed all Rachmaninoff's hopes, for Tchaikovsky, besides advising Sergei and patronizing his work, had promised him to have *Aleko* performed on the same night with his own *Yolanthe* and to play his *Rock* during the European tour Tchaikovsky was to make the following season.

Just as Tchaikovsky after Nicolas Rubinstein's death composed a trio for piano, violin, and cello and dedicated it "To the Memory of a Great Artist," so did Rachmaninoff compose a trio in memory of the man he most admired.

This composition, however, was not Rachmaninoff's first experiment in this form of chamber music. As early as 1892, while still a student at the Conservatory, Sergei composed a *Trio Élégiaque* in G minor which though never published was performed at a concert the following year. The composition was very Tchaikovskian—but for the fact that during its fifteen minutes its meter changed twelve times!

This time Rachmaninoff wrote his second *Trio Élégiaque,* which, except for the title, had nothing in common with the first composition. It is somber and tragic in character. The second part resembles Tchaikovsky's Trio Opus 50, being written in a form of variations, and it is hardly coincidental that the theme of the variations resembles that of the Tchaikovsky trio.

Despite the amount Rachmaninoff composed during the summers, which he usually spent out of the city on the country estates of either his friends or his relatives, the Satins, he was constantly worried by the lack of money.

"During the coming winter," he wrote to Slonov (September 3, 1894), "I shall have to nourish myself by calmly sucking my thumb. I am not joking. I have nothing even to live on, let alone any money for a real spree. To scheme, to count every kopeck . . . I just cannot live that way. Sometimes I absolutely have to forget for the moment everything that disturbs and worries me. For a moment I need to forget everything that hurts me. Of course, to scheme, to plan and count kopecks, at such a time just does not suit me. Therefore I will have to find a way of adjusting myself, of cutting down expenses. But what am I talking about? I will not have enough for an average man's living. Even that is too expensive for me. To cut down my expenses is virtually impossible. I shall have to concoct something extraordinary."

The "something extraordinary" that Sergei was to resort to in desperation was to take a position as piano teacher in the Maryinsky school for girls upon his return to Moscow. Sergei Rachmaninoff, who had proved his mettle in all the other branches of music, completely failed as a teacher. Those who excuse him because, as a perfectionist, he could not stand listening to the efforts of beginners give little credit to his intelligence. It is true that his stony expression as he listened "scared his pupils and killed in them every desire to play for him," but this bespoke less an incapacity to teach than a total lack of interest. He would have been stimulated if his position had been that of piano teacher at a school such as the Moscow Conservatory, where the pupils were talented; but the Conservatory doors were closed to him partly because of the old Safonoff-Zverev feud and partly because Safonoff, ever since Sergei had preferred Siloti's piano class to his, had not considered him a pianist. It was unfortunate that Sergei's uncompromising adherence to the principles of Zverev alienated him from Safonoff, who was, after all, a remarkable musician with a wide knowledge and great imagination and who eventually became Russia's most eminent conductor. As it was, Sergei was forced to teach boys and girls who, though they paid him well, were taking piano lessons only as a passing fancy.

Eventually, however, the school's directors realized what the situation was, and Sergei was made a sort of musical inspector in the Ekaterin and Elisabeth Institutes, where his duties consisted only in supervising the examinations and the final concerts.

In the same year he tried his luck as a concert pianist. With an Italian violinist named Teresina de Tua, he was to make a tour of central Russia arranged on a professional basis by a manager. However, halfway through the tour Rachmaninoff found some excuse to blame the manager for a breach of contract, packed his bag, and, without a word to anyone, returned to Moscow to work on his first symphony.

For the last two summers he had toyed with a new idea for the symphony. Carried away by Byron's *Don Juan*, he thought of writing a symphonic poem with "Two Episodes" à la Liszt, but later gave up the whole plan and composed instead a Gypsy capriccio, probably influenced by his friend Ladygensky, whose sister was a famous Gypsy singer. It has been supposed that the initials "A.L." on the dedication page of the First Symphony are those of Madame Ladygensky, but when he came to compose the symphony it was based not on Gypsy music but on old church motets.

In Moscow, during these turbulent years of financial and later mental insecurity, Rachmaninoff was very close to Yury Sakhnovsky, the same friend who had taken care of him when he was ill. Except for Taneyev, most of Sergei's friends were rather prosaic trade-musicians, and Sakhnovsky, like Taneyev, was an exceptional man, though in another way. Eight years older than Sergei, and wealthy, he would have been considered a very handsome young man had it not been for his extreme stoutness—he weighed over two hundred and sixty pounds. Well educated, brilliant and witty, he spoke four languages besides his own and was intelligently devoted to music. But he never made anything of his gifts; he felt no desire to achieve distinction in any field and was content to lead the life of a *bon vivant*. Indeed, even if he had wished to put his talents to good use, they would have been hopelessly swamped in his uninterrupted stream of orgies. He was lewd in the absolute sense of the word. One of the many poems he wrote—though masterly in its technical aspects—contained not a single printable word. He possessed a rich and rather exceptional vocabulary, and was quoted with gusto at stag parties.

But it would be unfair to consider this side of Sakhnovsky exclusively. He was a man of the world, he had traveled a great deal, he was well informed about everything that was going on, particularly in artistic circles, he owned a huge library of books and music, and he had an open mind. Though a conservative, he had tastes that were really advanced by comparison with those of his Moscow colleagues. He was a great admirer of Rachmaninoff's talent and, being older and better informed, had a definite influence on him. It was he who introduced Sergei to the "forbidden" music of Wagner and who also developed in him an understanding of the new Russian music of "The Mighty Five." It was through Sakhnovsky's good offices that Mitrofan P. Belayeff learned about Rachmaninoff's First Symphony and asked for the first performance of it at his symphonic "Concerts of Russian Music" in St. Petersburg.

.VI.

First Symphony and Marriage

SERGEI RACHMANINOFF considered that the failure of his symphony to please the St. Petersburg audience at its first performance, on March 15, 1897, was the greatest calamity that had ever befallen him. Sitting on an iron fire escape which led into the gallery of the Hall of the Nobility,[1] Sergei listened to his symphony.

"It was the most agonizing hour of my life," he said later as he remembered how he had stuck his fingers into his ears to keep from hearing his own music, "the discords of which absolutely tortured me." After the last chord sounded through the hall, he fled to the streets and rode aimlessly up and down the long boulevards of the capital.

The next day the press tore Rachmaninoff's composition to pieces, but Nicolay Findeisin, a critic with definite authority, suggested they should not be too hasty in judging Rachmaninoff's work and thus repeat the case of Tchaikovsky's Fifth, which was discovered and praised as "a new creation, magnificent and sublime," only after Arthur Nikisch performed it. Though Findeisin thought Sergei's symphony was not well

[1] The Carnegie Hall of St. Petersburg.

61

constructed and very uneven, still he found in it pages of a daring new trend certainly worthy of merit.

Rimsky-Korsakov, in talking to Rachmaninoff about the performance, said: "Forgive me, but I do not find this music at all agreeable," while César Cui, the venerable critic, old archenemy of the Muscovites, a man whose sarcastic articles had harmed more than one composer, (incidentally, including himself) spoke his mind with characteristic venom.

"If there was a conservatory in Hell," Cui wrote in the St. Petersburg *News*, "and if one of the talented pupils there was commissioned to compose a symphony based on the story of the 'Seven Egyptian Executions,' and if he composed one resembling that of Rachmaninoff's, he would have brilliantly accomplished his task and would have brought ecstasy to the inhabitants of Hell." Cui said further that he thought Rachmaninoff's symphony lacked themes and that, with its diseased and perverted harmonizations, it created a morbid atmosphere. He added, a little more generously, that while Rachmaninoff shunned banality, he most probably felt deeply and strongly and tried to express his emotions in new musical forms. Cui laughed at the very idea upon which the symphony was based. According to Sophia A. Satin, the manuscript carried a Biblical quotation, the same as Tolstoy's *Anna Karenina*,[2] thus suggesting that the symphony was thought out under a literary influence.

Two months later Sergei gave a full account of his feelings in a letter to his old friend Alexander V. Zataevich:[3]

For a long time I have not been writing letters, my dear friend Alexander Victorovich, neither to you, nor to anyone

[2] "Vengeance is mine; I will repay, saith the Lord." Holy Bible, Romans 12, xix.

[3] Alexander V. Zataevich (1869-1936), composer-ethnographer.

else. The chief reason lies in my weakness, which keeps me lying down all the time. This is my yearly spring state. I lie on my back and even read only occasionally. Also I cannot compose. This is the way it usually goes until I go to the country, where I quickly recover and begin to work. I am dreaming about my departure. I did not thank you for your congratulations for my birthday. I was touched that you remembered. And I also did not tell you of my impression of the first performance of my symphony. I am going to do this now, though it is still difficult for me since I cannot comprehend it myself. One thing is true, that I am indifferent to my failure, that I am not discouraged by the abuse of the newspapers, but that I am deeply grieved and very upset by the fact that the symphony, which I loved and still do, displeased me from the first rehearsal. "Then," you would say, "it was badly orchestrated." "But I am sure," I shall reply, "that good music can be recognized even through a bad orchestration and besides I do not consider the orchestration so bad. Therefore there remain but two suppositions. Either I, like so many composers, am partial to my composition, or this composition was badly performed. And this was actually the case. I am astonished that such an extremely talented man as Glazunov could conduct so badly. I am not speaking of his technique in conducting (this is not to be expected of him); I am merely speaking of his musicianship. He does not feel anything when he conducts. It seems as though he does not understand anything. I remember when once at a dinner party Anton Rubinstein was asked how he liked the singer N, who sang in his Demon, Rubinstein, instead of answering, made a sign with his knife. I should do the same.

And so I assume (I do not insist, but assume) that the performance may have been the reason for the failure. If this symphony was known to the public, the conductor would have been blamed (I continue to assume), but if the composition is both unknown and badly performed, then the blame is bound to fall on the composer. This is the right point of view, particularly since this symphony is not a decadent work, as they now use the word, but on the contrary somewhat new. Therefore it should be played according to the precise indications of the composer. In this way the composer may perhaps be reconciled with the public and the public with the composition (because then the audience could understand the piece). Wouldn't this be the reason why the symphony disappointed some of my friends who went with me to St. Petersburg, while they spoke of the symphony differently when I played it to them? As you see, at this point I feel that it was all the fault of the performance. Tomorrow I may change my mind. Yet I am not going to disown my symphony and I will look at it again after it has taken a rest for a half year. I will correct it and perhaps even publish it; or perhaps I will lose my partiality of opinion. Then I shall tear it up. . . . [But Sergei did not tear up the score and instead arranged it for four hands.]

Sergei Rachmaninoff's First Symphony was actually far from startling. When fifty years later this symphony was played in Philadelphia, on March 20, 1948, it proved how much we have advanced in the realm of "modern" music rather than how "shocking" and modern Rachmaninoff's symphony was. The American version of it differed from the original because of one or two cuts and a certain amount of rescoring which was done by Eugene Ormandy, who conducted the work. Only a blind worshiper of Rachmaninoff would find this symphony unusual and worthy of the standard programs; and though it has some pleasant tunes, I can see how even fifty years ago it was bound to make a weak impression.

It was true that Alexander Glazunov was no great conductor and it was also true that Glazunov never did care for Rachmaninoff's compositions. Glazunov said more than once that Rachmaninoff's music was antipathetic to him, that "there is a lot of feeling in his music, but no sense whatsoever," and that he despised his music for its naked emotionalism, its Gypsyism. He even found it lacking in technique. When sometime in 1932 the two composers met again in Paris and Rachmaninoff presented him with the score of his Fourth Piano Concerto, Glazunov "forgot" it in a taxi and did not apparently regret it.

It has been generally accepted, though never wholeheartedly, that this unfortunate performance in St. Petersburg was the cause of such a mental depression that for years Rachmaninoff lost his creative ability. These years have been kept shrouded in mystery, and Rachmaninoff himself always avoided speaking of them. They remain as though they had never existed. (There is a similar gap in Scriabin's biography: there were years in his life that he also preferred never to mention, or was perhaps told not to mention.)

"When you are my age, you will realize that people know about you only what you tell them," Rachmaninoff said to me on the eve of his seventieth birthday. I often wondered whether Rachmaninoff really believed this naïve statement.

Rachmaninoff in his youth was very different from the portrait that has been painted of him. He was a young man with a very passionate nature, easily carried away, sentimental, spoiled by early success, flattery, and fame, and with none of the strength of will and equilibrium which he fully developed later. It was absurd to blame one failure (even if Rachmaninoff himself was perhaps sincerely convinced of it) for that depression which was to remain with him in one form or another for the rest of his life. The effect of the incident of the symphony was only the first major manifestation of the logical progress of the growth and development of his nature. These emotional upsets over the success or failure in his relationships were characteristic of him from his childhood to the day when, outwardly sure of himself, he lacked sufficient stamina and manhood to face disappointment. This uncertain balance was in line with his constant self-doubt. And he let himself be nursed into a further depth of depression by taking to that common cure—drink.

According to Sergei's own analysis of his state, something "snapped" in him that night at the concert hall in St. Petersburg. If anything snapped in him, it snapped because the years at Zverev's, the Gypsyism, and the continuation of a dissipated life in the company of such giants in alcoholism as Sakhnovsky, Slonov, and their friends told on the large-framed but frail and sensitive Rachmaninoff.

"Rachmaninoff is drinking," people said in Moscow. And men like Sakhnovsky, who were close to him, knew that the effect of the symphony was only an additional blow to the one he had already suffered, caused by an unhappy love affair. Rachmaninoff was then in his early twenties and it was his first love. Sakhnovsky knew her and knew that she sang Gypsy songs exceptionally well, and that there were difficulties on her side of the love affair. He even told Sabaneyeff her name but unfortunately Sabaneyeff has forgotten it. Since so little is known about this "first love," it is therefore impossible to evaluate how deeply his true emotions were involved.

Rachmaninoff returned to Moscow a changed man after the fatal performance of his symphony. He gave up his room in the Hotel America and went back to the Satins'. His depression had reached its lowest depths. He saw his future only as a piano teacher and not even as a member of the Conservatory and spent weeks bemoaning his fate. Then suddenly he received a call to test his ability in another branch of music.

Savva I. Mamontov, a railway magnate and a patron of the arts, had founded an opera house of his own and he offered Sergei the post of second conductor. Since Rachmaninoff's experience as a conductor consisted only of two performances of his *Aleko* in Kiev in November, 1894, E. D. Esposito, the principal conductor at the opera, suggested that he should start with Glinka's *A Life for the Tsar*, an opera well known to the cast and the orchestra.

Rachmaninoff felt that he could conduct, although he admitted he had but a hazy idea of the technique of conducting. At that time there were no classes in conducting at the Conservatory nor could Sergei have learned much from the conductors he heard. Therefore, armed only with his knowledge of the score (he knew the opera as well as anybody) and his solid musicianship, he plunged with complete confidence into one of the most difficult of operatic scores. But at the first stage rehearsal, as soon as the soloists and the chorus on the stage joined the orchestra, which he had kept well under control, everything went topsy-turvy. Esposito, an experienced conductor not too pleased with Rachmaninoff's appointment as his second, gloated with delight at Sergei's confusion, and even Mamontov's helpful hand with the cast and some occasional advice thrown to the conductor's desk did not save the situation.

As Sergei was given only one rehearsal, the scheduled performance of the opera had to be given over to Esposito, who turned up his nose and conducted a flawless performance of

67

A *Life for the Tsar* without a single rehearsal. Sergei almost collapsed again, for this new failure impressed him with an idea that he was not fit for this branch of music either.

He sat in the hall with his eyes glued to Esposito's baton. He learned that the chaos at his own rehearsal had resulted from his forgetting to give any cues to the singers, that he was much too preoccupied with his orchestra, trusting the chorus and the soloists to know more than just their own parts. In short, he learned enough from Esposito's performance to prove to Mamontov that he was worthy of his confidence in him. On October 12, 1897, Sergei Rachmaninoff for the first time officially appeared before the Moscow public at the conductor's desk. He conducted Saint-Saëns' *Samson and Dalila* and the press acknowledged him with approval in his new role, though, of course, they mentioned a few mishaps.

However, with every new performance Sergei gained more confidence and respect and probably would have kept his post had it not been for an unfortunate performance of Rimsky-Korsakov's *May Night*, which was severely criticized. Rachmaninoff was not given sufficient time to prepare the opera. The chorus was not ready for the performance and this music was new to the orchestra. Besides all the other complications resulting from moving the opera into a new house (the old building having burned down), the acoustics were so bad that even the expert singing of Chaliapin and N. I. Zabyela could not rescue the performance.

Sergei realized that Mamontov's enterprise required a conductor of greater experience who could put on a spectacle with a minimum of rehearsals since Mamontov wanted a very varied repertory. Sergei resigned. Besides his first tests in conducting, he had "the experience of his life," as he said himself, in meeting and working with Feodor Chaliapin, who was then the star at Mamontov's opera. But his deep depression left him only spasmodically. Then a sudden engagement for a few concerts relit a hope that had seemed to be dying.

He took a short trip to London in 1898, where he had been invited five years before when Siloti had played his Prelude in C-sharp minor there. He was presented to the English audience in all three capacities, as composer, pianist, and conductor. He conducted his *Rock* and promised to return to London with a concerto better than his first one, which he played there at his debut. But no sooner had he returned to Moscow than he again fell into the depression which was sapping his strength and torturing him into despair.

In the spring of 1898 he wrote to Zataevich: "I can easily answer your question as to what I have composed. Nothing at all. But I am going to. . . ." and later in October of the same year he wrote him: "I do not know whether you know that I am living in the country, where I intend to spend all winter so that I can have quiet and work. It is absolutely impossible for me to achieve either of these things in Moscow. Besides, my doctor advised, or should I say ordered, this country life. Not long ago I was ill and even went down to the Crimea to recuperate. Now I am here at Ivanovka [the Satin estate]. I have started to do a little work and my health is improving. I live alone though I have three close friends. All three are enormous St. Bernard dogs. I converse only with them and in their company I am not afraid to walk in the surrounding woods. Once a week I go to Moscow to see my relatives and friends, to show myself and incidentally to give a few piano lessons. I have not written a thing, but with God's help I hope I will. When I will compose something, I shall let you know."

Sergei was neither a Moussorgsky who was willing to be burned at the stake for his ideas, nor a Taneyev who found refuge in his own laboratory of sounds. He had no desire for any radical innovation in music, no lofty ideals about Russian National music. Unlike Moussorgsky, who blossomed in the company of his fellow-composers, Sergei did not seek a close contact with his contemporaries. Of all the Moscow musicians Alexander Scriabin was the only other young composer from whom a great deal was expected. But Sergei could find no comfort in friendship with this former classmate, who was floating in a world of his own imagination, for they had grown apart as they matured, and their characters were no longer those of their adolescence.

Rachmaninoff and Scriabin had first met at Zverev's, on one of the Sundays that Zverev used to reserve for poor but promising students. The two were classmates under Arensky, and they shared a tendency to shirk Taneyev's lessons. But their paths were even then diverging, owing to their different temperaments.

At the age of fourteen, Alexander Scriabin had already formed his conception of the place music should take in human life and the role his own music was to play; and his life's work was one continuous and logical progression toward realizing this conception. He never reached it, but the effort raised his creative work to a unique plane in no man's land. Though his early compositions echoed Schumann and Chopin he had his definite likes and dislikes in musical literature. One of the dislikes was Tchaikovsky.

For the Muscovites, Tchaikovsky was what Papa Haydn was for the Germans: he could do no wrong. Rachmaninoff idolized him from the day he first saw him at Zverev's. When Sergei started to write music, one of his first works was a piano arrangement of Tchaikovsky's "Manfred" Symphony, which Zverev showed the composer with great pride. Rachmaninoff studied Tchaikovsky's works and was so influenced by the older Russian master that some of his own compositions remind us of Tchaikovsky even more strongly than Scriabin's remind us of Chopin.

The very natures of Rachmaninoff and Scriabin had become diametrically opposed.

Rachmaninoff was an introvert, closed in upon himself and modest, while Scriabin was of an expansive nature, spoke freely of all his artistic plans and could not hide his feeling of superiority to those around him. He was proud and arrogant even in his relation to his former comrades. Rachmaninoff spoke little; Scriabin loved to talk. Rachmaninoff had no desire to compose anything extraordinary; Scriabin thought of nothing else. Rachmaninoff was sentimental and very friendly, while Scriabin was sensual and rather cold. Rachmaninoff gained his popularity through his simplicity; Scriabin's was a complicated nature which did not evoke sympathy at first meeting: he was all a pose, like a man walking on stilts. Rachmaninoff was not interested in philosophy and knew very little if anything of other arts and sciences, while Scriabin became a philosopher-musician right from the start.

However, Rachmaninoff recognized Scriabin as an important and original composer in spite of their dissimilar tastes, while Scriabin was indifferent toward Rachmaninoff because he considered his music only an imitation of Tchaikovsky's, which he hated. He listened to Rachmaninoff's music with difficulty and only when it was necessary. While Scriabin was all *Vers la Flamme*,[4] all *Exstase*,[5] Rachmaninoff brooded in his gloom with only an ultimate vision of *Dies Irae*.[6]

Sergei's friends were worried and thought that Lev Tolstoy

[4] Scriabin, Opus 72.
[5] Scriabin, Opus 42.
[6] Medieval choral often used by S. Rachmaninoff in his late compositions.

could help him if he talked to him. Princess Alexandra Lievin, a close friend of the Satins' and Sergei's, wrote a letter to Tolstoy. "The young man will go to ruin. He has lost faith in his powers. Try to help him."

When Sergei arrived to see Tolstoy, he was playing chess with the pianist Goldenweiser, Sergei's old colleague from the Conservatory, who had become Tolstoy's disciple.

"I worshiped him then," Rachmaninoff remarked as he often told the story.[7] "My knees were trembling when I entered the room and Tolstoy made me sit next to him and stroked my knees. Then Tolstoy said, 'Do you imagine that everything in my life goes smoothly? Do you suppose I have no troubles, never hesitate and lose confidence in myself? Do you really think faith is always equally strong? All of us have difficult moments; but that is life. Hold up your head and keep on your appointed path. You must work. Work every day.' "

This sermon apparently had no effect on Sergei, for he referred to Tolstoy's words as "such and similar stereotyped phrases." However, he returned to Tolstoy, this time with Feodor Chaliapin.

"Chaliapin sang, as Tolstoy wrote," Rachmaninoff said. The two performed Rachmaninoff's song *Fate*, based on the opening theme of Beethoven's Fifth Symphony. All in the room seemed to have been delighted when suddenly everybody became silent. Tolstoy, who was sitting by himself in a far corner, looked annoyed.

"I have to speak to you," said Tolstoy to Rachmaninoff later. "I have to tell you how I dislike it all," and he began to

[7] Swan, A. J., and K. Swan: "Rachmaninoff: Personal Reminiscences." *Musical Quarterly*, v. 30, January-April, 1944.

deliver one of his customary abuses of Beethoven, Pushkin, and Lermontov.

"It was awful," Rachmaninoff continued the story. "At my back stood Sophia Andreyevna (Tolstoy's wife); she touched my shoulder and whispered, 'Never mind, never mind. Please do not contradict him. He must not get excited. It is very bad for him.'"

Later Tolstoy apologized: "I am an old man. I did not want to hurt you."

"How could I be hurt on my account if I was not hurt on Beethoven's?" Rachmaninoff said that he replied.

Sergei was then only twenty-six, but curiously enough he proudly repeated his saucy remark on more than one occasion even after he had reached the age of Tolstoy. Tolstoy's wife invited him every year to come to visit him, but Sergei never went.

"And just think, the first time I went to him, I went to him as to a god."

And what is even more astounding is that Rachmaninoff did not stop his story there, but went on describing how he had related the whole episode to Anton Chekhov, and how admirably Chekhov had explained Tolstoy's behavior.

"If it happened to be a day when Tolstoy was suffering from pains in his stomach," said Chekhov, according to Rachmaninoff, "he must have been unable to work and therefore have become very nervous. On such off days he is apt to say stupid things. But one should not pay any attention. It is not important!"

"What a man Chekhov was!" exclaimed Rachmaninoff.

There was nothing extraordinary in Chekhov's reaction, but Rachmaninoff's attitude suggests that even after half a century of experience in human intercourse Rachmaninoff still

73

did not take an objective point of view of his encounter with
Tolstoy, and apparently had never realized that when he went
to Tolstoy, he was only a talented youth with a few charming
pieces to his credit, a haughty member of the declassified
gentry without wealth or title, an egocentric nervous wreck
who expected from life nothing but a pat on the head each
time his Muse moved him to work. How naïve he was to think
that his song *Fate*, based on Beethoven's Fifth—"tak, tak, tak,
tak—fate knocking at the door," with this adolescent meta-
phor—should impress Tolstoy.

Tolstoy was speaking to him as to a grown-up man. What
Sergei needed was a nurse. In his childhood he missed his
father. Later he subconsciously found one in Zverev, only to
be rudely awakened to reality, and again in Tchaikovsky, both
of them as will-less as he himself; and now, with no firm
ground under his feet, he gave himself up to complete destruction waiting for a man to save him.

Dr. Nicolay Dahl was the man who pulled him out of his
crisis, but Dr. Dahl never really cured him. The depression,
the trauma which he tried to escape in dissipation, gnawed at
him his whole life, and his creative ability as well as his personal life followed a pattern as though it were written in his
palm.

It was Alexander Siloti who once again came to the rescue
of his cousin. He agreed to support Sergei for two years so
that he could devote himself entirely to composing, while his
cousins, the Satin sisters, finally persuaded him to see Dr.
Dahl.

Dr. Dahl was a psychiatrist who specialized in curing alcoholism through hypnosis. Dr. Dahl was also a great lover of
music. He played the violin very well and arranged evenings
of chamber music at his house. Men of different professions
(but mostly Dahl's colleagues in medicine, who played string

instruments for their recreation) played quartets and occasionally were joined by a student from the Conservatory. The students were eager to be called by Dr. Dahl "in emergency," for he paid them three rubles an evening—a handsome sum for a poor student—and Dahl enjoyed their company, for in this way he kept in close touch with the young musicians in Moscow.

From January till April, 1900, Rachmaninoff visited Dr. Dahl daily and, according to his own account, he sat in the armchair half-asleep while Dahl repeated the suggestive formula: "You will begin to write your concerto. . . . You will work with great facility. . . . The concerto will be of an excellent quality. . . ."

Whether Dr. Dahl made any other suggestions besides generally building up Rachmaninoff's belief in himself and bolstering his morale is not known, for the events of these years of the composer's life were later carefully screened, as I said before, by Rachmaninoff and those close to him, and the truth has never been completely revealed.

However, Dahl's treatments seem to have been miraculously beneficial to the composer's creative ability, and he also guided him into a new and happier path in his life. Here are three letters[8] written by Rachmaninoff to his classmate Nikita Morozov, which show that Sergei took a trip to Italy shortly after his séances with Dr. Dahl, finally putting an end to the turbulent years of his youth.

Varazze, Italy
June, 1900

I arrived here on the 11th. If I did not sit down at once to answer you, it was only because our house is in complete disorder.

[8] S. V. *Rachmaninoff*, Musgiz., Moscow, 1947.

Today at least I know which is my room and I got some paper and ink, thank God for that. All the time someone runs to and fro, moving and rearranging the furniture, cleaning and filling the rooms with dust—and the heat is such . . . Just a misery! . . . Right now my room is closed. I am not used to such disorder! . . . I have two things to tell you. First of all that I regret that I came here and did not go with you. [Morozov was also traveling abroad.] And then that I will not be able to go to Paris, because we[9] have spent more money on our trip here than we expected. I have the old depression again. Perhaps you could come here? But I doubt this because you do not like to change your plans once you have made them. Well, then, good-by until we meet again. Here is my address in case you want it: Italie, Varazze. Provincia di Genova. Maison Lunelli. Monsieur Sergei Rachmaninoff.

The unusual name "Maison Lunelli" was derived from the name of its original builder and owner, the engineer Vittorio Lunelli, a major in the army. "Maison Lunelli" (which still stands in a picturesque section by the sea) was often occupied by visiting painters and writers.

A week later Rachmaninoff wrote again to Morozov:

I was very happy to receive your letter, my dear friend Nikita Semenovich, and I am not in the least hurt by your consolations, as you say. On the contrary, I am very grateful to you for them. They always bolster me up. I have spent another ten days here since I wrote you my first letter and I still continue to regret that I did not go with you. The "house-regime" that we have here is not for me, not for my habits. I certainly

___
[9] It is not clear who was in Italy with him; there is no reference to this trip in any other source but these letters.

made a mistake, though I have a separate room. There is such a noise as one could find only in this house. The "General Kheraskov"[10] has not yet arrived. He got stuck in Paris, where he is extremely busy, it seems, with the feminine question. In the well-informed circles they say that it is doubtful that the "General" will solve this problem very soon, first of all because of its complexity and then because it happens to be in Paris, where one is preoccupied with this question more than anywhere else. He sends occasional telegrams in which he speaks of his arrival here somehow very vaguely. With his arrival I will have more fun, of course. . . . I have decided not to make the trip to see you now. I want to continue to work regularly. But I beg you to write me, if only occasionally, and particularly from Paris, where, I guess, you are going very soon. Also send me your address, just in case. Perhaps I will join you there, particularly since "Kheraskov" is there. Thanks for the postcard you sent me. Looking at the view, I can definitely say that it is far more beautiful where you are than where we are.

And almost a month later he wrote him from Milan.

July 18, 1900

Tomorrow I am going to Russia and nowhere else. My life here bored me to distraction and it is impossible to work even if only because of the terrible heat. I am writing you this just to let you know the address where I will spend the rest of the summer and where I will be waiting for your letter with the description of the Exhibition. I am delighted to depart from here, and I have a great desire to work hard upon my arrival home.

[10] "Apparently he means Y. S. Sakhnovsky, with whom Rachmaninoff was very close at the time."—E. Bortnikova, the editor of the letters.

In these letters one finds the last reference to his close friend Sakhnovsky. Sakhnovsky remained his admirer, but Rachmaninoff ceased to be his boon companion. Under Dahl's influence Rachmaninoff stopped drinking and for the rest of his life scarcely ever touched alcohol. During the years of 1907-1912 Yury Sakhnovsky, as a critic on the *Russkoe Slovo*, a Moscow daily, wrote favorable articles on Rachmaninoff and unfavorable ones on Scriabin, whom he did not like. Yet when in 1929 Rachmaninoff was told of Sakhnovsky's death, he showed no emotion.

On his return to Russia, Sergei wrote the last two movements of his future Second Piano Concerto. Incidentally, Sabaneyeff, who had known both Rachmaninoff and Morozov, told me that the second theme in the last movement came from Nikita Morozov. Sergei heard this melody which Morozov composed, and remarked: "Oh, that is a melody I should have composed." Morozov, who worshiped his friend, said calmly: "Well, why don't you take it?"

On December 2, 1900, at a benefit performance organized by the committee for the alleviation of the suffering of prisoners and given at the Moscow "Nobility Hall" (Princess Lieven and Sergei's aunt Madame Satin were members of the committee), Sergei played the last two movements of his concerto with Siloti conducting the orchestra. Encouraged by this first success since his unfortunate symphony, Sergei completed the concerto by adding the first movement, and played the concerto in its entirety the following year on October 27, 1901, at the Moscow Philharmonic concert. This was the first performance of one of the most popular compositions in piano literature.

But five days before its first performance Sergei was brooding over its qualities.

"You are right!" he wrote to Morozov. "I have just been playing the first movement of my concerto and only now it becomes clear to me that the transition from the first theme to the second is not any good, that as it stands now, the first theme is not the first theme but an introduction, and that no fool will believe when I begin to play the second theme that that is the beginning of the concerto. I feel that the whole first movement is spoiled and from this minute on it is repulsive to me. I am simply in despair. And why did you start with this analysis of yours five days before the performance of the concerto ! ! !"

Even without Rachmaninoff's comments any musician can see that his concerto was not a concerto written in strict sonata form. Nor did Rachmaninoff follow the modernists, but rather went back to the old Lisztian conception of a bravura piece with all the material for virtuoso display. Rachmaninoff's concerto, though excellently put together, is a series of romantic songs. Its popularity for almost fifty years seems to show that, though we negate romanticism and everything old-fashioned, we really are easily seduced by it.

On March 28, 1902, the concerto was played in St. Petersburg by Siloti with Arthur Nikisch conducting. It had a tremendous success and was repeated by the same artists in Leipzig at the Gewandhaus. At the same time Sergei composed one opus after another, including his cello sonata, probably his best work next to the concerto. His works gained in popularity, and the finest Russian artists chose his compositions for their repertory.

Ever since Sergei had left Zverev's *pensionnat* at the age of sixteen, the Satins' home had been his own. There, against a background of his success and failure, a friendship with his two girl cousins blossomed. No one offered him so much care and understanding or stood by him so staunchly in his darkest hours of depression. Now he decided to tie this friendship of thirteen years by an even closer bond.

On April 29, 1902, Sergei took the final step toward a new life. He married his first cousin Nataly Satin, who had been graduated as a pianist from the Moscow Conservatory. The announcement of his engagement had the effect of a bombshell in Moscow. There were all kinds of difficulties to overcome, particularly those which were created by the church. Rachmaninoff was not a churchgoer; and since there was no record of his confession, no priest was willing to marry him. Sergei stubbornly refused to go to confession. It looked almost hopeless. But fortunately one of Sergei's aunts (the mother of Anna E. Troubnikova) took matters into her own hands. As she was on good terms with Father Amphiteatrov,[11] the priest at the Archangelsky Cathedral, she promised to arrange everything if only Sergei would call on the priest.

"Against his will and only out of respect for his aunt, Sergei went to see Father Amphiteatrov. He returned very happy. 'If I had known what kind of a man he was, I would have gone without hesitation,' Sergei said in the family circle."[12]

However, there was one more barrier to be overcome. Since he was marrying his first cousin, he had to have the permission of the Tsar. This was usually gotten around by timing the sending of the petition and the ritual of the marriage at the same moment. The Rachmaninoffs were married on April 29, 1902, at one of the army chapels in the suburb of Moscow, with Siloti and Anatoly Brandoukov, the cellist, as their best men.

[11] The father of Alexander V. Amphiteatrov (1861-1923), Russian author and journalist, Russkie Vedomosty and Novoe Vremya.
[12] Anna Troubnikova in Ogonek, Soviet Magazine, 1946.

. VII .

The Bolshoi Theater in Moscow

For ten years, from 1894 to 1904, it had been very dull at the Bolshoi Theater in Moscow. It was true that its orchestra, ballet, and chorus were as good as those at the Maryinsky Theater in St. Petersburg, which meant that the ballet and the chorus were technically the best in the world. Yet there was no life in their performances. For a whole decade the critics had been pointing to the state of stagnation at the Bolshoi, to the necessity of "cleaning house" and calling for new and younger talent, but the directors were very slow about it. When Vladimir A. Telyakovsky, a retired cavalry colonel, became the director of the Imperial Theaters in 1904, he found going through their daily routines the same artists and directors whose names he had heard in his childhood when he was studying piano.

For a long time the Muscovites had regarded the members of the theater as just another branch of the civil service working in a bureaucratic institution, and they judged them not by their artistic merits but by whether or not they took bribes.

The same old Italian conductor, Ippolyt K. Altany, still sat at his conducting desk on a little elevated platform screened on three sides by old clothes in the form of a curtain, for he suffered from agoraphobia. Six years had passed since he had drilled the orchestra and the chorus into a precision unknown before in the theater, but that is as far as he could go. He was a good musician, an excellent worker, but not an inspired or inspiring performer. Yet there was nothing for which one could legitimately reproach him. This small man with the gait of a hunchback and little myopic eyes had his preferences in choosing artists, but he took no bribes and remained poor all his life. His second, the stage director, A. P. Barzal, on the contrary loved to have the artists treat him at the near-by tavern Alpenrose. He sometimes borrowed twenty-five rubles from the artists, though perhaps he did pay them back; he also was in need all his life. But the concertmeister, Herr Klamrot, who played first violin for fifty years, had an impeccable record. He used to come first and leave last every day during the half century of his services and when he played his solo part for the last time in *Traviata*, the whole house rose in tribute to the old man. He packed his instrument after the performance and went back to Germany.

Serge Koussevitzky had played the double bass and Eugene Plotnikoff the cello in the orchestra since 1892; then in 1889 Chaliapin, the iron-handed prima donna, joined the cast and the theater was never the same. Up till then Chaliapin was with Mamontov's private opera, but Mamontov had been arrested and put into prison "for illegal transfer of his capital from one Mamontov enterprise to another," whatever that meant. His opera house was going to pieces and Chaliapin accepted the new offer of ten thousand rubles a year from the directors of Bolshoi.

"We cannot pay so much to a basso," Telyakovsky was admonished from St. Petersburg. "We are not paying a basso, we are paying Chaliapin," replied Telyakovsky. And Chaliapin knew it.

The great Russian singer was already famous for his quarrels with practically all the conductors (except Nápravník in St. Petersburg and Rachmaninoff in Moscow), stage directors, artists, and even stagehands. More than once he refused for one reason or another to get dressed and go out on the stage, or would at other times undress and refuse to continue the performance.

Once during the performance of Dargomyzhski's *Russalka* he had a fight with the chorus conductor, Ulrych Havránek, took a cab, and went home after the first intermission. He was brought back with a great deal of difficulty. Usually after such quarrels Chaliapin insisted on apologizing and making up with the person with whom he had quarreled. But his friends had to keep him away from these good intentions because during the peaceful conversation when everything seemed to have been settled and forgotten, Chaliapin would bring up the subject of the quarrel all over again and pour out still more abuse. However, Chaliapin's prestige was so high that his influence in the theater was of paramount importance.

At this time the directors of the Imperial Theaters were planning a jubilee performance of Glinka's opera *A Life for the Tsar* for the hundredth anniversary of the date of Glinka's birth, and backstage intrigues and the polemics in the daily press revolved around the choice of the conductor. From St. Petersburg those with strong influence insisted that Mili Balakirev, an expert on Glinka's operas, should be called for the jubilee performance; while in Moscow musicians did not see any necessity for making changes and spoke of Altany's priority as an old conductor who through years of successful performances certainly had earned the confidence of the public.

Chaliapin favored inviting Rachmaninoff and his voice was heeded as well as his skirmishes were remembered. Rachmaninoff was offered the post of conductor at the Bolshoi and the leading of the Glinka performance.

Rachmaninoff himself had taken no part in this campaign. Yet he signed the contract when it was offered, even though he regretted the act months before taking up his duties.

After spending their honeymoon in Switzerland and Germany, and visiting the Wagner Bayreuth Festival, Rachmaninoff and his young wife settled down in their apartment on Strassnoy Boulevard in Moscow. A new life began as Sergei was nearing his thirties, that of a happily married man and later a most devoted father—a daughter, Irina, was born on May 27, 1904. Of his old friends, Nikita Morozov remained very close to Sergei. Morozov, who taught the theoretical courses at the Moscow Conservatory, had been Sergei's classmate and one of the three students who were graduated at the same time. He was probably the only friend to whom Rachmaninoff confided everything that happened to him in his artistic as well as his personal life (until Morozov died in 1925). The questions of program or forms of his compositions, the theoretical problems which he could not solve by himself, the choice of texts, translations and corrections of his scores, as well as the details of his home life, were always discussed by Sergei with Morozov, and Sergei listened to Morozov's advice. More than once he turned to him for encouragement and more than once he emphasized what his friendship meant to him.

While he was on his honeymoon in Switzerland, Sergei called for Morozov to come to Lucerne to visit them and, working on his latest opus, he wrote from Ivanovka, the Satins' country place:

I was very glad to receive your letter, my dear friend. I too have wanted to write you for some time, but I turned out to be even more lazy about writing letters than you, since after all you wrote me first. However, I have an excuse: I have nothing to write about. It has been a long time since I have had such a bad summer as this one and if I wanted to write about it I would have to speak only about our illnesses.

I was sick half of the summer, my wife was very ill until the fifteenth of July, and finally my little girl, except for the last two or three weeks, was ill all the time. Thus I could have worked only during the last two or three weeks, but I caught a cold and was laid up for the whole week. You can easily realize that there is no question of work: I have done nothing and I hope that I can do some more work during the month and a half that is left.

So, here is how things stand! I hate even to write about it, because when I begin to think that I have done nothing at all, I get very depressed. Apparently you also did not have very much fun this summer, since you decided to cut short your vacation. I explain your return to Moscow this way. Was it really so bad that Moscow seems better to you at this time of the year? And what can be worse than Moscow in the summer! Well, at least you have been working and have accomplished a lot. You are a lucky one. You would be very happy anywhere because your nature is such that you are satisfied and everybody and everything seems always better when the finished work is lying on the table. . . . Though you say you are too lazy to write letters, perhaps you will manage to write me a few lines again. You will make me very happy.

Yours,
Sergei Rachmaninoff

August 18, 1903

P. S. My regards to Vera Alexandrovna.[1]

[1] Vera Alexandrovna was Morozov's wife. She graduated as a pupil of Safonoff in piano from the Moscow Conservatory and became a piano teacher.

Though Sergei signed a contract with the Bolshoi Theater in the spring of 1904, he continued work on his opera at Ivanovka hoping to have it ready before the beginning of his new appointment.

Looking for a subject for an opera, Rachmaninoff turned to Pushkin's short drama *The Miser Knight*, the only one left in this selection of Pushkin's works which had not yet been set to music. Dargomyzhski's *The Stone Guest* and *Russalka*, Moussorgsky's *Boris Godunov*, Rimsky-Korsakov's *Mozart and Salieri*, and César Cui's *A Feast in Time of Plague* were all written after Pushkin's dramas.

While Rachmaninoff did not follow in the footsteps of the St. Petersburg group of musicians in his composing, in this particular case he was influenced by Dargomyzhski's idea of using Pushkin's text as a libretto for the opera. However, he deviated in one respect from the principles of the "new Russian school" as laid down by "The Mighty Five"—his music for the orchestra overbalanced that written for the singers. But *The Miser Knight*, an opera in three scenes, was not successful as a true drama for the simple reason that Pushkin's version did not offer much action. Pushkin's psychological theme— the "Miser Knight" as a slave of his passion—is illustrated by the music in the orchestra, thus making Rachmaninoff's work a sort of "symphonic opera."

Almost simultaneously with this opera, Rachmaninoff was working on his third opera, *Francesca da Rimini*, an episode taken from Dante's *Inferno*. Rachmaninoff was not the first musician to be inspired by this subject. Liszt's symphony and his sonata (*"D'apres une lecture de Dante"*) as well as Tchaikovsky's symphonic poem were all composed on the same theme. This time, however, it was Modest Tchaikovsky who wrote the libretto for Rachmaninoff's opera in one act with a prologue and an epilogue. Despite the difference of the subjects of *The Miser Knight* and *Francesca da Rimini*, the idea of passion dominating an unfortunate individual is the principal theme of both works. And in both cases it leads to disaster.

The weakness of this opera was ascribed to its poor libretto; actually it represented only another bold but unsuccessful experiment in creating a "new opera," a sort of "music drama," where the plot of the story was to be negligible.[2]

May I first of all ask you a favor [Rachmaninoff wrote to Morozov]. *I have just sent you the third scene of The Miser Knight and I beg you to read it carefully and correct the translation,[3] which is in some places (I marked them) made with surprising incompetence. I allow you to add notes wherever you like so long as the accent of the words will fall on the strong beat of the bar, and besides that there shall be no rests between the two syllables such as Oh-ne.*

I am terribly afraid that this letter will not catch you in Moscow. But if it reaches you without the music even an hour before your departure, will you please take them along with you to the sea where you are going, and make corrections there. I am writing about this to Gutheil, who is going to send you the music.

I agree in advance with everything you are going to do as long as you are willing to do it. I do not want to send it to Siloti; it will take too long. Then, please send the manuscript

---

[2] I must add here to Rachmaninoff's attempts at composing opera the following ten subjects, though none of them was completed: *Esmeralda, Boris Godunov, Mazeppa, Undine, Salambo, Mona Vanna, Minstrel, Fugitive, A Mysterious Island,* and *Uncle Vanya.*

[3] German translation for publication in Germany.

to Gutheil and he will forward it abroad for publication. For God's sake, please, do this for me.

Now, I will tell you what is going on here. Irina is feeling fairly well. On the advice of another doctor we decided to stop taking her temperature and instead we are weighing her. This weighing shows with mathematical precision that the little girl is gaining one pound and a half every week—a sign according to the doctor and also in my own opinion that there is nothing seriously wrong with her. Our doctor explains the high temperature as a consequence to the influenza. From several friends we have heard of the same thing in children's cases.

Thus I have stopped worrying in the last few weeks. . . . I am working a lot now. About ten days ago I sent one scene of Francesca to be translated.[4] But I refuse most stubbornly to think about the theater, though it does frighten me a little. I will not start on the theater for at least two or three weeks. On the whole I have an awful lot of work piled up and I have unfortunately very little time left. I am offering two thousand rubles as reward to anyone who will release me from my job at the theater. I would like to put an ad in the paper: "Lost last spring my peace of mind because of signing a contract. Will reward the one who will deliver it to the following address." Though I doubt that anyone will be able to find it.

What is this annoying affair with your money? And how is it that you, who have been gallivanting abroad for the last two months with such moral and material losses, cannot keep quiet and must go gallivanting for another month to the Baltic seashore? This is to be marveled at. I hope to see you soon. My regards to Vera Alexandrovna.

Yours,

July 2, 1904. Sergei Rachmaninoff

[4] German translation for publication in Germany.

A few weeks later he wrote to Morozov again.

Dear friend, only a few lines this time to thank you for the favor you did me by correcting my score.

About the rest I do not have to go into details because Natasha[5] has seen you and told you everything. In case she did not have time to call on you I will tell you in a few words that my little girl is ill again (though she had not yet recovered from her previous illness) and that in despair we decided to send her to Moscow, since Natasha had to go there anyway to be at Volodya's[6] wedding. Therefore I am all alone at Ivanovka.

Here is how far I have gotten with my work. Last week I sent the prologue to Francesca to be translated. This leaves me one scene and the epilogue to finish. I have not even begun to prepare myself for the theater and this now not only worries me but begins to torture me. On the other hand, if I start now to study the opera scores, I will never finish Francesca. I have decided to finish my opera first. On the whole I am terribly tired and would like to have a rest. But this is impossible because I have so much to do. And besides my little girl, my precious one, tortures me and I do not know when she is going to get well. I must declare that to be a father, composer, and a conductor all at the same time is very difficult and very painful.

You have apparently remained in Moscow. I congratulate you with all my heart. It is much better to sit quietly at home than to go visiting strangers. Now good-by until we meet very soon. Write me. I promise to answer more promptly.

Yours,
Sergei Rachmaninoff

[5] Nataly Rachmaninoff, wife of the composer.
[6] Vladimir Alexandrovich Satin, Rachmaninoff's brother-in-law.

Greetings to Vera Alexandrovna.

July 21, 1904.

Finally, on August 4th, he closed his letter to Morozov with: "Now I am going to submerge myself in the *Life for the Tsar.*"

During the two following seasons Rachmaninoff worked at the Bolshoi Theater, but the reaction of the press, musicians, and the public toward him in his new role as a conductor was divided. Though always recognizing in him a splendid musician, some thought that his conducting was very much like his piano-playing—cold and lacking in spontaneity—while others, basing their opinion particularly on his performances of the Russian operas, considered his interpretations epoch-making in the annals of the history of Russian opera.

Before he raised his baton for the first opera he was going to conduct, Rachmaninoff made several innovations right in the pit of the orchestra. Until then the conductor's desk had been placed right in front of the footlights with the violin sections on both sides of it while the rest of the orchestra sat behind the conductor, who faced the stage.

Rachmaninoff, following Richard Wagner's methods, asked to have the order of the seats in the orchestra rearranged to that which is now customary. He even stood while conducting— instead of sitting. Then he himself worked with every soloist on his part, accompanying him at the piano. This arduous but sensible innovation not only brought him into closer contact with the cast but inspired the artists, who felt, as Chaliapin expressed it: "With Rachmaninoff at the piano, I have to say instead of 'I sing,' 'we sing.'"

The year which he had spent at Mamontov's opera and the few concerts he had conducted in London were all the experience he had had so far, but this combined with the authority and the popularity his name gained through his vocal compositions and his appearances in concerts were sufficient to make the orchestra and cast follow him obediently.

Rachmaninoff carefully studied anew the scores of Russian composers and restored all their original intentions in regard to tempi, dynamics, and nuances which had been distorted through the decades by various musicians in the "search for tradition." He eliminated all the tendencies of soloists to gain cheap effects by rubatos and endlessly held high notes, and he brought the orchestra into prominence from its former role of a mere accompanying instrument.

Those who considered him a lyricist were surprised by his dramatic interpretations. He particularly showed this in scenes with recitative supported only by isolated chords in the orchestra—when the nuances of the sound created either the mood for the following lines or reflected what had just been said. His *fortissimi* sounded as mighty as Borodin's epic style and his *pianissimi* were as ghostly as Moussorgsky's weird death, but it was in the field of pure accompaniment that he was considered without equal. After his strict rehearsals with the singers, in which he carefully showed them either by playing on the piano or by explaining in his laconic way, they felt at perfect ease with him at the performance, so harmonious was their mutual understanding.

Particularly unforgettable were the performances with Chaliapin, for the two became close friends, and their combined artistic work knew no equal either in depth, strength, and brilliance of interpretation or in perfection of delivery. Rachmaninoff, who was better educated musically, had the last word in what was possible and what was not in the music they performed, while he profited from Chaliapin's knowledge of the theatrical.

He eliminated the cult of "operatic stars." He was demanding and autocratic but fair. And though all agreed that neither his gestures nor his interpretations had the slightest sign of affectation, some thought that his hand was not elastic enough or that he did not possess enough energy to carry the performance to the end with the necessary force.

Thus, no final word has been said about him as a conductor, for a great many insisted that despite all his qualities he was not a "born conductor," that this was always felt in his performances, and that one did not quite know in what role the public found Rachmaninoff most fascinating: as a composer, as a promising pianist, as an orchestra conductor, or as a strange and enigmatic man. His repertoire consisted mostly of Russian operas: Glinka's, Dargomyzhski's, Borodin's, Rimsky-Korsakov's, and, of course, Tchaikovsky's, in the interpretation of whose music he was considered peerless.

However, during his second year at the Bolshoi Theater Rachmaninoff lost the little interest and enthusiasm he had for his job. It must be remembered that this was during the first Russian Revolution of 1905. Rachmaninoff was a comparatively uninterested observer. He kept out of all that was going on and was only annoyed by political events which affected the theatrical life. At this time merely the name "Imperial" was sufficient to keep the public away from the Bolshoi Theater. Newspapers, posters, and programs often were not printed, while in the theater itself the constant ferment among the members made Rachmaninoff believe that he could not continue at his post.

Life within the walls of the Bolshoi Theater was only a small replica of what was going on in the city. The revolts and protests which crippled normal life in Moscow, with strikes affecting water supplies, electricity, telephone, and food, had an echo in the form of collective protests among the members of the theater. Everyone was signing petitions to the directors in regard to improvement not only of the material situation in their jobs but in regulating the degree of their subordination, their civil rights, the number of their working hours, and so on.

The petitions were sent not only by the members of the ballet, the chorus, and the orchestra, but by the workers, stage-hands, painters and carpenters, tailors and seamstresses. In these petitions they complained against the administration, their teachers, professors, chorus masters, conductors, and stage directors. All of the petitions ended on a threatening note of "if not . . . then we will strike. . . ." The threat of strikes moved like a dark shadow inside the theater building. Everyone was nervous, irritated, and at the same time frightened. And this was true of both the subordinates and the administrators. Everyone expected something to happen, tried to guess how all this was going to end.

The manifestoes no longer impressed anyone. Those who shouted "hurrah" on hearing them did not believe them the next day. Some considered this to be the right time to square personal accounts under the cloak of political theories. Everything was mixed and muddled. Men who were the worst enemies by virtue of their social position, political convictions, and personal interests walked arm in arm, while old friends and men of common interest found themselves in conflict with each other and could neither explain nor extricate themselves from the intrigues in which they were involved.

The military governor of Moscow, Admiral Feodor Douba-sov, whose mere word could close or open the doors of the theater, was much annoyed by these "unpleasant events," complaining that he had only eighteen to twenty thousand armed soldiers and Cossacks to subdue the Muscovites. His personal life was thrown out of gear because he was a great balletomane and now, on account of the "troubles," he had to remain at home dreaming of whom in the Moscow ballet he should bless with the privilege of being his next mistress.

Rumors ran through the city that the revolutionists had threatened to blow up Uspensky Cathedral, the State bank, and also the Bolshoi Theater, and the theaters closed their doors periodically, sometimes for as long as three weeks at a time. The directors were afraid to permit the performance of Glinka's A Life for the Tsar, for when the singer sang the stanza about giving his life for the Tsar, the gallery booed. And it was sufficient for someone during a performance to shout, "Down with the monarchy!" to make the whole theater become a battlefield where hats, coats, umbrellas, and galoshes flew through the air while fat merchants, indignant at the disturbance, stood in their boxes or struggled in the crowd, threateningly waving chairs as though they were made of feathers.

Chaliapin begged the directors to let him take his vacation and go to the South of Russia to nurse his health. But no one believed him ill and he received some letters threatening him if he should sing at the Imperial Theater and others threatening him if he should not.

Then, at the concert for the benefit of the pensioned old artists, he upset both friends and foes by singing Dubinushka, a revolutionary song. He had been recalled for an encore when someone shouted from the gallery, "Dubinushka!" Chaliapin stepped to the footlights and said that the song was a composition written for chorus and therefore he could not sing it alone, whereupon the house answered with applause and before he knew what had happened, Chaliapin was leading the whole house in the singing of *Dubinushka*. Those in the galleries were delighted, but the boxes were soon empty. An old artist, Nicolay N. Figner, kissed Chaliapin on the stage and on the following day denounced him before the directors.

The incident reached Tsar Nicolas II, and he was surprised that Chaliapin was not thrown out of the theater; but the shrewd Tsarina suggested leaving Chaliapin alone lest the strains of *Dubinushka* might be heard by a wider audience than that at the Bolshoi Theater.

The stream of telegrams from Moscow suggested that the time had passed to consider raising the salaries of the artists and the workers. Immediate action was imperative, but the petitions needed Baron Frederick's personal signature and he was away hunting with Nicolas II. At that time the directors of the Imperial Theaters had no confidence that Sergei Rachmaninoff could keep the theater men from striking, for he himself often spoke of the poor fees the musicians were paid.

Serge Koussevitzky, handing in his resignation from the double-bass chair in the orchestra, slammed the door with great noise in a long-winded protest against the conditions at the theater. What Koussevitzky said in his statement of over fifteen hundred words, published by the Moscow daily *Russkoe Slovo* and reprinted in the Moscow *Gazette*, was that the Bolshoi Theater, which claimed to be a temple of art, actually was a hell, and that the musicians, who were supposed to be artists, were forced to work like slaves. But the musicians took his declaration with a smile, for since his recent marriage he no longer needed his position at the theater. Also, the conditions of the musicians in the theater were only a part of the whole life of the "middle class" and, as Telyakovsky remarked, were in all fairness no worse than anywhere else.

95

Koussevitzky failed to mention that the musicians were paid their salaries all year round but worked only a little longer than six months, having their summer vacations as well as another vacation during Lent, when the theaters were closed.

Sergei Rachmaninoff, on the other hand, came to Telyakovsky to hand in his resignation on different grounds. At first he said the reason for his final decision was an engagement for a concert tour in the United States, but when Telyakovsky offered him the post of the principal conductor at the theater, he became more frank and confidential.

According to Sergei, the revolutionary spirit had a most detrimental effect on the members of the orchestra. The excellent discipline built by Altany had been gradually falling apart and after the events of the past winter had disappeared completely. He said that it was impossible to work with the orchestra under such conditions, since his ideals were doomed never to be fulfilled. He thought that unless the "harmful element" among the members of the theater was immediately removed, there would be no way of handling the orchestra and one would be forced to be occupied not with art but with petty incidents, personal affairs, and intrigues based on envy.

When Telyakovsky argued that the directors of the theater could not very well dismiss the musicians he had marked for immediate discharge (because there were men among them who had worked for seventeen or eighteen years and who needed two or three years of service to have the right to a pension), Rachmaninoff said that this did not concern him as the conductor. He repeated that these musicians were not only unfit to be in the orchestra but were harmful and that he would have to replace them if the directors still wished to have an adequate orchestra. It was up to the directors and the Government to make the necessary arrangement about their pensions. Pension them sooner if necessary, he said, but keeping them in the orchestra just because they had to finish their quota of years was absurd. He said the same in regard to the cast of the theater.

Telyakovsky, who valued Rachmaninoff very much as a musician and conductor, could not, however, find any basis for an agreement because Sergei refused every compromise. Telyakovsky was ready to agree with Rachmaninoff from the point of view of an artist, but as a director of a Government institution he saw no moral right to dismiss men who had put up with many privations during their long services because of the final reward—a pension for their old age.

From this interview Telyakovsky gained the impression that Rachmaninoff would not remain as a permanent conductor but would be willing occasionally to conduct those operas which particularly interested him. They decided to leave the final decision until the end of the opera season, and that night Rachmaninoff gave a magnificent performance of his two operas *The Miser Knight* and *Francesca da Rimini*.

But not everyone felt as friendly toward Rachmaninoff as Telyakovsky. Intricate intrigues were woven to get the conductor out of the theater. The actors as well as the orchestra musicians managed to inform Telyakovsky of their opinion of Rachmaninoff and to warn him how untrustworthy and dangerous he was. Dr. Lev Kasansky, a member of the board of directors, who saw everything in dark colors and who was more afraid of the word "politics" than of fire, came to Telyakovsky with his own version of the Rachmaninoff problem.

He saw in him a dangerous rival to Telyakovsky as a future director of the Imperial Theaters. Telyakovsky brushed aside the question of trusting or distrusting Rachmaninoff and remarked that in his opinion Sergei was an excellent conductor and a very valuable asset to the theater.

"That is just it," said Kasansky. "The more success he will

97

have, the more he will gain popularity and authority, the more dangerous he will become, and you had better be careful of him. You had better listen to me. I know these artists well. Even Chaliapin is afraid of Rachmaninoff!"

Dr. Kasansky became even more confused and upset when Telyakovsky told him that he liked Rachmaninoff so much that he was going to ask him to accept a position which he wanted to create especially for him—to be the head of all the opera affairs—but that he feared Rachmaninoff would not be interested in the post. Telyakovsky tried in vain to explain to Kasansky that though artists never refuse power and, as a matter of fact, seek it, yet when it involves responsibility they become less anxious to have it. When they have to answer letters, sign papers, discharge those who do not fit into the organization, cut down salaries of those who are useless but have powerful protection back of them, then these artists who seek power decline it, saying that this is not their business, that this is something for bureaucrats, the administrators, and that their business is only to evaluate and to say: "Here I do not need this one. Please engage someone else." But getting necessary sums of money cannot interest great artists—poets at heart. It does not concern them when the board of directors asks for an accounting while those who were discharged come to make scenes and throw fits of hysterics. . . . And yet, whether this is an artistic job or not, no theater can exist without it, concluded Telyakovsky. And in his opinion neither Nápravník in St. Petersburg nor Rachmaninoff in Moscow would ever be interested in such a position.

But Kasansky only shook his head and said that he was particularly worried by the forthcoming production of Rimsky-Korsakov's opera *Sadko*. He was sure that Rachmaninoff would do a good job of it and would gain more popularity. "I advise you to be careful with Rachmaninoff. Mark my words," said Kasansky.

Telyakovsky, who had done a great deal for the Imperial Theaters in engaging good artists and distinguished painters to design the sets, and who had managed to keep relative peace in the most temperamental branch of society, had to admit that on the whole in Russia one is afraid of nothing more than of an exceptional talent.

Whether Rachmaninoff was aware of all this or not, he eventually resigned, and a couple of years later when he was asked if he would return, he said:

"I will never return to Bolshoi Theater. They need a different man there. They all call Fedia 'Chaliapin the trouble-maker.' This is true. Feodor is a trouble-maker. They are terrified at the mere thought of him. He might swear and he might hit someone. And Fedia has a mighty fist. And he knows how to stand up for himself. Well, what else can one do, if you please? They have a regular tavern backstage. They yell and they drink, and only swear in the worst language. Where is there a place for art, for an opportunity to work? They need Chaliapin the trouble-maker, from whom they all hide in every corner.

"No, that is no place for real work: there you have nothing but constant irritation and hostility. Under such conditions one cannot create anything. It is too bad. For one could create a lot of good there. . . ."

Most of the outstanding men in Russia were considered trouble-makers. Some were destroyed by society, as were Lermontov and Pushkin, some exiled by the Government, as were Dostoevski and Herzen, some excommunicated by the Church as was Tolstoy, and some, like Metchnikoff, left their country in time, deciding that the work they wanted to do was too difficult under existing conditions because their main energy had to be spent on the struggle for the right to work and not on the work itself. All the outstanding men were branded as guilty. All of them were in the way. None of them was wanted.

In Moscow the Government authorities, fearing public demonstrations, did not dare to have the performance of Glinka's A *Life for the Tsar* without a strong guard of soldiers, and in St. Petersburg the insurrection scene in Moussorgsky's *Boris Godunov*, in Rimsky-Korsakov's new version, was deleted. Rimsky himself was dismissed from his position as a leading professor at the Conservatory because he was accused of siding with the students, the revolutionary element. Hundreds of students were expelled. Glazunov and Liadov resigned, while Madame Esipov, the famous piano teacher, went abroad. The Conservatory was closed.

The affairs in Moscow were not any better. Taneyev resigned in protest against Safonoff's repressive attitude toward the students of the Conservatory. The Moscow Conservatory was closed too, and Safonoff went abroad.

The seeds of Rachmaninoff's eventual and permanent desertion of Russia were well sown.

. VIII .

Retreat to Italy

WHEN IN THE MIDDLE OF MARCH, 1908, Rachmaninoff went abroad, he did not know that this was the beginning of a long series of journeys in search of peace for his work. It was obvious from his attitude at the Bolshoi Theater that Rachmaninoff was not affected by the revolutionary spirit which was then sweeping Russia. It is hard to tell what political views he held at a time when politics were affecting everyone's life, for Rachmaninoff's choice of newspapers—*Russkie Vedomosty* and *Novoe Vremya*—throws a somewhat confusing light on his political ideas. The *Russkie Vedomosty* was a liberal paper. It did not cater to the tastes of the crowd. Its careful selection of articles of serious content and reliable information gave the paper the authority which it enjoyed. Well-known men in the arts and sciences were contributors of long standing, including Tolstoy, Saltikov-Schedrin, Uspensky, Chekhov, Korolenko, and Chernyshevski. Association with this paper, even if merely as a reader, served as a sort of a "passport," as they said at the time in Russia.

As for the *Novoe Vremya*, it was a reactionary daily paper

which was then calling for the most outrageous reprisals for anything liberal. Perhaps Rachmaninoff wanted to know the worst fate that was to befall Russia.

But from the remarks in a letter to Morozov in which he expressed a lively interest in the debates in the first Russian Duma (Russian Parliament), one gains the impression that his convictions were akin to those of the Cadets—a party which advocated a constitutional monarchy. Thus Rachmaninoff certainly did not believe in the possibility of the overthrow of the Government and regarded the events of 1905-6 as merely temporary revolts and unpleasant outbreaks from which, for personal comfort, one should stay away. He also undoubtedly realized that since the whole musical and theatrical life, as well as his colleagues, were involved in these "unpleasant events," he would have to take a firm stand or choose the easier way— leave the country and wait until it blew over.

Rachmaninoff lived in a world of his own, a small one but his own: his music and his small family. He took this world to Italy. In Florence, after looking in vain for a suitable apartment, the Rachmaninoffs finally settled down in Madame Lucchesi's boardinghouse. The two rooms which they occupied were comfortable and cheap. And Madame Lucchesi offered the composer another room in the cellar (whether free of charge or not was not clear) where there was an upright piano on which her brother played. She said Rachmaninoff could use it from nine to one and from three to six. He found this arrangement satisfactory because he thought that while he finished rewriting the scores of his operas *The Miser Knight* and *Francesca* he would not need a piano and then he would have to spend only a week in the cellar before moving to the sea on the first of May.

Rachmaninoff was enchanted with Florence; and though he

did not take time to visit a single gallery, he enjoyed its parks and cathedrals and found the view from Michelangelo Place better than any picture. Almost immediately upon his arrival he started on a new project for an opera based on Flaubert's novel *Salambo*. Its tragic tale, developed against a background of complicated circumstances, with its romantic heroes perishing in a conflict with reality, impressed Rachmaninoff much in the same way as it had Moussorgsky, whose first attempt at writing an opera had also been based upon *Salambo*.

Like Moussorgsky, Rachmaninoff wrote his own scenario; but as for the libretto, he wanted it to be not the usual operatic one but a book for a dramatic play with Flaubert's text arranged in verse. He first asked Morozov to contact Svobodin, a friend of Sakhnovsky's, but later (when Svobodin failed to do any work) he chose his old friend Slonov. However, whether because of Morozov's criticisms of the scenario or because of the difficulty of collaboration by correspondence or because of the misfortune of constant illness in his family, he never did compose the planned opera.

Meanwhile, his own remark that "to be a father, composer, and a conductor all at the same time is very difficult and very painful" must have come into his mind more than once, for he was barely away from Russia six weeks when he was faced with making decisions about his own future and the support of his family. The loose ends of his affairs which he had left hanging in mid-air when he left Moscow now demanded his immediate attention and he wrote to Morozov for advice.

Florence, April 21, 1906
. . . Now, Nikita Semenovich, listen to me carefully. For the next season I have a contract, not signed yet, to work in the theater for five months, from September first to February

first. The fee is 8,000 rubles. I also have an offer (also not signed) for ten symphonic concerts. The fee is 4,500 rubles. I have three more concerts of Russian music (at the circle of "Amateurs of Russian Music" organized by M. C. Kerzin) for a fee of 900 rubles and two benefit performances without pay. I must add to this that starting with September first I shall not have a kopeck left. This I add to clarify everything. Now here is what I might have: last night I received a cable concerning a contract for America for the next season with conditions on which I insisted in my correspondence with the manager. Besides that I hope to compose something in the near future, though I never hope very much.

Now here is the question. Will you weigh everything that I "have" and everything that I "might have" and tell me frankly if I should send all that I "have" to the devil and remain with what I "might have"? Think it over, Nikita Semenovich, and let me know. You, a man of decision, could not possibly understand what tortures I live through when I realize that this question has to be decided by me and me alone. The trouble is I am just incapable of making any decision by myself. My hands tremble! Think it over and write me quickly. The decision, as I see it, must be taken this year— that is, right now. If I depend on what I "might have" I could even live abroad, that is if I could control my homesickness for Russia. On this question mark I will close my letter.

He added in a postscript that he had just received the contract for his signature from the Moscow office of the Imperial Theaters. "Fate is knocking on the window. Tuk, tuk, dear friend, stop chasing happiness!" Rachmaninoff was quoting from his own song, *Fate.*

A week later the Rachmaninoffs moved to the seashore to

Marina di Pisa, five miles away from Pisa, where they rented a small cottage for the sum of nine hundred liras. It pleased the composer particularly because of its cleanliness.

"I think," he wrote to Morozov, "one finds cleanliness in Italian homes just as rarely as one does in the compositions of all these modern composers." The little cottage, with its beautiful view and the sea within fifty paces of its door, had five rooms, and though there was not enough linen and silver, still, since they had one extra room, he begged the Morozovs to come to visit them.

But Rachmaninoff was homesick. He ran to open the door himself each time he heard the bell, hoping it was the postman. His two Russian newspapers were forwarded to him, but the news at home only made him more restless, more confused, and he could not keep his mind on his work.

. . . *A few days ago I wrote to the directors of the Imperial Theaters* [Rachmaninoff wrote to Morozov], *asking them to postpone for another month the date of my definite answer; and since it is very probable that after the month elapses I shall still be unable to sign the contract, I told them to look for somebody who could replace me. I have sent the same kind of letter to your office* [the directors of the Russian Musical Society] *concerning the symphonic concerts. I find it very difficult to compose anything after such a long time of doing nothing. I must say that this confuses and upsets me in many ways because of the decisions for my future plans. It looks as though nothing will come of the plans concerning America. It seems as though they would like to exploit me there. But I gave them an ultimatum with one month's time to decide. By the way, I need America if I am going to give up everything in Moscow. (Where did you get the information*

that Safonoff is engaged for three years to conduct the Philharmonic concerts?) All this put together confuses and worries
me. Without one thing or the other I cannot manage to live.
What then should I give up? I am clinging to America because
this tour will take only two months of my time and will give
me a large sum of money. But what if they will fool me there
and if I will not be able to compose anything here? There I
go with my old refrain. . . .

Why don't you say something about yourself? Frankly, this
interests me, and you behave as though you have your mouth
full of water. Write me!

The month of May passed and Rachmaninoff still could not
bring himself to work. To make matters worse, first his wife
and later his little girl became ill. He was their nurse and at
times his anxiety over the health of his daughter drove him to
despair. He found that the doctors in Pisa were incompetent
and he had to call in a doctor from Florence whose treatment
of the child, while it brought some improvement, still did not
cure the mysterious disease.

"You cannot imagine how weak she is," wrote the unhappy
father to Morozov. "Of that healthy girl only a memory is
left. It is hard to describe how we have suffered."

Three weeks later the Rachmaninoffs decided to return
home. Their little Irina was definitely not getting any better.
She had fever constantly, she could hardly eat anything, and
the weary parents feared complications. Besides, their Floren-
tine doctor was going to leave them and go abroad.

"But will we get to Moscow?" worried Rachmaninoff. He
had read in the paper that there was trouble on the Warsaw-
Vienna railroad. "What an affair! We cannot remain here and
it looks as though we shall not be able to leave. It seems

that there is nothing left for one to do. Will we see you in Moscow?" he wrote pathetically to Morozov.

Back in Ivanovka, in the peaceful atmosphere of their own home, they recovered from their ailments and Rachmaninoff only regretted the time he had wasted in Italy. However, though he forced himself to work regularly, he progressed very slowly. He abandoned the idea of writing the opera *Salambo* and he composed "small pieces, deciding to polish them up regardless of their qualities." But in less than six weeks "events were happening with head-whirling speed," as he said, once again demanding his decision.

He received a letter from the office of the Russian Musical Society saying that the project of the symphonic concerts was "hanging in mid-air." Having just accepted this appointment before leaving Italy, he was apparently hurt by the letter, and immediately resigned from the project. This decision, coupled with his resignation from his post as a musical inspector at the Ekaterina and Elisabeth Institutes, left him without any immediate prospect of earning money. The only solution for this problem, he thought, was to compose. But as he felt that he could not concentrate in Moscow, he discussed the matter with his relatives and decided to go abroad again, to Germany this time, Leipzig or Dresden—cities with a musical atmosphere—where he hoped to live on the money he would get for the small pieces he had lately been composing.

"What can I do," he wrote to Morozov, "if all my plans, because of my indecision, need encouragement from those near me, whom I love and trust? A man such as I never does anything by himself and loves to be pushed into action. And here I am again, grateful to you for your push. Now I can be frank with you and tell you that I have refused everything that was binding me to Moscow, and that I will go abroad for the whole winter. I am very happy that you approve of my plan. I am working as hard as usual but I progress very slowly. Things do not come easily to me. Often I feel very unhappy. My Natasha is in bed again. Yesterday she played tennis, fell down, and tore a ligament in her instep. She is going to be laid up for a week, though the sharp pain is already gone. She lies in bed and sings sad arias. . . ."

In November, 1906, Rachmaninoff went with his family to Dresden, where they spent the next three years, only returning for their summers to Ivanovka. And thus began a second period of restless wandering in search of inner quiet.

. IX .

Dresden

ACCORDING TO RIESEMANN, Rachmaninoff chose Dresden for
their residence because on a previous visit to the town
he had been impressed by a performance of *Die Meistersinger,*
his favorite Wagnerian work. The discipline and "the mighty
inspiration" of the production made him believe that among
all the German cities Dresden had the musical atmosphere
he was seeking for his own work. Besides, Leipzig with its
famous Gewandhaus orchestra, which Arthur Nikisch was
conducting, was only two hours away, and to Rachmaninoff,
Nikisch as a conductor meant what Tchaikovsky meant to
him as a composer.

The two-story Garden Villa on Sidonienstrasse 6, with all
its six rooms on the sunny side, stood, as the name indicated,
in the middle of a garden and was just the kind of a home
Rachmaninoff had always wanted to have. It was a very simple
matter to arrange his quarters so that he could have quiet
and privacy for his work, but to have it furnished and properly
appointed almost involved him in lawsuits and certainly influenced his feelings toward the inhabitants of Dresden.

In all of Dresden there were only two stores that rented furniture, and as the rent for the furniture was almost as high as that for the villa, Rachmaninoff decided that in the end it would be cheaper to buy everything for his household. However, he made the mistake of taking a fancy to a red armchair which he ordered to be sent to his address. When on the following morning Rachmaninoff changed his mind and went back to the store to cancel his order, the salesman insisted that the deal was closed. After two days of arguing, Rachmaninoff found the chair delivered at his home. He refused to accept it and the storekeeper threatened to start a lawsuit.

Life in Germany seemed to him far too expensive. He certainly saw no sign of the low prices he had heard about before he came to Dresden. He complained that groceries were too dear, but . . . so was the music. For a decent place in the opera one had to pay as much as one would for a brace of ducks. "Are all of them thieves," thought Rachmaninoff, "or is it just I who have such bad luck?"

However, Rachmaninoff liked the small city on the banks of the Elbe even though, generalizing from such small incidents, he thought that the inhabitants were dishonest and vulgar, and even though it did not inspire him with a desire to seek social contacts. The Rachmaninoffs lived to themselves, receiving almost no one and not going out into Dresden society.

"I work a great deal and I feel very well," wrote Rachmaninoff to Slonov. "In my old age this kind of life pleases me very much, and right now suits me well."

Rachmaninoff was thirty-three years old and when he said "in my old age," he was neither jesting nor posing. He felt old. He meant just what he said.

". . . I am not striving to get anywhere, I do not want anything more than I have, and I am not envious of anyone.

All I wish is that everyone in my family be well and that my work may progress successfully. Though the latter is not yet the case, who can stop me from hoping?"

But Rachmaninoff diligently went to concerts and the Dresden opera. Richard Strauss's *Salome* impressed him. "Strauss is a very talented man and he certainly knows how to dress everything up," thought Rachmaninoff. Watching the performance, Rachmaninoff suddenly imagined one of his own operas being given at the Dresden opera house. It made him feel awkward and embarrassed, he said, almost as though he were forced to face an audience undressed.

Rachmaninoff also heard four oratorios—Beethoven's *Missa Solemnis*, Handel's *Samson*, Bach's B-minor Mass, and Mendelssohn's *St. Paul*—and, of course, he did not miss the symphonic concerts at the Gewandhaus in Leipzig, where Nikisch was conducting. However, he did not care for the piano concerto by "someone called Dovel" (Rachmaninoff meant MacDowell) played by the famous Teresa Careño. In fact, it upset him so that he coughed and sneezed for the next three days. On the other hand, nothing gave him so much pleasure as *Die Meistersinger*, and he went to hear this favorite opera each time it was performed. Rachmaninoff also was seen at a performance of the *Merry Widow*, laughing like a little boy.

Yet this seemingly happy life did not find its reflection in his compositions. He was working on several projects at the same time, sometimes starting on a new important work without having finished the last one. On one of his visits to a Leipzig picture gallery he was much impressed by Arnold Boecklin's[1] then striking though now rather banal canvas "The Isle of the Dead." It is a picture of a quiet sea. A small boat with a white-robed passenger and a coffin is rowed up to an

---

[1] Arnold Boecklin, German painter (1872-1901).

island of blue-green cypresses with a large rock containing mysterious recesses. This painting inspired him to compose a tone poem—a musical form of "painting in sound" in which he had tried his prowess once before when he wrote his *Rock*. *The Isle of the Dead*, drawn in the most somber orchestral colors, can easily be divided into three episodes: first, the Sea, which is somewhat reminiscent of the introduction to Rimsky-Korsakov's *Sadko*; then the Isle; and finally, Death itself.

In this composition Rachmaninoff introduced, for the first time, the medieval choral *Dies Irae*. Two reasons have been advanced for the strong attraction this particular melody held for him which made him return to it again and again in his compositions.[2] Some maintain that Rachmaninoff thought of the *Dies Irae* as a sort of *memento mori* and that despite its ominous foreboding it exacted an extreme activity while yet alive. Others think that Rachmaninoff, in his gloomy preoccupation with the word "fate," finally came to the conclusion that Fate can be conquered only by Death.

Yet this constant thought of death might have been a reaction caused by his feeling that he had "aged terribly" and was terrified that "he would soon join the devil," so that for weeks at a time, while he was working, he would suddenly be seized by a fit of depression, apathy, and revulsion to everything he had done, and, in fact, "to everything else." His eyesight gave him trouble because of the strenuous work of writing, and he developed headaches. He slept badly and complained that he was becoming "unglued"—"I have a pain here, and it hurts me there."

"I have been working here for five months and five days," Rachmaninoff reported in a letter to Morozov. "I have accom-

[2] Rhapsody on a theme of Paganini (1934), Symphony No. 3 (1937), Symphonic Dances (1941).

plished a great deal, but unfortunately I still have nothing finished, nothing polished."

This failure to complete anything was not caused entirely by his mental state. Contrary to the general assumption that as a composer he had the technique of writing at his finger tips, Rachmaninoff at times needed help—and not only with the orchestration of his works.

Dear friend Nikita Semenovich [he wrote in a hurry to Morozov], will you solve the following problem for me, or at least help me to solve it? Here it is: first comes the first theme— I will call it the principal theme. Then comes the second theme, not a long one, which returns to the principal theme in that theme's original tonality, but stated this time in a more condensed form. The close of the principal theme is the same tonality as the theme's beginning. Now comes theme III, which is developed in detail and which forms something whole and complete in itself and which is written from beginning to end in the same tonality. Then follows a sort of development—a development of the principal theme, which returns again to a plain statement of the theme. Then begins a sort of a recapitulation: first theme I, then theme II (of course both themes this time in a different tonality than at the first appearance). And finally we return to the principal tonality and principal theme.

Now, here I have a question to ask you. What am I supposed to do now? In what kind of form am I writing? Is there such a form? Is it possible that after all I have just described I must go to the Coda? This somehow does not satisfy me. Or do I need a new theme? Of course, this must be one of the damned Rondo forms. I do not know a single Rondo form. Be so kind as to answer my question immediately. And

*then, please, point out to me all the five accursed Rondo
forms in Beethoven's Sonatas. I will buy them all and compare them. Only please do this in a hurry, because it troubles
me and delays me in my work.*

Three weeks later, on December 21, 1906, Rachmaninoff
wrote to Morozov: ". . . I will carefully guard your letter about
the Rondo form. It will be useful to me in the future if I again
come up against something of this kind; and besides I will save
your letter as a souvenir of my first lesson in form, a lesson
which was given to me only in my old age."

But despite everything, he had written the first two movements of his first piano sonata and he played them to his friend
Oskar von Riesemann, who—so Rachmaninoff thought—did
not like the work.

"You know," he wrote to Morozov, "I begin to think that
everything I have written lately pleases no one. And I myself
begin to wonder if perhaps it is not all complete nonsense. My
sonata is certainly wild and endless. I think it is forty-five minutes long. The length of this work was caused by the program,
or the idea, which guided me—three contrasting characters
from a literary work."

Rachmaninoff was speaking of Goethe's *Faust*. In this sonata he wanted to express Faust's disappointment, his brief
meeting with Marguerite, and the demonism of Mephi-
stopheles. His sonata in its content had more weight than the
salon pieces which he had been writing heretofore—the preludes, songs, and *moments musicaux*.

But Rachmaninoff was not going to supply any kind of a
program for his sonata, though it seemed to him at times that,
if he did disclose the basis for his work, it might clarify it.
However, he was sure that no one was going to play the sonata

because of its difficulty and length, and because he himself doubted its musical merit. At one time he wanted to make a symphony out of it, but this was impossible because of its purely pianistic style. Thus since Rachmaninoff left it in its original difficult and lengthy form as a sonata, it is still awaiting a "discoverer" of its full merits. Actually, both in its length and its majestic conception it resembles the B-minor Sonata of Liszt.

Rachmaninoff was so secretive about the several compositions he was working on that he learned of the existence of his second symphony from the newspapers long before he had finished the work. It was Alexander Siloti's fault. He came to visit Rachmaninoff and kept on prodding him about his work. Rachmaninoff told him that he was going "to have a symphony," whereupon Siloti invited him to conduct it in the fall at one of his concerts in St. Petersburg and announced this to the press.

Twelve years had passed since Rachmaninoff had written his first symphony, which caused him so much pain. But his second symphony, like his first, turned out to be a somber composition, very Russian, though without direct quotations of folk melodies. It is typical of Rachmaninoff that all four parts are bound together more or less by the same thematic material, and in this respect it shows more the influence of Borodin and Taneyev than of Tchaikovsky.

After writing a first draft, Rachmaninoff was so bored with it, and so unhappy about its qualities, that he left the manuscript in his desk and only completed the composition upon his return to Ivanovka the following summer. He swore that once he had finished work on this second symphony and corrected his first symphony, he would never again compose in this particular musical form.

"To hell with them!" he said to Morozov. "I do not know how to write symphonies, and besides I have no real desire to write them."

He also kept secret the work on his new opera, the first act of which was all finished.

"I have very little faith in my composing in general," complained Rachmaninoff, "and in choosing the right subject in particular. Only when I am well started on my work, only then do I become sure of the final result and almost without noticing it reach the end of the composition. But sometimes both the music and the subject suddenly begin to bore me terribly, and then I send the whole thing to the devil."

Now in Dresden, as in Italy, Rachmaninoff again turned to a dramatic subject, and apparently this time his new choice—Maeterlinck's *Mona Vanna*—satisfied him, for, as he referred to it later, he never had been so happy while composing. In November of 1906, very shortly after his arrival in Dresden, Rachmaninoff wrote to Slonov:

Dear friend Mikhail Akimovich, not a soul must know what I am going to tell you. Please be so kind as to take Maeterlinck's Mona Vanna (third edition, the translation of Matterna and Vorotnikova) and open the book at page twenty-seven (Vanna's entrance), and try to make one scene in verse out of the following six pages without—if possible—leaving anything out. . . .

Slonov very quickly sent the libretto of the first scene and Rachmaninoff, who was working with unusual enthusiasm, asked him to send the rest of the libretto, but for some reason Slonov did not finish his task until the beginning of January,

1907, and Rachmaninoff, who had already written some parts of the opera, suddenly stopped working on it.

Concerning the fate of the opera, Sophia Satin wrote the following to A. A. Troubnikova, the composer's cousin, on March 25, 1946:

It will be of interest to musicians and the members of the Museum that the opera which Rachmaninoff intended to compose was more than half written. He did not finish the work because Slonov held up the libretto of Mona Vanna[3] for a long time, and what he did send him was rejected by Sergei. Therefore, I think, he had completed two scenes and would have finished the opera, but he could not wait any longer for Slonov, and so put this work aside and never returned to it. What a pity, for he had seldom been as enthusiastic about a subject for his work as he was about this opera. We hope that the manuscript is safe in Switzerland, and Natasha[4] will get it when she goes there this summer.

After Rachmaninoff gave up his work on Mona Vanna, he contemplated doing an opera using one of Turgenev's subjects. Often in his conversations with friends he spoke of his love for the purely Russian atmosphere of the old Russian country estates and he even mentioned a possible subject for such an opera in Turgenev's A Quiet Backwater or A Song of a Victorious Love. Besides these, he thought of making an opera out of Chekhov's Uncle Vanya, and it is probable that his song Let Us Rest was written in connection with this plan. And finally there were even reports in the newspapers that he was

---

[3] Written in M. A. Slonov's handwriting, the first act of the libretto of the opera Mona Vanna is in the archives of the State Central Museum of Culture in Moscow.

[4] Mrs. S. Rachmaninoff.

composing an opera called *Minstrel*, with a scenario which Chaliapin had written for him after a poem of Maykov.

Toward the spring of 1907, Rachmaninoff had to lay aside his pen for several engagements he had accepted because, as he said, his resources were coming to an end. Besides, the Rachmaninoffs were expecting their second baby and they decided to return for the summer to their country place in Russia. But before he could return home, Rachmaninoff had to go to Paris, where he was scheduled to appear as both conductor and pianist.

Rachmaninoff did not cherish this idea. Though he promised to let Morozov know why he was not happy about this particular engagement, he either never wrote the letter or the letter has not survived. However, one might suspect that Rachmaninoff, who never liked an open competition, realized that this time he was going to be thrown into the arena, so to speak, with odds against him on all three counts: as composer, conductor, and pianist.

Sergei Diaghilev, who probably did more than anyone else for propagandizing Russian art, had organized his "Russian Seasons" in Paris and announced Five Historical Russian Concerts for the month of May. Diaghilev did everything on a large scale, and he engaged such artists as Rimsky-Korsakov, Glazunov, Scriabin, Rachmaninoff, and Chaliapin, as well as Josef Hofmann and Arthur Nikisch, to impress the audience at the Grand Opera in Paris.

"If the theater were to burn down tonight, the best artistic brains and the most elegant women in Europe would perish," Diaghilev would remark before each triumphant first night.

Despite the almost traditional preference shown by Parisians toward the music which came from the Petersburg group rather than Tchaikovsky's disciples, Rachmaninoff won their praise for his performance of his second piano concerto.

"The ovation he received after he had finished playing," reports Oskar von Riesemann in his *Rachmaninoff's Recollections,* "continued until he sat down again to give an encore. At that moment, just as the audience had settled down to an expectant silence, a shrill and penetrating whistle came suddenly from the gallery. . . . But the friendly and astonished smile with which Rachmaninoff looked up to the gallery charmed the audience into renewed demonstrations of enthusiasm, which would not cease until the first strains of the Prelude in C-sharp minor calmed down their excitement."

Thus, despite his fears, Rachmaninoff scored a triumph which set a Rachmaninoff pattern for his pianistic career. From then on packed halls stamped their feet and shouted "bravo" after every appearance until finally he would either play his Prelude in C-sharp minor or have the hall attendant come out and close the piano.

. X .

The First Tour
in the United States

WHEN RACHMANINOFF RETURNED to Ivanovka, the lilacs were still in bloom and the roses which his sister-in-law Sophia Satin had planted at the entrance of the estate enhanced the picture which was so dear to him.

Rachmaninoff had spent many summers in Ivanovka. At first it had been hard for him to get used to the monotonous view of flat fields which stretched out for miles around that part of southern Russia. He, who had been brought up in the north, missed the rugged beauty of Oneg, where he was born, and that of Borisovo, his grandmother's estate. But with time he got used to the southern Russian landscape and grew very attached to it. Rachmaninoff loved Russian earth, Russian peasants, and the country life—the farming, the planting, and the harvest. He spoke of the weeds as though they were his personal enemies, and he often worked in the field behind the plow. He was interested in every aspect of farming and bought new implements to improve it. Like his father, he had a great love of horses. An excellent rider, he loved to break in young horses and he was interested in bettering the quality of the cattle they had.

Upon his return from Paris he did nothing for weeks, but he had a good reason.

"My dear Nikita Semenovich," he wrote to Morozov on June 16, 1907, "I was very glad to receive your letter last night. I am answering you only a few lines.

"First of all, my Natasha, thank God, feels well and is expecting my future son from day to day. The midwife, who has already arrived, is also waiting. I am waiting, too! In fact, all Ivanovskies are waiting and once it will be all over, all of us will be very happy. . . ."

And he closed his letter with: "When my son is born, I will let you know."

Three days later Rachmaninoff became the father of his second daughter, Tatiana.

As the winter season approached, Rachmaninoff was again faced with an old familiar problem.

It has often been reported that Rachmaninoff said: "I never could decide which is my true calling—a composer, pianist, or conductor. At times it seems to me that I should have been only a composer and then again I think I am only a pianist. Now, when the larger part of my life has passed, I am troubled by the thought that by having dispersed myself in so many fields, I did not find my true calling."

Thus in 1908, when Rachmaninoff began touring European cities, appearing as either a pianist or a conductor, he was still uncertain as to which career to espouse. For at this time, when he was most immersed in composing, he regretted every hour he could not devote to it; concertizing interested him only as a means of support.

". . . I met Buyoukly[1] here. Do you remember him?" Rachmaninoff wrote from Warsaw. "He has created a furor. He is

---

[1] V. I. Buyoukly, a pianist, a pupil of P. A. Pabst, who was graduated from the Moscow Conservatory and played with sensational success in Warsaw.

playing here tomorrow. And my friend Zataevich is afraid that I will have an empty hall. My concert for some reason is billed as 'extraordinary,' but he—that is, Buyoukly—probably will make his concert extraordinary. Speaking frankly, I do not care. All I want is to receive my money and leave as soon as possible, because it is very dull here."

Rachmaninoff still hoped that a visit to the United States would solve his financial problems, but the negotiations with a New York manager which had started several years before were long drawn out, and months and months passed while contracts with new alterations of conditions traveled back and forth across the ocean. Meanwhile, Rachmaninoff led the life of a concertizing virtuoso, a life about which he complained yet which he must have enjoyed up to a certain point. Here is a typical letter written en route. It is on the whole a cheerful letter—for Rachmaninoff.

My dear friend Nikita Semenovich, eight days ago I wrote you from Berlin. I do not know if you received my letter. . . . I have three concerts. Last night I played here in Amsterdam. Tomorrow I am playing in The Hague and day after tomorrow I play again in Amsterdam. I play my second concerto with the same orchestra which is traveling everywhere. The orchestra is excellent. Mengelberg conducts all the concerts. He also conducts in Frankfurt am Main, where I am going to play the same concerto again with him next week. He accompanies wonderfully. It is a pleasure to play with him. But despite this pleasure I am terribly tired. Today I am at last sitting alone in my hotel room. It is seven-thirty in the evening. I will write a few letters, drink some tea, and go to bed.

But you know, after all, I am not any good at these concert tours, and I often wonder whether I should not cancel my trip to America, which I probably will not be able to stand. Ten days ago I again sent my new conditions to America. I am willing to go for twenty-five concerts, but mit Privilegium auf mehr, and at the rate of 1,000 rubles per concert. And now I am afraid they will agree. Then what? Despite the large material profit, which will console me to a certain degree, it will be very hard for me to bear this hard labor since such short trips as I have made in Europe tire me so. Now, I hope to be home on the 14th. On Thursday, the 17th, in the evening I am going to Frankfurt, where on the 18th in the morning I have a dress rehearsal and the concert at night. I will return home after the concert and then I have three free weeks; then I will return to Russia and will be free until the summer. This will delight me.

And how are you? Did you hear Carmen with Nikisch? Probably not. That is bad. And do you know that Nikisch struck my symphony from his two programs (in Berlin and in Leipzig), though the symphony was already printed on the programs? The explanation? Probably because he saw that the symphony was dedicated not to him but to Taneyev. Because last May in London, when I saw him, he asked, "Was macht meine Symphonie?" I told him then it was being published. He bought the symphony, and there it said, "To Taneyev." I think this is the reason, because now in Berlin he did not even want to see me. I will tell you about it when I see you.

Well, so you did not hear Nikisch. Well, did you see Kitesh? Did you try to get the tickets for Stokman? You will probably answer no to all my questions.

How is Verushka? My little girls have been "falling apart" lately. The eldest one is suffering from nothing else, if you please, than insomnia. She cannot fall asleep before ten o'clock, often wakes up during the night, and gets up early in the morning. *She looks like a lemon now. The youngest is still "making teeth!" And the teeth are growing enormous. In the daytime one does not hear her, but at night she also sleeps badly and screams very often and very loudly. This young lady possesses a powerful voice. They are torturing their poor mother. And the nurses quarrel and each one blames the other: "It is yours who woke mine up, and not mine, yours . . . ," etc.*

On the 25th, according to the European [Julian] calendar, we will "do" the Christmas tree. We have already planned all sorts of surprises. It would be nice if you could come to us for the New Year.

They have brought me my tea. . . . Good-by! Best of luck. Take care of yourself. Write me!

Yours

S. Rachmaninoff

Amsterdam, December 11, 1908.

Finally, when Rachmaninoff was back in Russia enjoying his summer at Ivanovka, he received a cable from America saying that his manager had died.

. . . It looks as though even this time I am not going to get to America [Rachmaninoff wrote to Morozov]. *In this cable I was informed that from now on my managers are going to be the wife of the deceased assisted by someone else. I decided to tempt fate once more and sent them my contract at once, asking them all, including "the wife," to sign my contract as a guarantee for me.*

Now, I presume, that once they will get back my contract they will be happy that they have gotten rid of at least one of the artists who was left on their hands and will destroy it.

To hell with it! I will be delighted! Meanwhile, last week I received a notice from a New York bank that Wolfsohn[2] had deposited twenty-five hundred dollars into my account for the last five concerts according to our contract. He certainly managed to do it in time! Perhaps he died from vexation. Thus my America is in complete confusion again. . . .

However, six weeks later this American confusion was cleared up.

My dear friend Nikita Semenovich, I have not written you for a long time and you are probably angry with me. I beg your pardon, though except for my work I cannot find any good excuse for not writing you. I would have written you but business letters were in my way, letters in connection either with publishing or the office of the Musical Society or my own artistic activities, which once called for your just remark that I had become a "Flying Dutchman."

It would not be bad at all for me to get a secretary, if only the amount of business correspondence I have would correspond to the amount of my material means. But before getting a secretary I would like to buy an automobile! I want one so much, I just cannot tell you! All I need is a secretary and an automobile! Otherwise I have everything I need.

Today I changed some of my plans so that I could write letters. Thus, I work a great deal. You, of course, would like to know the net results and I have nothing to say, except that I did not finish anything, that I have very little time left, which worries me, that I am not contented with what I have already done, that it is very difficult for me to compose,

2 Henry Wolfsohn, Rachmaninoff's manager.

etc., etc. *The usual story. I can add that I am not lazy—my sole consolation.*

And then about my health. It looks as though it were improving. I feel stronger. I should go to weigh myself, but I cannot find the time to do it. I am too busy. I have probably gained ten pounds. This is consoling. But what is not consoling is that—I am going to America, after all. The devil take her. I feel I could even give up the idea of a secretary just so that I would not have to go there. This is how much I do not want to go there! Perhaps, though, after I return from America I will buy myself an automobile. Then it will have been worth it. . . .

Sunday afternoon, November 28, 1909, Sergei Rachmaninoff played his third piano concerto, which he had composed during the past summer[3] especially for his debut in the United States, with the New York Symphony Orchestra conducted by Walter Damrosch.

The New York *Herald* reported on the following day: "Mr. Rachmaninoff was recalled several times in the determined effort of the audience to make him play again, but he held up his hands with a gesture which meant that although he was willing, his fingers were not. So the audience laughed and let him retire."

The critics unanimously agreed that the third concerto was not as striking in its originality as Rachmaninoff's second, that in parts it was vague and groped for form and theme, and that it was so loosely put together that one was more interested in the statement than in its development, which was both moody and indefinite.

[3] There is no record, either in *Rachmaninoff's Recollections* or in any of his letters, concerning his work on this piano concerto.

A critic of the *Sun* wrote his review with such insight and fairness that after the forty years of the concerto's career there is not much that one can add, despite the development and changes of our musical tastes. Here are some excerpts:

. . . The concerto was too long and it lacked rhythmic and harmonic contrast between the first movement and the rest of the concerto. The opening theme in D minor is tinged with melancholy of a sort typical in late years of a good deal of Russian music. This is the melancholy of inactivity, of what may be the resignation or submission or distrust of one's powers, and it does not rise, as did Tchaikovsky's, to the pitch of surging passion or high tragedy. . . . Russia's present-day composers have been charged before now with failing under the stress of recurring periods of political and social unrest. Rachmaninoff has been looked to among the younger men as likeliest after Glazunov to attain abroad nationalism of idea and expression. He has not done so in this concerto unless the outside world is laboring under a delusion as to what real Russia is. . . . The new concerto, then, may be taken as a purely personal utterance of the composer and it has at times the character of an impromptu, so unstudied and informal is its speech and so prone, too, to repetition. . . . The same mood of honesty and simplicity and the single pursuit of musical beauty, without desire to baffle or astonish, dominated Mr. Rachmaninoff's playing of his new concerto. The pianist's touch had the loving quality that holds something of the creative and his execution was sufficiently facile to meet his self-imposed test. Sound, reasonable music this, though not a great or memorable proclamation.

This concerto, which has gained even more popularity since Vladimir Horowitz has included it in his repertoire, Rachmaninoff—according to his own story—learned on the boat on his way to New York, using a dumb piano; and at the concert Walter Damrosch and the musicians played from the manuscript.

Rachmaninoff followed his debut in New York by a series of

appearances as pianist and conductor. He conducted his second symphony in Philadelphia and Chicago, his *Island of the Dead* in Chicago and Boston, and played recitals with programs consisting exclusively of his own works.

After this three-month tour the consensus of the press was that Rachmaninoff, who had been received with the enthusiasm that befits an honored guest, had left the impression of a pianist with great if not supreme gifts, a conductor of marked ability, and a composer of indubitable talents, who took a serious and dignified attitude toward his art.

In Boston he was offered the position of conductor of the Boston Symphony, but the mere thought of leaving Moscow made him decline the invitation. And here is what Rachmaninoff wrote to his friends at home.

I am weary of America and I have had more than enough of it. Just imagine: to concertize almost every day during the three months! I have played my own compositions exclusively. I was a great success and I was recalled to give encores as many as seven times. This was a great deal, considering the audiences there. The audiences are remarkably cold, spoiled by the guest performances of first-class artists, those audiences which always seek something extraordinary, something different from the last one. Their newspapers always remark on how many times the artist was recalled to take a bow and for the large public this is the yardstick of your talent, if you please.

. XI .

Marietta Shaginian

IT WAS REPORTED that upon his return from the United States, Rachmaninoff intended to stay in Russia. He declined a very lucrative offer for another tour of the United States because he felt too lonely when separated from his family for such a long time. He preferred remaining in Russia, where his popularity was steadily growing.

It is interesting to note that during all his travels Rachmaninoff never made any contacts with the composers in the Western world. All Russian composers without known exception since the time of Glinka and Dargomyzhski had sought such contacts as soon as they crossed the border. But not Rachmaninoff. And there is no record left of the attempts made by his Western confreres to get into closer relationship with him, because his purely businesslike attitude of a visiting virtuoso and his known aloofness to any social functions forbade any close approach to him. His interest in the contemporary foreign music, in "what was going on," he satisfied by occasionally going to concerts or the opera, and at home in Russia since being married he had withdrawn from his circle of old friends

—Sakhnovsky, Slonov, and Chaliapin—into his own family circle, where those who could have had any influence on him were confronted with a family wall.

Two years after his return a new influence—which was not made public until after the composer's death—entered his life via a romantic if not an unusual channel. I am speaking of his relationship with Marietta Shaginian, the Russian authoress. Outside the circle of his musical friends hers was the only advice he followed in the choice of material for his compositions and she was the only woman outside of his family whose relationship with him has been documented. It started with a fan letter written by her to Rachmaninoff some thirty-odd years before the publication of the correspondence which revealed this unknown chapter in his life.

The publication of these letters had as startling an effect as had at one time the announcement of Rachmaninoff's marriage to his first cousin, Nataly Satin. Even his schoolmates and those who thought they knew him intimately throughout his life knit their eyebrows trying to remember what possible relation Marietta Shaginian could have had to the composer.

Today the sixty-one-year-old Marietta Shaginian is a Soviet authoress of note who has been decorated with the Order of the Red Banner. "Marietta Shaginian was one of the first authors," reads her official record in the Soviet Encyclopedia, "to turn from the religious as well as exotically erotic-bourgeois intellectual interest in her art to the proletariat and to support the revolution with her artistic ability." In 1919 she became a social worker and organized the first school for spinning and weaving in the region of the river Don. Several of her novels are based on the lives of workers connected with hydraulic and electric power plants, in which she took a great interest.

But thirty-seven years ago—that is when she belongs to my

story—Marietta Shaginian was just one of the many intellectual girls who attended courses in philosophy and literature at the universities and were to be seen at the art exhibitions and the concert halls. Her thick black hair, dark eyes, prominent nose, and full mouth bespoke her Armenian descent, while the serious expression on her face reflected a strong will, a sharp mind, and a thirst for knowledge. A daughter of Sergei Shaginian, one of the members of the faculty of the University in Moscow, Marietta was a studious girl who quoted Hegel and Kant, and whose enthusiasm for Goethe even led her to make a pilgrimage to Weimar. She was already known among literary circles for her numerous articles on art, literature, and music as well as for her short stories, which had appeared in periodicals for the past nine years, and a book of poems published when she was seventeen.

Marietta Shaginian writes skillfully and with conviction. Although she sees Moscow now through the prism of an honored Soviet citizen, I quote her article which was published with Sergei Rachmaninoff's letters as a sort of commentary on the Moscow of that time.

"The youth of our generation used to refer to the first fifteen years of our century as timeless," she wrote. "Time seemed to have stopped, seemed to have moved outside of history. In the very air, in the mood of the people there was an expectation— the seemingly passionate desire for something to happen so that the rhythm and movement of history might again become perceptible. . . . The artists and students became neurasthenic, suffered from a deep inner crisis, and were seeking help and clarification for their problems from those who were as doubtful and helpless as themselves. This is why personal intercourse became so important in their lives: it substituted for a union with the collective.

"Complete strangers wrote letters to each other and a great deal of spiritual strength was spent that way," continued Madame Shaginian, as her thoughts took her back to the Moscow of 1912. In her memory Moscow was then "so small that it would be hard to imagine it now. The building of the Noblemen's Club, now 'The Home of Professional Unions,' seemed a giant standing against the bottleneck of Tverskoy Street which led to the Tverskoy Chapel where the small one-story shops—the famous Okhotny Ryad—crowded into the little crooked streets. Moscow was also small because that group of people who went to concerts, expositions, and theaters was always the same. Everyone knew everyone else. And everyone knew the other's tastes, opinions, and social position, and somehow one did not expect anything new or startling from this group."

Marietta belonged to that small Moscow. She was not a professionally trained musician; she knew and loved music like so many of her generation who were educated in the so-called "closed pensions"—that is, in private boarding schools for girls. In these schools there was always a music room where the girls diligently practiced two hours a day. The picture of the long empty corridors of the building remained forever in their memory, the smell of the evening tea with milk, the long, trembling sound of the bell calling them to prayer in the morning, and the dreary, monotonous cascades of scales and exercises coming out of the music room.

Music was obligatory. It included choir-singing, piano or violin lessons, and later elementary theory and harmony, so that when the girls were graduated, they spoke proudly of "reading scores," while all they could do was to follow the music with their eyes on the printed page.

But after they left school, whether they chose to become

musicians or not, the girls continued to be interested in the musical life of Moscow and one could always see them in Nobility's Hall in the specially reserved standing room, the so-called "back of the *colonnes*" places, which cost only fifty kopecks apiece. There, "back of the *colonnes*," everything was known about the favored musicians. There the Moscow youth created their idols and whispered stories and legends, and hearts beat faster and the blood rushed to their cheeks at the mere mention of a favorite name.

In 1912, Sergei Rachmaninoff was one of these favorites. They greeted his concert appearances with ovations and often waited far into the night to see him leave the hall or get into the large black carriage which took him home. Sometimes the police had to be called to help to extricate the young "Rach-maninostok"—those young ladies who had hidden themselves in his carriage.

Rachmaninoff's admirers walked home elated by his music, but they also worried about him. His "all-buttoned-up" appearance made them think of him as a West European, and his haughty manner, emphasized by his height, kept them at a distance when their excited and loving natures wanted to approach him with warmth and comfort. They heard that he was not well, that it was hard for him to play, that he was not happy, that the well-known Dr. Dahl gave him hypnotic treatments, and that because of this he had dedicated to him his second concerto.

"At that time (1912) they did not clean the heavy snow from the streets in Moscow," wrote Marietta Shaginian. "The winter silenced the street noises; inside the houses one did not feel the city's shivers. Full, deep, cottonlike quiet enveloped the nights of Moscow. Heavy snow was lying on the pavements, the roofs and the eaves of the houses; the gardens looked as though they were dressed in silver and along the wide avenues sleighs glided softly through the snow.

"In February, 1912, such a snow storm was raging that one almost felt lost even in the center of the city. One felt as though one were swept onto the Russian steppes, into Pushkin's *Snow Storm*. It was during one of these February nights that I wrote a letter to Sergei Rachmaninoff, whom I did not know at the time. I sent my letter to catch him in St. Petersburg, where he had gone for a concert, and I signed it 'Re' [D in the musical scale] to conceal my true name. Later on, even up to the last days of our friendship (which lasted from February, 1912, until July, 1917) I remained 'Re' for him. He never called me anything else."

Unfortunately, no letters of Marietta Shaginian have survived, but here are fifteen of the letters written to her by Sergei Rachmaninoff which she was willing to have published.[1]

Marietta Shaginian, a poetess, an author, but above all a clever woman, chose these letters in such a way as to give a glimpse of their relationship, allowing the reader to use his own imagination by reading between the lines.

As for her article, it must be remembered that it was written for publication in 1946, when Marietta Shaginian was an honored Soviet poetess. Therefore a great deal of what she attributes to Rachmaninoff, particularly his restlessness because of the political situation in Russia at the time of their friendship, is probably a product of Marietta Shaginian's fantasy. What Marietta Shaginian failed to say was that at the age of twenty-four she had fallen in love with Sergei Rachmaninoff as so many young girls—music enthusiasts—had done. Behind those avowals of common intellectual interest, those arrangements of texts for his compositions, and a sort of mother complex of

[1] *Novy Mir*, Moscow, 1943, No. 4.

guarding and worrying over him, she was a young woman in love who did not have the audacity to say right out, "I think I am the woman for you."

As for Rachmaninoff's side of the story, it is all told in his own words in his letters. However, even from this scant material it is obvious that Marietta Shaginian occupied the composer's mind more than usual and that she had a definite influence upon him. A woman with a strong will of her own, Marietta Shaginian took the reins into her own hands right from the beginning, and their correspondence became firmly established with the following letter which Rachmaninoff wrote in St. Petersburg, obviously answering several letters from a persistent young admirer.

My dear[2] Re—

Thank you for your charming letter which I received yesterday. I would like very much to talk to you only I am so busy, I have so much to do, I travel so much, and I am so tired that I can "talk" only very rarely. This time I am trying to be very exact because of the ultimatum you delivered to me at the end of your letter. Write me here (I am going to be here until the end of next week). What is the matter with you? Are you ill? Why do your letters leave such a sad impression?

S. Rachmaninoff

February 14, 1912

My dear Re—

You are not going to be angry with me if I ask you to do me a favor? And if it is not going to be too hard for you,

---

[2] "My dear" is used in the personal English sense of the word rather than the American formal.

will you do it? Now here I am going to tell you how you can help me. I need texts for my songs. Could you suggest something? I imagine that "Re" knows a great deal in this field; she knows almost everything, or perhaps even everything.

Whether it is going to be a contemporary author or one who is dead is immaterial. So long as the piece is original and not translated and not longer than eight or twelve—sixteen lines at the maximum. And here is something else. The mood should be rather sad than gay. The light, gay colors do not come easily to me.

I am going to wait for your answer. Thus until the next letter. I hope that you feel better now, that you are well.

S. Rachmaninoff

P.S.

I do not write you anything about myself because I do not know how to write it and I do not like it. And it was the truth (and not a lie!) when someone told you that I am a most ordinary and uninteresting man.

March 15, 1912
Marietta Shaginian wrote in her article:

The early literary tastes of Rachmaninoff were more or less haphazard and as he needed texts for his songs our correspondence immediately became a sort of intercourse between musician and writer. He asked me to help him and I often copied, prepared, and arranged verses, poems, and texts of Russian poets for him, classic as well as contemporary. The latter, by the way, he did not particularly like. Nevertheless, I succeeded in making him realize the value of some works by Alexander Block (*In my garden*), Andrey Belyi (*Grasses waved so tearfully*), Vallery Bryousov (*The Pied Piper*). Rachmaninoff wrote these songs after my arrangements of the texts.

Usually I tried to "read" them to him. Before I actually met him personally I tried to do this in my letters. I tried with every possible means, such as drawing graphically the rhythm of the verses, the wave of it. . . . I used the method of comparison, and by all sorts of analogies I explained the inner sound of the verse. In one of my letters I also analyzed Pushkin's *Muse* for him. Rachmaninoff dedicated this song to me.[3] (Later Nicolay Medtner, hearing me recite the *Muse*, became very enthusiastic and also composed a song which he dedicated to me.)

Sometimes I became impertinent enough to make suggestions to Rachmaninoff regarding his music: "What I would have done were I in his place." Rachmaninoff followed my advice.

My dear Re—

I received your letter and your book (I did not receive your letter in Charlottenburg). Thank you very much for everything. I read everything you sent me. Only Baratynsky's *Spring* will be of use to me. The Oriental Melodies are good but cannot be used as texts for songs, as you yourself so justly remarked. I have not had time yet to see everything that you marked with the little crosses that look like signs of sharps (Re sharp?).

I am going to force myself to copy everything that you recommend, so that I will have it ready this summer, when I plan to start work.

Now, concerning the contents of your letter I will answer all your questions in a businesslike fashion. First of all a few words about your injustice. In your last letter you were not always just toward me, my dear Re. Here is an example. After you had mercilessly criticized The Little Verses of Galina, you remarked—and not without poison in your tone—that I love to use "these little verses." In reality I used them two or three times out of fifty-one. . . . And here also you warned me not to seek a cheap theatrical success for my songs! This

[3] Dedicated to Re on June 6, 1912.

is even worse! Do you think it was necessary to say this to me, my dear Re?

Then concerning Sakhnovsky—I do not protest against your criticism of him personally, or his writings. But why do you suspect me of taking all these articles seriously into account and even of being influenced by them? Thus it seems that as soon as Sakhnovsky wrote that I was the troubadour of "horror and tragedy" I changed my trend immediately and declared to you that "light colors do not come easily to me," and now you tell me not to believe Sakhnovsky.

To tell the truth, I do not read Sakhnovsky's articles (I know that they are favorable). I do not read them because all of them are unconvincing to me. Deep inside me, to be honest about it, I rather prefer to believe and to listen to my heart because there is no critic in the world who is more doubtful about me than myself. . . . I write so little about myself (or do not write at all) because I hardly know you, my dear Re. Let me first get a better look at you, or perhaps hear more from you.

You ask me about my children! You say that it will give you great pleasure if I tell you something about them. All right!

I have two daughters, eight and four years old. Their names are Irina and Tatiana, or Bob and Tassinka. They are two disobedient, badly brought up, but charming and very interesting girls. I love them terribly! They are the dearest and the brightest things in my life! (And in brightness there is silence and happiness! You are right when you say this, my dear Re!) And the girls love me very much. Once, some time ago, I got angry at the youngest and told her that I would stop loving her. She began to pout, left the room, telling me that if I stopped loving her, she would run into the woods! I feel the same way about them. All these last weeks both girls and I have been ill. We all had influenza with more or less serious complications. Now we are almost well. On the 24th of March in the evening, when your roses were brought to me, I had just returned to my room after a consultation with the doctor at the bedside of my daughter—the one who wanted to run into the woods. . . .

Your letter of the 24th just arrived. Tassinka and I are very grateful to you.

S. Rachmaninoff

March 29, 1912

Where did you hear, my dear Re, that I love the young girls who study at the Conservatory or those who go to the Philharmonic concerts? One seldom meets such people, who are so sure of themselves outwardly and are so poor inwardly. What can be worse than this?

You ask me what I love beside my children, music, and flowers? Anything you like, my dear Re! Even crab soup, if you like, only not our musical young ladies.

My dear Re, I did not have time in Moscow to write you and want to do this now in Tambov, where I have to wait some time for a train to take me to our country place. I want to write you, if only a few lines, a few words of gratitude for your dear, funny letter and for the book with the poems which you copied with so much energy and patience. I would say that you have Boborikin's[4] ability to work if I were not afraid of a poisonous sermon from you.

I am going to the country. My family will join me in about a week. I shall be awaiting your address and then I shall write you. Until the next letter! I wish you happiness.

S. Rachmaninoff

April 28, 1912

[4] Peter D. Boborikin (1836-1921), a prolific journalist and author.

In 1912, Marietta Shaginian became a close friend of the family of Emil Medtner, the philosopher. The Medtner family consisted of four brothers: Karl the businessman, Emil the philosopher, Nicolay the composer, and Alexander the viola player. Every one of them (except the businessman) was considered by his brothers as a "genuis." Instead of the icon, a mask of Beethoven hung in the corner of their sitting room, because "for the next thousand years the Fifth Symphony will remain the greatest creation in the Art of sound." So pronounced brother Emil.

The two eldest brothers, Karl and Emil, married the two sisters Bratenshy. Anna Bratenshy, who married Emil, later left him for his brother Nicolay and eventually became his wife.

Marietta Shaginian spent many weeks as a guest in their house, where Nicolay Medtner, the composer, also lived. "A cultured German family, an organized life with the obligatory reading aloud, speaking two foreign languages—German and French—a library of philosophical works the equal of which I never found anywhere in Moscow, and finally the music played and discussed in their home made this period of my life 'my Athenian period,' as I used to call it. This was my schooling in literature, science and art. I am very indebted to the Medtner family."

Marietta Shaginian wrote this in her autobiography, and at the time of her correspondence with Rachmaninoff she tried to persuade him to join their circle.

About this same time Marietta Shaginian wrote an extremely long article, "Sergei Rachmaninoff—a musical-psychological study," which was published in the magazine *Trudi i Dni* (1912). Though a good story teller, Marietta failed completely in this essay for the simple reason that no amount of high-sounding ideas shrouded in quotations from great thinkers and aesthetes could hide her lack of real knowledge of music and psychology. One wades through page after page of analyses, hyperboles, and axioms, interspersed with the most complicated phraseology, before one finds a breathing spell where she attacks those critics who dared to compare Rachmaninoff with Tchaikovsky. She ascribes to Rachmaninoff a position in the musical world to which he never aspired, and attributes to him qualities which were but the flight of her own imagination. Not competent herself in musical analysis beyond banal generalities, she repeats almost to the letter what Emil Medtner, under his pen name Wolfing, wrote in his articles on music.

The following letter was not Rachmaninoff's comment on Shaginian's article about him, but one of the regular letters in their correspondence.

Besides my children, music, and flowers I also love you, my dear Re, and your letters. I love you because you are clever, interesting, and you do not go to extremes (this is one of the most important conditions for anyone to be "attractive" to me), and I love your letters because I find in them your faith, love, and hope in me—the balm with which I cure my wounds. You described me remarkably correctly though with a certain amount of timidity and uncertainty. How do you know me so well? I cannot stop wondering. From now on, whenever I have to speak of myself, I can always refer to you and quote from your letters. Your authority in this matter is indisputable. . . . I am speaking seriously. There is only one thing that is not so good: since you are not sure that the portrait which you are painting from your imagination resembles the original like two drops of water, you seek in me something that is not there and you want to see me as I do not believe I will ever be.

My "criminal spiritual humility" (from the letters of Re) is unfortunately very obvious, and my "ruin resulting from the narrow-mindedness and philistinism" which surround me (also from the letters of Re) appears to me as it does to you to be in the very near future. All of this is true. And it is true because I have no faith in myself. Teach me to have faith in myself, my dear Re! Perhaps just half as much as you have in me. If I ever had faith in myself, that was a long time ago, a very long time ago—in my youth! (Then I was a disheveled musician—a type definitely preferred by you to the kind that neither you nor I like.)

It is not without a reason that for the past twenty years my only doctors have been the hypnotist Dr. Dahl and my two cousins (one of whom I married ten years ago and whom I also love very much and beg you to add their names to the list of those I love). All these people, or better said, doctors, taught me only two things: to be brave and to have faith. Sometimes I succeed in doing it. But my sickness sits in me so firmly and with the years has developed even deeper. It will be understandable if eventually I will decide to give up composing and will become either a pianist, a conductor, or a country squire—perhaps, even an automobile racer. . . .

Yesterday it occurred to me that what you wish to see in me you can find close to you in somebody else—in Medtner. While describing him as well as you do me, you would like to attach to me everything that belongs to him. It is significant that half of every letter is devoted to him. It is significant also that you would like particularly to see me in his, in "their" society, in this "holy place, where they argue, defend, receive confessions, and repudiate" (from the letters of Re). Would

I not also see and meet there "the youth of our time who write verses with such ease and, helas, very far from real poetry" (from the letters of Re)? These are the "disheveled," I am sure! It is fortunate, however, that the central figure, the subject, is this time well chosen. Indeed, Medtner himself is not "disheveled" the way you would like to see me. And I have no prejudice against him. On the contrary! I love him very much and I admire him, and speaking frankly (as, by the way, I always do with you), I consider him one of the most talented among the contemporary composers. He is one of those rare people—as a musician and a human being—who grows in stature as one knows him better. This is the fate of few and I wish him all the best. Yes, this is Medtner—young, healthy, strong and energetic, armed with a lyre in his hands! And I? I am mentally sick, my dear Re, and consider myself unarmed and already fairly old. If I have anything good, it is hardly in my future. . . .

As to what concerns the society of Medtner—well, let it be. I am afraid of all of them ("criminal timidity and cowardice!" —from the letters of Re) and would prefer this "essence of true art" (from the same letters of Re—your letters). And why do I write all this to you, my dear Re? "Alone with my soul" I do not like the content of this letter.

To close, just a few words of a different order. As I am always attentive to your words and wishes, I am writing you this letter "during a sleepy spring evening." Probably this "sleepy evening" is responsible for this unpardonable letter, which I beg you to forget very quickly. . . .

The windows are closed. It is cold, my dear Re, but according to your instructions, the lamp on the table is lit. Because of the cold, the cockchafers that you love so much and whom I detest and am terrified of have, thank God, not been born. My windows have big wooden shutters which I close with iron bolts. I feel more secure that way during the evenings and nights. This is again, of course, my "criminal timidity and cowardice." I am afraid of everything: mice, rats, cockchafers, bulls, burglars, I am afraid of the strong wind which blows and howls and wails in the chimney. I am afraid when the raindrops beat against the windowpane, I am afraid of the dark, and so on. I do not like old attics and I am ready to believe that ghosts live there (I am sure you are interested in all this!), otherwise how can one explain that I am frightened even during the daytime when I am alone?

Ivanovka is an old estate which belongs to my wife. I consider it my own, as I have been living here for the last twenty-three years. It was here, right here, a long time ago, when I was very young, that I worked so well. However, this is an old refrain, and what else is there to tell you? Better nothing at all. Good night, my dear Re. Farewell and try to cure me also. . . . I probably will not write you soon again.

S. Rachmaninoff

May 8, 1912

My dear Re—

A few days ago I finished my new songs. Half of them are written after poems from your copybook. Here again is the list, in case you are interested: A. Pushkin: Storm, Arion, and Muse (the latter is dedicated to you); Tyutchev: You Knew Him, I Remember This Day; A. Fet: What Happiness; Polonsky: The Music of the Dissonance; Khomyakov: The Resurrection of Lazar; Maykov: It Cannot Be, written on the death of his daughter; Korinfsky: In the Heart of Every One of Us; Balmont: The Wind. Fortunately I could not use the verses of Galina because I did not have them. . . .

On the whole I feel very happy about these songs and I am very happy that I succeeded in writing them without much suffering. I wish to God that my future work would be like this. . . .

I received the Anthology which you sent me. But I like very little in it. In fact I was horrified by most of the poems. Very often I saw remarks written on the margins by Re: "This is good," or "All this is good," and I tried for a long time to understand what it was that Re thought so good! Often I remembered the remark made by M. Shaginian, in a little book I received: "It is sometimes very difficult to explain the sense of a poem."

Good-by, dear Re. Take care of yourself. Where are you now?

S. Rachmaninoff

June 19, 1912

My dear Re—

Unfortunately I can write you only a few lines—just answer your questions.

Thank you for your article. There is a lot that is interesting and your remarks are so true. You are particularly right when you refer to your own letter to me. But in the final account you are wrong. My "weight" is exaggerated. In reality I weigh less (and less every day).

And now I will turn to your instructions—you always have some for me. Well, tell me for instance, how can you, my dear Re, blame me for the stories the reporters write about me in the newspapers. And how could you, who "feel me as a musician," not recognize in me a man who is far removed from newspaper gossip and who hates all these passages, so favored by tenors. Your complaints against Berlioz and Liszt convince me that you do not like their compositions. It only remains for me to regret that I do not feel about them the same way, or that you do not feel about them as I do.

Your reproach, that I have forgotten you, makes no sense. I remember you very well, and I love you very much. This is by now a hackneyed truth. If I do not answer your letters promptly, it is only because of my large correspondence and all sorts of business. . . . I have no tuberculosis. I am just tired, very tired, and I live on my last strength. (Yesterday at the concert, for the first time in my life, on one of the fermate I forgot what to do next and to the great distress of the whole orchestra I tried for a long time to remember what was coming next. I wish to God I could leave soon. My songs will be published in about a month. Muse is dedicated to Re. . . .

I did the right thing in writing E. Medtner a short note thanking him for sending me his book. Then I had only received the book and hadn't had time to read it. Now that I have read it I have nothing to add. I do not like the book. I feel in every line of the book the clean-shaven face of Mr. Medtner, as though he were saying, "It is all a lot of nonsense what is said here about music, and it is of no importance anyway. The most important thing is, look at me and see how intelligent I am." And this is true! E. Medtner is an intelligent man. But I would much rather learn this from his biography (which probably will soon become public) than from a book on "music" which has nothing in common with him. I am impatiently awaiting the book you promised me. Couldn't you suggest something new and Russian that is interesting? (But not the "Anthology" type.)

You have disclosed your name to me. I must confess to you that I have known it for a long time. I discovered it purely by chance. . . . Good-by! I wish you all the best, and from my heart.

S. R.

November 12, 1912

The book by Emil Medtner to which Rachmaninoff referred was published in Moscow in 1912 by the "Musaget," the publishers of the magazine *Trudi i Dni* (*Works and Days*) to which E. Medtner and Marietta Shaginian contributed many articles. Medtner wrote under the pen name "Wolfing" and this book, *Modernism and Music*, consisted of a collection of his critical and polemical articles written in the years 1907 through 1910, with the addition of articles written in 1911, numbering altogether four hundred and forty-six pages.

The first part of the book included critical articles on composers as well as performers (mostly German and Russian) and short essays, if one may term them such, on the science of criticism, different styles, "Modernism and artistic truth," dilettantism, music and ideas, the cult of the child prodigy, the behavior of performers on the stage, Apollonism and Dionycism, etc., along with "vogue" and its influence on music and the "Judaism" in music to which most of the book was devoted and on which most of the criticisms were founded. Medtner's book, published in 1912, reads as though it were dictated by the *Gauleiter* of music in Nazi Germany.

It is not surprising that Rachmaninoff did not like the book: Medtner praised him as a pianist but not as a composer.

During this flirtatious correspondence, which lasted for nearly ten months, Marietta Shaginian signed her letters with the obviously invented name "Re" and even sent her own books to Rachmaninoff without telling him that Shaginian, the authoress, and "Re" were the same person.

Sergei Rachmaninoff played his part like a gentleman and did not let her know that he understood her coquettish game.

". . . Our correspondence resulted in our meeting at the end of 1912 and it then turned into a friendship," wrote Marietta Shaginian.

My dear Re—

We are leaving in an hour. Let me say "Au revoir" to you and express to you my happiness in meeting you and at last seeing Re with my own eyes. I will await your letter and your book. You can send it to Berlin, Musikverlag, Dessauerstrasse, to Sergei Rachmaninoff.

. . . I will be in Berlin for about a week. Where I shall go from there I still do not know. I am repeating again that you can send all letters care of the Gutheil's music shop; they always forward my mail.

All my best wishes, and from the depths of my heart.

S. Rachmaninoff

December 5, 1912

I am very grateful to you, my dear Re, for the little book which you presented to me. I certainly like a lot in it. But I will not comment at length because first of all I am afraid of you and then I have looked at it too superficially to report to the author. One thing I definitely do not approve of—I am speaking of the introduction to the reader. I would rather hear this information not from you but about you and written by someone else. I am afraid that many after reading it will become prejudiced. However, please forgive me. You can judge this better than I.

Just a few words about myself. . . . After a month spent in Switzerland my health improved, but in six weeks here I have lost everything I gained in Switzerland. I have been working very hard and I still am. It is such a pity that I am tired again, sleep badly, and feel weak. By the way, this is the reason why I did not answer your letter for such an unpardonably long time. (Though I said "unpardonably," I still trust to your kindness and believe you will forgive me.)

148

What are all these misfortunes that are happening to you, my dear Re? Why do you say "you have suffered so"? Does this still continue to this day? Write me.

We will be here for another month and we hope to be in Moscow for Easter. Until then I have a great deal, a great deal to do.

Greetings and best wishes from my heart.

S. Rachmaninoff

March 23, 1913

At last I received your letter, my dear Re, and I know where you are [Rachmaninoff wrote to Shaginian, who was in Steinach-am-Brenner in the Austrian Tirol]. If I had not got this letter, I had already decided to write you today and to address it to "the one" with whom you would like me to be such friends.

Rachmaninoff was referring to Emil Medtner when he spoke of "the one" or "it," and Shaginian's "mission" was her endeavor to bring Rachmaninoff into the Medtners' circle.

"The one" or "it" probably knows all about you. A strange thing! I love you and want to see you, hear you, and read you, but I am afraid of "the one." As though you were answering me, I read in your letter "I consider my mission to be accomplished" (what mission? and when did you accomplish it?). Ah, here you have the "it," this is something for you. "Why don't you become friends?" Thank you very much. In reply to you I must say that I accept with regret and surprise the first part of your statement and definitely refuse the second part.

Now I turn to your questions. There are only two, and I have little time, considering that my bags are packed to leave!

My children, thank God, are well. I myself have been working every day for the last two months. But sometimes the work becomes unbearable. Then I take my car and drive as far as twenty-five miles deep into the country. I breathe the air and bless the freedom and the blue skies. After such an "air bath" I feel much better and have more energy. [Rachmaninoff had at last bought himself a car after he returned from the United States.]

A few days ago I finished a poem for orchestra, chorus, and solo voices, the text of Edgar Poe's The Bells, translated by Balmont.

Before we leave I have still another work to finish. From October on I have concerts and tours, and tours and concerts. This is a "mission" I would like to see someday "accomplished."

Good-by, and best luck to you in your travels!

S. Rachmaninoff

June 29, 1913

My dear Re [Rachmaninoff wrote to Shaginian in Moscow]—

I have no envelopes, therefore forgive me for writing you a postcard. An hour ago your articles and your letter with your address reached me. I am taking this opportunity to ask you a favor. Today I received an offer from the Committee for the 350-year celebration of Shakespeare to do a scene from King Lear.

Tell me, please, if there is a new translation of Lear. If there is none, let me know which of the old translations is considered the best. Is there an edition of King Lear in a separate volume? Could I ask you to send me one copy immediately? Though I have no envelopes, nor Shakespeare, at least I have a conscience and I promise immediately to send you the price of the book in stamps with my most sincere gratitude.

How is your health? I am very industrious in the country.

S.R.

August 30, 1913

My dear Re—

I will try to do everything as you ask me. We will see each other at Medtner's, if he will ask me. I am free on Tuesday.

Au revoir!

September 12, 1914   S. R.

As I was clearing my writing table today, I reread some of your letters, my dear Re [Rachmaninoff wrote to Shaginian, who had moved from Moscow to Nakhichevan on the Don with her mother], and while reading them, I felt toward you so much gentleness, gratitude, and besides something so bright, so good, that I wanted painfully to see you at once, to hear you, to sit next to you, and to talk to you frankly and intimately, to talk to you about you, about myself, about anything you would like. Or perhaps, keep silent! But above all to see you and sit next to you. . . . Oh, where are you, my dear Re? And when, when will I see you?

S. R.

September 20, 1916

Of her encounters with Rachmaninoff, Marietta Shaginian says in her article:

We used to meet at our house or at Medtner's, where I often visited for a few weeks, or at Rachmaninoff's on Strassnoy Boulevard or in the North of Caucasus in Mineralny Vody, while he took a cure in Essentuky and I lived in Kislovodsk.

151

When my sister and I moved to Nakhichevan on the Don to live with my mother, Rachmaninoff, whenever he passed Rostov on the Don on his concert tours, always either came to visit us or, if he did not have enough time, called me to come to him in Rostov.

My dear Re [wrote Rachmaninoff to her in Nakhichevan]—
May I come to you tomorrow (Friday) between five and six in the evening? Give me an answer.

S. Rachmaninoff

Thursday, November 5, 1916

Of this last visit with her in Nakhichevan, Shaginian says in her article:

The last time Rachmaninoff came to us in Nakhichevan was in 1916. Then he was suffering from a fear of death. I remember how he begged my mother to tell his fortune and how long he was going to live. One of the books of Artsibashev[5] which he read had made a tremendous impression on him.

"One cannot live if one has to die. How can you bear the thought that you are going to die?" While he was saying this, he was eating salted peanuts, which he liked so much that we always had some ready for him. Then he looked into the empty plate and said: "Because of the peanuts my fear has disappeared. Do you know where it has disappeared to?" My mother gave him a whole bag of peanuts to take along with him as a talisman against the fear of death.

My dear Re [he wrote to Marietta Shaginian in Nakhichevan]—
Only today and very late I arrived in Rostov. Tomorrow

[5] Mikhail Artsibashev (1878-1927), Russian novelist. On his mother's side a great-grandson of Kosciusko. His first novel, *Sanin*, 1907, showed him in revolt against all social restraints.

morning I am leaving and will not return. I want to see you but I cannot go to you. Perhaps you will consent to come to me today before the concert in the Music School? We will be alone, I promise you. About six-thirty in the evening? We could spend an hour and a half together. I will play and you, you will talk to me. All right?

I am sending you my songs.

Sincerely devoted to you,

January 26, 1917

Yours,

S. R.

P.S.: Give me an answer.

I quote the following from Marietta Shaginian's article which was published with Rachmaninoff's letters.

Rachmaninoff was an important composer, but he was one of the greatest pianists [wrote Marietta Shaginian]. "Our epoch did not know another virtuoso who was more brilliant or stronger in the art of interpretation. His playing was demonlike. When he was at the piano, he could convince you of anything. He could convince you that one of his trifles, something like his E-flat minor *Moment Musical*, had no equal in the whole of musical literature —so strong, so categorical was his power over his listener.

Once during an intermission such a storm of wild enthusiasm reigned in the hall that it was almost impossible to get through the crowd. When we entered the green room, we found Rachmaninoff in a terrible state. Before we had a chance to congratulate him, Rachmaninoff, angrily biting his lip, began to complain that he was getting old, losing his mind, that he belonged to the scrap heap, that one should prepare an obituary for him telling everyone that there had been a musician, but now nothing was left of him, that he could not forgive himself for . . . , etc., etc.

"Didn't you notice that I missed the point?[6] The point came down, do you understand?" he said.

[6] Rachmaninoff meant the climax.

Later he told me that every piece he played had a construction with a culminating "point." And that he felt that one should measure and divide the whole mass of sounds so as to give depth and force in such gradation that this high point would flash, as, for instance, when the ribbon falls down at the end of a race, or when a glass breaks to pieces from a sudden blow. This culminating point could be, depending on the composition, at the end of the piece or in the middle; it could come as thunder or very quietly, but the interpreter should approach it with absolute calculation and exactness; otherwise the whole structure of the piece would fall apart, the piece would become soft and scattered into bits, and the listener would never get the impression of the whole that he should. Rachmaninoff added: "And I am not the only one who feels this way. Chaliapin also feels the same way. At one of his concerts the audience was wild with enthusiasm while Chaliapin backstage was tearing his hair 'because the point came down.'"

It did not matter what kind of an audience was listening to him, he always gave his best, it was always Rachmaninoff even if played to an almost empty hall. Once he sat down at the piano he created the piece and delivered it to his listener. He would burn himself out performing and then, white, looking like a squeezed lemon, exhausted from the work, he would lie half dead during the intermission.

Beside the inner creative work which he did in order to prepare himself for a performance, he worked eight hours a day on his technique, no matter where he was. And here is how he usually worked before his concert. He used to take phrase after phrase, or one measure at a time, and run it up and down on the piano as an arpeggio over and over again.

I very often sat next to him while he worked this way because he would ask me to tell him stories. And I was so hungry to hear the whole piece, for I felt as though he were giving of a familiar face at first only the nose and next the chin and then the eyebrows. Once I could not control myself any longer and I told him about it. He answered me half jokingly: "You see, at first one has to iron out every little corner, take apart every screw, so that later it will be easier to put it all together into one whole."

I saw Rachmaninoff for the last time in July, 1917, in Kislovodsk. I had just married, and my husband and I saw an announcement of a concert—a benefit performance. All those participating on this occasion were celebrities and the prices were very high.

Sitting next to my husband in the last row, I felt as though I were looking at the stage through the reverse side of binoculars, looking at the diminutive picture of something endlessly far away, disappearing, past.

First Merezhkovsky[7] came on the stage. Small and "black," he made a speech lisping about "Bolshevism" and then, flashing his eyes and suddenly raising his voice to a high pitch, he spoke of "Bolshevism" as though it had originated with the antichrist and the beginning of the reign of Peter the Great. . . . Then after him the announcer of the program led in the tall elderly Hippius[8] by the arm. She read, in the quiet voice of an undine, some kind of poem from a piece of paper in her hand. Later she dropped her pince-nez in her bust and, gazing with her half-blind eyes around the stage, suddenly looked lost. It was painful to see how helplessly she searched for an exit, how she almost fell to the ground when she missed a step on the stairs leading off the stage. . . .

Next Rachmaninoff appeared, dressed in tails with a white cape over his shoulders, nervous and seething with anger. Rachmaninoff did not want to accompany Koshetz,[9] and Koshetz pouted and refused to sing without him. Rachmaninoff finally consented.

We saw him during the intermission. That night in Kislovodsk was full of peculiar smells—a smell of roses and the southern earth was mixed with perfume, a smell of cigars with poplar trees. Swarms of midges were fighting in the bright light. The members of the orchestra paced back and forth on the stage, waiting for the beginning of the second part of the concert.

[7] Dmitri S. Merezhkovsky (1865-1941), Russian novelist and critic. About 1900-02 Merezhkovsky evolved a mystic, neo-Christian or apocalyptic teaching, based on the equal sanctity of flesh and spirit as opposed to the cult of the flesh as represented by paganism, and the cult of the spirit as revealed by ecclesiastical Christianity.

[8] Hippius Zinaida (1869), Merezhkovsky's wife. One of the leading poets of the Russian symbolist movement of the nineties.

[9] Nina Koshetz, well-known soprano.

Rachmaninoff was scheduled to start it with the *Marseillaise*, but he purposely drew out the intermission while he sat with us on a bench in a garden. Somehow he could not find the courage to say good-by. I never saw him again.

. XII .

Musical Feuds in Moscow

SINCE MARIETTA SHAGINIAN'S LETTERS reflect only a small part of his life at this period, I shall continue my story where I left it—with Rachmaninoff's return to Russia after his first visit to the United States in February, 1910.

"Only in Russia will he find his own environment and only here will he find the true ground for his artistic development," Nicolay Kashkin wrote in an article in the *Russkoe Slovo* in 1909. No one could then have known how true and prophetic were these words.

Sergei Rachmaninoff returned home with the full intention of staying in Moscow and devoting himself to conducting. Moscow celebrated his return home and Rachmaninoff who, while in Dresden, had declined the offer to replace the ailing Arthur Nikisch because of the time involved in the preparation of the programs—time which he wanted jealously to save for composing—now accepted the permanent post of conductor with the Philharmonic Society.

At first Rachmaninoff conducted only the works of Russian composers, but soon he added the compositions of Mozart,

Beethoven, Wagner, Liszt, and Richard Strauss to his programs. The enthusiasm with which the audience greeted each of his appearances grew in a steady crescendo, and the reviews in the newspapers and magazines read like headlines about the march of a conquering hero. Finally Sergei Rachmaninoff was compared to the greatest conductors in the West and acclaimed as a conductor "by the Grace of God."

But Rachmaninoff's success as a conductor coincided with the appearance of a musician well known in Moscow circles, who was now putting in a bid for the title of champion in his new role as an orchestra leader. Serge Koussevitzky, the former double bass from the Bolshoi Theater, where he had played under Rachmaninoff's baton, returned to Moscow after an absence of four years abroad. No complete understanding of Rachmaninoff's behavior in Russia and later of his attitude toward Serge Koussevitzky in the United States—an attitude which somewhat changed the course of Rachmaninoff's career and consequently his life—is possible without a picture of the confused and often bitter fight being waged in the musical life of Moscow, a life that was never too harmonious at the best of times.

There were three principal figures in this picture: Koussevitzky as conductor, Scriabin as composer and pianist, and Rachmaninoff himself, who was all three—conductor, composer, and pianist. I have received the opinions of a number of men who took part in the musical life of Moscow at that time. Unfortunately, these opinions must be largely discounted because of their violent feelings, which prevent an objective point of view even today. There is, however, one reliable source— Leonid Sabaneyeff's *My Recollections of Scriabin*, on which a large part of the following account is based. Sabaneyeff was a close friend of both Scriabin and Koussevitzky. He saw

Scriabin almost daily during the last five years of his life, while Koussevitzky singled out Sabaneyeff as "the only critic-musician" after Sabaneyeff had written a "just" (in the words of Koussevitzky) review of Koussevitzky's Moscow debut as a conductor.

Rachmaninoff also held Sabaneyeff in great esteem even though Sabaneyeff was a "Scriabinist" and even though he wrote critically about Rachmaninoff. Years later in France, through a firm belonging to his daughters, Rachmaninoff published Sabaneyeff's book on Taneyev and, had it not been for World War II, would also have published the Sabaneyeff book on Nicolay Medtner. Rachmaninoff spoke to me about Sabaneyeff's book on Scriabin, and there is a reference to his interest in this book in an article by Alfred Swan.[1]

Sabaneyeff's *Recollections* was widely read in Moscow and abroad and generally acknowledged as authentic. A large portion of it is devoted to reports of scenes in which the author himself had taken part, including conversations given verbatim which the author heard, and thus provides a very vivid and authentic account of the relationships between the musicians involved.

Koussevitzky returned to Moscow as a man of power, for shortly after leaving the Bolshoi Theater he had married the daughter of the millionaire Konstantin Ushkov, chairman of the largest tea firm in Russia. Now he was going to conduct the orchestra of the Music Society, which was mostly composed of musicians from the Bolshoi Theater—Koussevitzky's former colleagues. But he managed to stir up resentment and ferment with beneficent results as well as envy and heartbreak —sometimes in the same men. The Muscovites particularly resented the fact that with his arrival on the scene the two

[1] *Musical Quarterly*, v. 30, January-April, 1944.

competitive organizations, the Moscow Philharmonic and the Russian Musical Society, suddenly had to face a newcomer who was ambitious, independent, and rich.

Koussevitzky was suspected of trying to "swallow" both organizations as well as all the music publishing firms. He was also suspected of trying to organize his own publishing house and to establish a complete monopoly over the music business in every form. The fact that he had already founded a publishing house in Berlin added grounds to their suspicions, and they were ready to believe the rumors that Koussevitzky planned to build his own concert hall and have his own orchestra. No wonder, then, that at his debut Koussevitzky played to an almost empty hall. But Koussevitzky knew how to attract an audience. Soon after his debut he launched his new protégé, Alexander Scriabin, and thus started an artistic battle which could only be compared to that of "The Mighty Five" which had been waged at the end of the last century.

In 1908, Alexander Scriabin was living in Lausanne, Switzerland, trying to make both ends meet because since the death of Mitrofan Belayev, his patron and publisher, his income had been cut down to one half of what he used to receive from the publishing firm. It seems that among the revenues which Belayev left in his will to his publishing firm was a certain sum to be derived from an apartment house in St. Petersburg. But after Belayev's death the house not only did not bring the expected revenues but needed extra expenditures on upkeep and repairs, and finally became a liability because of a large fine, when an old woman was hurt in an elevator in the house. The committee which took care of the publishing firm cut down the fees to their contributors and Scriabin was stretching out his last seventy-five francs, which he had borrowed from his landlord, when Serge Koussevitzky appeared on his doorstep. After paying his respects to Scriabin's talent in a lordly manner, Koussevitzky lent his ear to Scriabin's woes and dreams.

Scriabin told him, as he was telling everyone else, that he was writing a *Mystery* (a Passion play) which would end the world "as we know it." Brushing aside any notion one might have had of him as a composer of "music for music's sake," or "music for a career's sake," or any other sake, Scriabin, intoxicated by the grandeur of his own vision, made a most involved disclosure (never quite clear even to himself) of the "Last Festival," at which he planned to lead mankind to a specially erected temple on a lake somewhere in India. The vision was clothed in a language justified by his dream, a language cluttered with quotations from Nietzsche and mixed with pronouncements of the Hindu prophets and his own belief in the divinity of man and himself. The gist of Scriabin's idea, if stripped to the bone, was that the creative spirit of the universe which had been trampled down by materialism would have a resurrection and then reign supreme. Not music alone but all the arts were to be part of his *Mystery*, where the material and spiritual polarities would eventually meet in an act of love from which would come a return to the primordial state of chaos, followed by a "new breath of Brahma."

However, less world-shaking, and easier for the layman to understand, was one of Scriabin's simpler explanations of his *Mystery*. After Koussevitzky's superb performance of his *Extase*, when exalted friends were riding together in the conductor's black limousine to celebrate the composition which Koussevitzky had just declared as "the greatest piece in music," Scriabin said to Sabaneyeff:

"Frankly speaking, I love this festive mood after the concert. . . . I never want to go home. . . . I want this Festival to continue, to become bigger, wider, and to grow and to multiply itself . . . to become eternal and to conquer the whole world. This is my mystery . . . when it will involve the whole of mankind."

But at the time of Koussevitzky's visit in Lausanne, he spoke of it to him as he usually did to others. Scriabin spoke gently, almost in a languishing voice, at times half-closing his eyes as though he were looking far into the distance. He would be deadly serious in what he was saying, while a happy smile lit up his face, with its childish, excited, brilliant eyes: ". . . One has only to start. . . . For I will have there seven days. But they are not going to be just ordinary days. . . . Just as during the creation of the world the seven days meant the passing of whole eras, whole lives of races, so then will. . . . But they will also be at the same time just like our days. . . . Time itself will be accelerated and in these days we will live through millions of years. It will be like a curve." Scriabin would illustrate with his hand. "The time will gradually quicken its tempo, because it has been slowed up by the process of materialism. But then dematerialization will set in. First of all, time will be affected. . . . What strikes me as significant is that in observing nature I see that the vegetation, the trees and flowers, are silent and immovable. They drink as though in chorus the juices from the earth and the sun's rays. . . . And all around them lives the world of animals, that world which is in constant movement from the slowest motion to the most rapid, from a straight line to a curve. It is a dance of movement against a background of the motionless vegetation. . . . Did this ever occur to you? . . ." Scriabin would keep silent for a while and then continue.

"In nature the animals correspond to the activity of the masculine and the vegetation to the feminine, will-less, passive. These are polarities. There might be some kind of love act between the two—some kind of polar act." Scriabin would explain further. "All the animals and vegetation are nothing but the creation of our psyche. They are symbols, but what wonderful symbols! . . . Don't you feel that, for instance, the animals correspond to the caresses of men and women during their act of love and that every caress has its corresponding animal, or even a whole class of animals? For instance, the birds correspond to the light caresses that have wings . . . and then there are the torturing kind of caresses—these are the wild beasts. How mistaken are those who believe that the wild beasts are just wild beasts! . . . The caresses of mice are very bad." Scriabin was terrified of mice, and here his vision would be affected by the common superstition. "The mice correspond to disaster and something terribly unpleasant. This is sure. They probably have also another existence and another significance. . . ." Scriabin would take a deep breath and sit motionless for a long time, without any expression on his face. Then he would breathe out the air he had just swallowed. "This is the purifying breath," he would say. "The insects, the butterflies, the moths, all are but the flowers come alive. These are the caresses without a touch. . . . They were all born in the sun and the sun nourishes them. . . . They are the caress of the sun—the one closest to me. . . . With what unison in the Weltanschauung one is faced, if one looks at things this way! In science everything is divided, analyzed. There is no synthesis. . . . But how else can it be, how else can I invite this world to my 'mystery'? Because the animals, birds, and the insects have to be there. And how will they be there if they are not a part of my being? . . . How wonderful, what real happiness it is to torture the world with millions of eagles and tigers, to peck at it with caresses and to burn it with the caresses of the wings of tiny moths and the bites of the snake!

... As in my *Extase*, for instance. On this last day of my 'mystery,' at this last dance, I will divide myself into millions of tiny moths—not only I, but all of us. . . . Perhaps, by the end of the 'mystery,' we will cease to be human but will become caresses, beasts, birds, moths . . . snakes. . . ."

Scriabin argued his thesis as the natural, inevitable, and logical sequence to the "principle of the whole." He also added that he would need at least five years in order to write it. Apparently he was sure that by the end of this time his diabolical plan to destroy a society based on the bourgeois weal would be ready, and that then he would square his account with this harsh and miserable world.

Koussevitzky listened to him solemnly and attentively but probably understood nothing Scriabin had said; for more than one man had been puzzled by Scriabin's fantastic projects, and Koussevitzky could never have been accused of being a mystic. He probably thought that Scriabin was speaking of some kind of large composition he had in mind which he, Koussevitzky, could publish with his new firm, conduct at one of his concerts, and forget after a good supper. For two years later Koussevitzky said to Sabaneyeff: "It was only Alexander Nicolaevich [Scriabin] who thought that something extraordinary must happen. It was only he who expected that after the performance of *Extase* everyone right then and there would be suffocated with ecstasy. But in reality we all, including him [Scriabin] went to a restaurant where we supped well and with pleasure. The same would have happened with the *Mystery*. We would have played and then had supper."

But at that time in Switzerland one thing was clear to Koussevitzky, and that was that Scriabin needed a certain "fixed sum"; this was the customary and gentlemanly way to put it.

Koussevitzky agreed to pay him five thousand rubles a year to relieve him of financial worries. For this Scriabin was to let Koussevitzky publish his magnum opus or any "small composition" he might write. Perhaps because Koussevitzky entirely missed Scriabin's plotting against the world and his prophecy of its end, and because of Scriabin's firm belief in it, the two musicians neglected to have their agreement written down and signed. At any rate, a few years later the world still remained Koussevitzky's kind and not Scriabin's, and this arrangement played a decisive role in their relationship.

From then on Koussevitzky regarded Scriabin as his personal property, while Scriabin considered the whole matter, including Koussevitzky's appearance, as though by divine intervention, as a logical product of his creative power combined with a certain amount of good luck that his choice also happened to be an orchestra conductor.

Besides all the publicity and promotion which the conductor gave to Scriabin and his compositions, he paid him at the beginning of their association what was called "Chaliapin's fees" —one thousand rubles per performance—whenever Scriabin was his piano soloist.

But by proclaiming Scriabin the genius of Russia, Koussevitzky split the Muscovites into two camps not of equal strength. On one side, headed by Taneyev, was a party of "conservatives," which still did not recognize either Wagner or Brahms and was against the Petersburg group and "The Mighty Five." This party had powerful members in the press—the critics Nicolay Kashkin, Semeon Kruglikov, and Yury Sakhnovsky. The other party, far smaller in number (the so-called "modernists" and later "Scriabinists"), were divided among themselves in their tastes and choice of composers, and had Vladimir Derganovsky, Alexander Krein, and Leonid Sabaneyeff as their representatives in the press. The two parties fought bitterly for their cause and became personal in their accusations and slander.

Rachmaninoff, through no fault of his own, was involved in this "artistic civil war," which had been ablaze almost from the time he returned from the United States. He did not ally himself with any party by any act or public utterance, though every word said in the warring camps was reported instantly and he was aware of everything that was going on. He "kept outside" but he felt very deeply about it and there is no question in my mind that his feelings toward Koussevitzky were far from sympathetic. For when, in 1941, Koussevitzky proclaimed Dmitri Shostakovich as a new Beethoven, Rachmaninoff, with an expression of disgust rather than anger on his face, said to me: "Yes. This is not the first time that he has discovered a second Beethoven. He did this once before. You know who I mean? . . . Scriabin. And do you remember what happened then? Just read Leonid Sabaneyeff's book!"

It is true, however, that while Rachmaninoff was in Dresden, without leaving his own publisher Gutheil he joined Koussevitzky's publishing enterprise in Berlin in the capacity of an adviser on the board of directors along with his close friends Nicolay Struve and Oskar von Riesemann. But he did so from a sense of duty and because he approved Koussevitzky's noble idea to promote the works of young Russian composers. Rachmaninoff was also the soloist at Koussevitzky's debut in Berlin in 1909, and played again with him in London. But from the way he spoke of "him" (Koussevitzky was referred to by musicians as "he" and "him"; it originated in Scriabin's house) and by the way he added "to play with him again," one feels that Rachmaninoff derived very little pleasure from this association.

But the affair Koussevitzky-Scriabin and the fact that the conductor and Rachmaninoff were in opposing musical camps was only one side of the story. Rachmaninoff could not approve of Koussevitzky's revival of the "star system"—the dividing of artists into different grades. This was a practice Rachmaninoff had fought against years ago and involved dividing musicians according to rank based on social position and even bank accounts, as well as all the intimidating paraphernalia of secretaries, special privileges, intrigues through friendship, etc. And though, with Chaliapin, Rachmaninoff was one of the two musicians to whom Koussevitzky could not talk down, his resentment was so long-lasting that as late as 1929, when they were both in the United States, he let the conductor know that he would be just as happy if Koussevitzky would not perform his work.

As for Scriabin, Rachmaninoff was sincerely grieved that the criticism and abuse in the press gave the impression of a personal feud with his old colleague. He took the first opportunity to prove the contrary and engaged Scriabin to play his own piano concerto at one of the Philharmonic concerts. This may have appeased the minds of those who were worried over their personal relationship, but as far as the hostile press was concerned, it only added fuel to their conflict; for this time they argued the technical points of the performance of the two musicians.

One more composer was drawn into this quarrel and sided with Rachmaninoff. His name was Nicolay Medtner.

Nicolay Medtner, according to his own brother Emil, the philosopher, can be considered as a Russian composer only through pure misunderstanding. "One can hardly point out another composer who in his creative ability remained so wholly outside the 'influence of the environment' where he was born and brought up," insisted Emil Medtner. "Every note in his compositions shows his racial origin, and not only the Russian critics but also those abroad consider Medtner as a German composer." But the Muscovites accepted Medtner as one of their own perhaps because in his music they found something in addition to the German classical tinge that might have come from Taneyev.

Medtner himself neither knew, understood, nor was even interested in modern music. He did not like the French composers and he refused to accept anything composed after Brahms and Wagner. When a few years later he heard Sergei Prokofiev (February 5, 1917), he remarked: "If that is music, then I am no musician." Yet Medtner belonged to that circle of modern Russian writers and poets who congregated at his brother's home. Despite Shaginian's persistent efforts to bring Rachmaninoff into their midst, Rachmaninoff resisted with all his might, probably because, as he said to her, of his "criminal shyness," nay his inferiority complex, which guarded him from such an arena of spiritual and philosophical gladiators as was at the Medtners'. Rachmaninoff's close friendship with Medtner belongs to a later date.

Medtner was indifferent to Scriabin's work of the later period and Scriabin seldom looked through Medtner's works, for their classicism only depressed him. Scriabin, who believed that there should be no music "per se," but that music had only one *raison d'etre*—a sort of nucleus, a part of a whole of the *Weltanschauung*—found that Medtner's music was crowded with notes for no particular purpose. "I do not understand how one can in our time write 'just music.' This is so uninteresting," he said.

And from Rachmaninoff as a composer Scriabin did not expect anything new or interesting, though as a pianist he ranked him very high and only reproached him with the quality of his tone.

"Though he plays with a beautiful tone," said Scriabin, "everything he plays has that same lyric quality as his own music. In his 'sound' there is so much of materialism, so much meat . . . almost some kind of boiled ham."

Since all three composers were first-class pianists and most of their music was written for that instrument, it is only natural that Scriabin was particularly critical of the quality of the piano sonority. Scriabin had an almost magical touch, especially bewitching when he played softly, superbly using his pedal for an ephemeral effect. He hated pianists who played "as though they were washing laundry or smelling the instrument," and especially when they played his compositions with the same approach and touch as if his piano pieces were Rachmaninoff's or Tchaikovsky's.

The Moscow composers lived far from what might be called the life of a happy family. Medtner lived within the circle of his brother and his friends, Rachmaninoff with his own family, while Scriabin received hardly any calls from the "conservatives," Gretchaninoff or Medtner. During these years Rachmaninoff called on him twice and Taneyev came to see him once. But all of them respected Taneyev and they went to the outskirts of the city to see him in his little house, which still had neither heat, electricity, nor running water, the house with the sign permanently attached to its front door "Sergei Ivanovich is not at home," regardless of whether Taneyev was in or out. There they were scorched by the sarcasm of their host, who shook his head and muttered into his beard, as he bade them farewell, that "murky waters are flowing in music."

However, despite the divergences in their musical aims, despite their freely voiced criticisms of each other, they all, to a man, distrusted the ambitions and the power of Koussevitzky and the effect he might have on their work.

Though the critics had reached the zenith of their praise of Rachmaninoff as the conductor and pianist who knew no peer, they tore him to shreds for his latest piano compositions, spoke of him as "outdated," "a living corpse," and reproached him for the Gypsyism and the "salon" in his music, for his bad taste, and for his being the "idol of the crowd," which, by the way, he was.

Rachmaninoff had to admit that at this time, except for his large choral work *Liturgy of Saint John Chrysostomus*, he composed mostly short piano pieces (Preludes, Opus 32, and *Etudes Tableaux*, Opus 33) and thirteen songs (Opus 34), among which his *Vocalise*, a song without words, gained as much popularity among singers as his second piano concerto with pianists.[2]

I have heard musicians attributing a special significance to this song. They claim that its dramatic conception, as it was interpreted by the famous Russian singer A. Negdanova, to whom the song was dedicated, was a cry of Rachmaninoff's tormented soul and that the fact that the song is without words only emphasizes all the more the speechlessness of a deep emotion.

"I have finished only the Liturgy (to your great surprise)," Rachmaninoff wrote to Morozov. "I have been thinking about the Liturgy for a long time and for a long time I was striving to write it. I started work on it somehow by chance and then suddenly became fascinated with it. And then I finished it very quickly. Not for a long time (since my work on *Mona Vanna*) have I written anything with such pleasure. That is all. And then, of course, I have good intentions and good

---

[2] *Vocalise* has been arranged for every instrument including double bass.

wishes. But worst of all is the business with my small piano pieces. I do not like this occupation and it comes to me with difficulty. No beauty, no happiness."

Thus Rachmaninoff's rather meager output was put in the shade by Scriabin's symphonic works. Besides, Rachmaninoff could not have insulated himself from every sound. He must have heard the persistently growing rumbling of a new musical volcano, Sergei Prokofiev, whose presence was announced at his first public appearance with *Diabolical Suggestion*,[3] this thunder and lightning which set both conservatives and Scriabinists fighting a new and perhaps more formidable foe.

Meanwhile, Serge Koussevitzky, whose concerts were steadily growing in number, was taking over the field which hitherto had been Rachmaninoff's own—that of presenting the works of the Russian composers. Rachmaninoff never was a fighter, nor was he a match for Koussevitzky in a field where competitive tactics decided the issue. He preferred to withdraw from the field and say nothing, though no one was fooled by this dignified silence. It is a matter of conjecture whether all this, combined with the harsh criticism of his latest compositions, made Rachmaninoff resign from his post as conductor and again seek seclusion for his own work, first in Switzerland and then in Rome.

[3] S. Prokofiev, Opus 4.

. XIII .

Farewell to Russia

BUT RACHMANINOFF'S RETIREMENT did not last long. After one month in Switzerland the Rachmaninoffs moved to Rome. There the family lived in a small boardinghouse while he spent every morning in solitude in a small apartment on the Piazza di Spagna which once had been occupied by Modest Tchaikovsky, and where his brother Peter—the composer—had visited him many a time.

"Nothing helps me so much as solitude. In my opinion it is only possible to compose when one is alone and there are no external disturbances to hinder the calm flow of ideas. These conditions were ideally realized in my flat on the Piazza di Spagna. All day long I spent at the piano or the writing table and not until the sinking sun gilded the pines of the Monte Pincio did I put away my pen."[1]

In these cool, quiet rooms, Rachmaninoff composed his Choral Symphony, *The Bells*, after Edgar Allan Poe's poem.

This composition was suggested to him in an anonymous letter, and Rachmaninoff never found out who wrote it. Mik-

---

[1] Oskar v. Riesemann: *Rachmaninoff's Recollections.*

hail Bukinik, the cellist and a contemporary of Rachmaninoff's
at the Moscow Conservatory, told me that the idea had come
from his pupil Maria Danilova, a shy young woman who had
studied the cello with him. A great Rachmaninoff enthusiast,
after reading Balmont's translation of Poe's poem, she was so
impressed by it, so sure that music should be written to this
poem, that she could not find peace until she had written to
Rachmaninoff. She almost collapsed when she heard the composition a year later, but she guarded her secret as did her
teacher, to whom she had confided her story.

Just as Edgar Allan Poe's poem embraced four phases of
human life, so is Rachmaninoff's Choral Symphony divided
into four parts.

Hear the sledges with the bells—
    Silver bells!
What a world of merriment their melody foretells!
  How they tinkle, tinkle, tinkle,
    In the icy air of night!

Hear the mellow wedding bells—
    Golden bells!
What a world of happiness their harmony foretells!
  Through the balmy air of night
  How they ring out their delight!

Hear the loud alarum bells—
    Brazen bells!
What a tale of terror, now, their turbulency tells!
  In the startled ear of night
  How they scream out their affright!

Hear the tolling of the bells—
    Iron bells!
What a world of solemn thought their monody compels!
    In the silence of the night,
    How we shiver with affright
    At the melancholy menace of their tone!

It is obvious from the content of the poem why it would
appeal so much to Rachmaninoff. However, for his *Bells*
Rachmaninoff did not use the original Edgar Allan Poe poem
but Constantin Balmont's translation into Russian, which was
very free and had some of Balmont's own added verses about
the "ringing of child's laughter," "the days gone astray," etc.

In his orchestration Rachmaninoff used four different tex-
tures of the sounds of bells: silver for the first part of the poem,
golden for the wedding, somber copper for the tocsin, and iron
for the call of death. Rachmaninoff, who loved his *Bells* best
of all his compositions, gave the best of himself both in inspiration and in his skill in orchestrating. He dedicated *The Bells*
to Willem Mengelberg, the Dutch conductor, and to his
Concertgebouw Orchestra in Amsterdam, with whom Rachmaninoff always played with particular pleasure.

But Rachmaninoff had no luck in Rome. His two little girls
caught typhoid fever, and the family moved to Berlin because
Rachmaninoff had more confidence in German doctors. After
six anxious weeks the Rachmaninoffs returned to Russia and,
except for a short trip to England for a few concerts, Rachmaninoff did not go abroad again because of the first World
War, which broke out in August, 1914. In fact, he almost
canceled his concerts in England because of the fear of death
from which he was suffering at the time. The sudden death
from a heart attack of Raoul Pugno, the famous French

pianist, who was found alone in a hotel room in Moscow, made such an impression on Rachmaninoff that he was afraid to go to London alone lest a similar fate might befall him.

When on February 8, 1914, Rachmaninoff introduced his new composition *The Bells* at the Philharmonic concert in Moscow, the success was unusual even for him. At the end of the performance he was presented with laurel wreaths, flowers, and gifts while the audience gave him a tremendous ovation. One must remember that though the feud between the Rachmaninoff, Medtner, and Scriabin parties was still alive, it had lost some of its verve, because Scriabin broke with Koussevitzky, his chief supporter, while the latter, now firmly established as a conductor, was championing music by another Russian modernist, Igor Stravinsky. Furthermore, Koussevitzky gave three concerts in 1910 devoted entirely to the music of J. S. Bach, which upset Scriabin seriously. The fact was that these two willful musicians, right from the start of their friendship, had regarded each other as tools for their individual plans and therefore their friendship never did have a solid basis that could be expected to last. They had ceased to be friends even before the famous trip on the Volga when Koussevitzky took his orchestra to tour the cities along the river on a specially chartered boat loaded with caviar and wine. Scriabin went along as a soloist. But Scriabin's friends intrigued and influenced him against Koussevitzky, and such small matters as where they should celebrate the last Koussevitzky performance of a Scriabin work—whether it should be at his home or in a restaurant—caused friction between the two musicians. Scriabin was accused of being temperamental and behaving like a sulking child, while Koussevitzky was accused of tactlessness.

It seems that Koussevitzky paid Scriabin only one hundred

rubles per concert for his eleven appearances on the Volga tour, and that when Scriabin complained to him, Koussevitzky explained that the tour was very expensive, that all the musicians—some with their wives, including Scriabin's—were all living on his bounty, and added that "Scriabin was not worth more than a hundred rubles."

Later, when Koussevitzky, discussing his plans for an Italian tour, offered Scriabin five hundred rubles per concert, the composer wanted more. Koussevitzky thereupon told him that he could get any pianist to play as well for two hundred rubles. This, and other quarrels, put an end to their friendship, and Koussevitzky sent him a bill for the fifteen thousand rubles which had been paid to Scriabin according to their oral agreement made in Lausanne three years before, when Scriabin promised to set the world on fire with his *Mystery*.

Mikhail Pressman, an old friend of both Rachmaninoff and Scriabin, repeated to Alexander Siloti Koussevitzky's remark that Scriabin was not worth more than one hundred rubles, and Siloti immediately arranged for Scriabin to have a new publisher, P. Jurgenson's firm. But when Scriabin received Koussevitzky's bill for fifteen thousand rubles he felt as though he had been hit on the head with a hammer. He began feverishly to compose in order to pay the debt.

Koussevitzky never did collect the fifteen thousand rubles. On the contrary, he paid Scriabin for every new composition which he sent to his firm, and the two exchanged notes and checks with almost Chinese etiquette, saying, "Please accept . . ." and "I did not mean" this or that. Several attempts made to reconcile the two probably would have succeeded if Scriabin's friends had not upset his final decision by such remarks as "Oh, why start this Ushkov business all over again?" I am sure that Scriabin felt his loss. Despite his caustic remark to Sabaneyeff, "How can a man with such a face as Sergei Alexandrovich [Koussevitzky] understand my music? He is much too *terre à terre*, much too materialistic," Scriabin agreed that no one could perform his works so well as Koussevitzky.

Thus ended the historical quarrel of the two outstanding musicians in Moscow at that time. "A great deal of it was due to misunderstandings exaggerated by the artistic ego of these two prima donnas," concludes Leonid Sabaneyeff in his book.

Fantastic as it may seem, Scriabin did believe that he had "created" Koussevitzky. "Where would 'he' be without me?" he shouted in his high-pitched voice. "I could get along without him, but 'he' would never have amounted to anything. . . ." And Scriabin could not understand that his "creation" had rebelled against him by conducting works of other composers and even by giving a whole cycle of J. S. Bach's works. "Now, the Bach was entirely unnecessary," complained Scriabin.

And finally he hurt the pride of Koussevitzky, who did not want to be treated merely as his patron but considered his fostering of Scriabin's works as an artistic mission. Koussevitzky's merit in this respect was indisputable, but Scriabin was too easily influenced by intriguing friends.

In a very few years Koussevitzky had launched himself well on the road to success. During the summer of 1915, Koussevitzky bought out the K. Gutheil music publishing firm, and he shuttled back and forth with his orchestra between the two capitals, St. Petersburg and Moscow, giving more concerts than any other organization. Koussevitzky popularized Scriabin's works long after the two men had ceased to be friends.

While Rachmaninoff did not take sides in this quarrel any more than he had done during the whole Koussevitzky-Scriabin affair, his sympathies were with Scriabin. He declined

Koussevitzky's invitation to be soloist on his third Volga tour and their relationship remained civil though always distant. However, both musicians combined their talents during the war, giving benefit performances in the principal cities of Russia to help the Government in this wartime emergency and for war relief.

When on April 27, 1915, Scriabin suddenly died from blood poisoning, Koussevitzky and Rachmaninoff joined in aiding the deceased's family, which was in financial distress. Koussevitzky gave a Scriabin memorial cycle of four concerts in Moscow, with Rachmaninoff playing Scriabin's piano concerto at one of them. All the proceeds were given to Scriabin's family and Rachmaninoff toured the large cities of Russia playing the music of his deceased colleague and turning over to the family all the profits from the concerts.

The audience warmly responded to Rachmaninoff's gesture. It was the first time since Rachmaninoff had been graduated from the Conservatory that he publicly played the works of another composer. But the Moscow critics remained hostile to him and criticized the way he interpreted Scriabin's works.

A year later, to Rachmaninoff's astonishment, a committee for the preservation of Scriabin's memory sent a delegation asking him to accept a prominent position in their circle and to arrange concerts of Scriabin's music with his participation as either pianist or conductor. Rachmaninoff declined their advances and told them that he himself would choose the manner in which he would commemorate the composer. "I think I have proved my loyalty and keenness by the concerts I have since arranged," said Rachmaninoff in his *Recollections*.

With Scriabin's death the Koussevitzky-Scriabin affair came to a close, but the bitter memories of it remained for life with Moscow musicians and, of course, with Rachmaninoff.

But to return to Rachmaninoff's own compositions. In the first year of the war, in the winter of 1914, he composed *The Vespers*. Next to his *Bells*, he said, he liked this composition best.

Ever since his childhood Rachmaninoff had been attracted by the melodies of the service of the Russian Orthodox Church and, like Mikhail Glinka, Rachmaninoff dreamed of combining the liturgic cantilenas of the Russian Orthodox Church with the European fugue style. The writing of this, probably the most impressive composition in the literature of the Russian Church, Rachmaninoff owed to his association with Kastalsky, the composer of sacred music whose "wealth of color and sound," in Rachmaninoff's opinion, "may entitle him to be called 'the Rimsky-Korsakov of choral music'"—and with Stepan Smolensky, an authority on the medieval notation in which the Russian ancient sacred music was written.

In his *Vespers* Rachmaninoff used nine chants from the sacred music in their original keys and dynamics, and added six chorals of his own. The Mass was presented at Nobility Hall by the Moscow Synodical Choir, which usually sang at the Uspensky Cathedral in the Kremlin, and it had such success that it had to be repeated five times before crowded houses.

"My favorite passage in this work is the fifth hymn, 'Lord, now lettest Thou Thy servant depart in peace' [Luke 11,29]," Rachmaninoff said in his *Recollections*. "I would like this to be sung at my funeral." But for some reason this wish was not remembered either at his funeral or at the services which were held after his death.

While resting from his concert work in the summer of 1915 in Ivanovka, Rachmaninoff composed six songs (Opus 38) on the texts of Russian "symbolist" poets, which Marietta

Shaginian had chosen for him. Besides, Rachmaninoff apparently was inspired by the voice of Nina Koshetz, whom he had heard at the performance of Taneyev's Mass. These songs surprised everyone not only because they were written on the text of the symbolists but because of their freshness and the promise of a new inspiration in his art. Rachmaninoff dedicated this opus to Nina Koshetz and also gave concerts with her, acting as her accompanist. This was the first and last time since the days of his youth, when he accompanied Feodor Chaliapin, that Rachmaninoff was known to play for a singer.

In February, 1917, the Russian Revolution broke out. The Russian public heard Rachmaninoff for the last time in Kislovodsk during the summer of that year, which Shaginian describes as the time she saw him last. Rachmaninoff retired to his country estate in Ivanovka. But, as he said, "The impressions I received from my contact with the peasants, who felt themselves masters of the situation, were unpleasant. I should have preferred to leave Russia with friendlier memories."

During the second phase of the Revolution, "the Bolshevik coup" in October, Rachmaninoff was living in his Moscow apartment, working on the rewriting of his first piano concerto as well as working on a new composition—the fourth piano concerto—but he told Oskar von Riesemann, "almost from the very beginning of the Revolution I realized that it was mishandled. Already by March of 1917 I had decided to leave Russia, but was unable to carry out my plan, for Europe was still fighting and no one could cross the frontier."

Rachmaninoff was a great Russian patriot. He proved this during both World War I and II, but his patriotism did not go as far as "my country right or wrong," and the upheaval in 1917 evoked only revulsion in him. Rachmaninoff had but a superficial knowledge, if any, of the true history of Russia and of the social struggle going on there as well as in the whole world. Economics and politics were vistas to which his innocent intellect never reached; and closed within himself as a rebel against fate, he did not have the stamina to stand up under the chopping down of the "Cherry Orchard," as it were, and to witness the disappearance of the last remnants of his world.

His memories were still fresh with the squabble of musicians, their petty intrigues, the Koussevitzky-Scriabin affair, as well as his own unpleasant experience with the critics who belonged to the Scriabin fanatics. Now, during the Revolution when every restraint was thrown off, he sought quiet from the clamor that he was sure was not going to spare him.

What would have happened if Rachmaninoff had not left Russia is a matter of conjecture. His fears for his own and his family's welfare were definitely unfounded. He was influenced by the general hysteria of the class of people with whom he associated, and many regretted their fateful decision later. As a matter of fact, Theodore Komisarjevsky told me that he was delegated on behalf of the Bolshoi Theater to see Rachmaninoff and ask him to return to the opera house.

"I am surprised at you," he said to Komisarjevsky. "If you wish to stay in this brothel, go ahead, but I will not."

"Then," as Rachmaninoff relates in his *Recollections*, "an entirely unexpected event, which I can only attribute to the grace of God and which, in any case, was the happy dispensation of a well-disposed fate, came to our rescue." Rachmaninoff was offered a tour of ten concerts in Scandinavia.

With a small suitcase in his hand, Rachmaninoff walked out of his home in Moscow and took a train to St. Petersburg. There, after he had made all the necessary preparations for their departure, he was joined by his wife and their two daughters. Though he was going out of the country legally (he was given a passport and visa), besides the necessary luggage he was not permitted to take with him any more than five hundred rubles for each member of the family. "But at the time money seemed quite unimportant compared to the fact that we were saved," Rachmaninoff said later.

The Rachmaninoffs were going to Sweden via Finland, but as the trains did not run across the border, the family had to travel in a peasant sleigh through a raging snow storm.

It is well known that when Mikhail Glinka was leaving Russia, he stopped his carriage, and after taking a last look at St. Petersburg, spat on the ground, and said: "May I never see this accursed country again!" I am inclined to believe Oskar von Reisemann, the author of *Rachmaninoff's Recollections*, who compared Rachmaninoff to Glinka by saying: "Rachmaninoff would have liked to kneel down and kiss the soil of his native country, which was dearer to his heart than anything in the world."

.XIV.

Exile in the United States

O N DECEMBER 8, 1918, in Providence, Rhode Island, four
weeks after the Rachmaninoffs had arrived in New York
on a small Norwegian boat, Sergei Rachmaninoff started on the
second half of his career as a concert pianist, a career which
spanned over fifty years, evenly divided into two periods:
the Russian, 1892-1917; and the American, 1918-1943. It is a
record of rapidly growing popularity from what the music
critics call "followers" to sold-out houses.

After they left Russia, the Rachmaninoffs spent one year in
Denmark and Sweden before the composer made his final
decision to leave Europe, where World War I was still in
progress. The news of his departure from Russia had reached
the United States and Rachmaninoff received offers for piano
recitals as well as invitations to accept the posts of permanent
conductor of the Cincinnati Symphony Orchestra and of the
Boston Symphony, replacing Karl Muck. Once again Rachmaninoff was faced with the old problem of what to be: composer,
conductor, or concert pianist. But he had brought no fortune
with him out of Russia, and as his immediate concern was

to take care of his family, his problem was already solved this time for him by an old friend, who, on the eve of Rachmaninoff's departure from Moscow, pointed to his hands and said: "There is your capital." Rachmaninoff declined the offers to conduct and came to the United States as a pianist.

Yet with all the concerts Rachmaninoff had played in Russia, with all the experience he had had as a concert pianist, he did not have a sufficient repertory for programs, since hitherto he had played chiefly his own compositions and therefore, as he said, would have "played himself out" in a very short time. Thus, at the age of forty-four, Rachmaninoff took his seat at the piano to build up both his programs and his virtuosity with the same determination he had used in his student days when his ardent desire was to be graduated from the Conservatory with the Great Gold Medal.

I have heard from musicians that Rachmaninoff, even at a much later date, occasionally liked to consult his colleagues and played for Josef Hofmann and Josef Lhévinne. But I am sure that his own memories of Anton Rubinstein were his guiding star in this field, for he spoke of Rubinstein as a pianistic marvel born to master the instrument. On more than one occasion Rachmaninoff said that in his opinion no one ever surpassed the artistry of Anton Rubinstein.

Of all the concert pianists Rachmaninoff ever heard, Anton Rubinstein left the deepest impression upon him. When he gave his historical concerts in Moscow in 1885, Rubinstein presented a complete survey of the works of Bach, the old Italians, Mozart, Beethoven, and Chopin, up to Liszt and the contemporary Russians. "I stored up wonderful memories with which no others in my experience can compare," said Rachmaninoff in his *Recollections*.

"It was not so much his magnificent technique that held one

spellbound, as the profound, spiritually refined musicianship, which spoke from every note and every bar he played, and singled him out as the most original, the unequaled pianist of the world. Naturally, I never missed a note, and I remember how deeply affected I was by his rendering of the *Appassionata*, or Chopin's Sonata in B minor. Once he repeated the whole finale of the Sonata in B minor, perhaps because he had not succeeded in the short crescendo at the end as he would have wished. One listened entranced, and could have heard the passage over and over again, so unique was the beauty of tone which his magic touch drew from the keys. I have never heard the virtuoso piece Balakirev's *Islamey* as Rubinstein played it, and his interpretation of Schumann's little fantasy *The Bird as Prophet* was inimitable in poetic refinement: to describe the diminuendo of the pianissimo at the end as the 'fluttering away of the little bird' would be hopelessly inadequate. Inimitable, too, was the soul-stirring imagery in the *Kreisleriana*, the last (G minor) passage of which I have never heard anyone play in the same manner. One of Rubinstein's greatest secrets was his use of the pedal. 'The pedal is the soul of the piano!' said Rubinstein. "No pianist should ever forget this."

But whether consciously or subconsciously, Rachmaninoff also realized that the old-fashioned way of virtuoso playing was on its way out, and he created his own style. Curiously enough, although a lyricist and a romantic through and through, he created a new school of playing which can be compared only to monumental, finely chiseled sculpture.

"There was a great difference in Rachmaninoff's playing in the United States as compared to that in Russia," Kirena Siloti, the daughter of the famous pianist, told me, and she assured me that this was the opinion of many musicians who heard him at these different times. The soft lyrical approach gave way to a new conception built on an iron rhythm and power. But the dominating feature remained—Rachmaninoff the man and the composer.

Sergei Rachmaninoff was not one of those pianists with a "speciality" in which he excelled, as far as the works in the musical literature were concerned. One did not go to hear Chopin or Beethoven as played by Rachmaninoff. One went to hear Rachmaninoff play Chopin or Beethoven. For it mattered very little what he played. It was a Rachmaninoff performance. Some may hold this against him, but what one looks for in a performer is a personal matter.

Four years passed during which Rachmaninoff not only found a foothold in this country but in a relatively short time gained complete financial security, so successful was his concertizing. Except when he was on tour he lived with his family in New York City, and yet he did not acclimatize himself sufficiently to call this country his new home.

Rachmaninoff was a Russian and he was going to remain a Russian. And I am sure that, with the rest of Russian émigrés, he believed at that time that the Bolshevik rule and their own exile were only temporary. He took no interest in the literary or theatrical life of this country, but this is understandable since Rachmaninoff never really mastered the English language. He told me only a few months before he died (that is, twenty-five years after his arrival in this country) that Sinclair Lewis's *Main Street* was the only book he had read in the English language. The English classics he read in Russian translation. As a Russian he was also used to a different kind of theater—the classical repertory of drama and comedy. The regular Broadway shows had no attraction for him.

Rachmaninoff told me that when they first arrived, Mrs. Rachmaninoff and he went about in society, but, he added,

"I am not much of a society man, and so I was asked less and less." Even among musicians he saw mostly Russians, with Fritz Kreisler as an exception. Rachmaninoff was homesick. "Even the air does not smell here the way it does in Russia," he said to me.

He was overjoyed when in January, 1923, the Moscow Art Theater, headed by Konstantin Stanislavsky, came to New York City. He had always been a great admirer of this organization with which Anton Chekhov, his favorite author, was so closely connected. With his family he attended all their performances, but he derived even more pleasure from the informal meetings with his old friends, the members of the cast, either at Alexander Siloti's or his own home. The evenings spent with Stanislavsky, the actress Knipper-Chekhova, the widow of the author, the actors Kachalov and Moskvin, and Mikhail Fokine, the choreographer, brought him once again close to his beloved Moscow.

Rachmaninoff wiped away tears of joy with the back of his hand as he listened to one of the members of the cast sing the old Russian folk songs to the accompaniment of an accordion. Often the guests closed these happy gatherings with an improvised chorus and the composer at the piano. When the time came for the company to return to Russia, Rachmaninoff went to the boat to bid them farewell. As the boat sailed away, those who saw his tall, bent figure knew how he was feeling as this part of his life was again torn away from him.

A year later the Moscow Art Theater came back to New York for a second visit and this time the lyric branch of the theater included in their performances Rachmaninoff's first opera, *Aleko*. Though Rachmaninoff told Youlia Fatova, the actress who was singing the leading role in his opera, that he not only was not coming to listen to his *Aleko*, but that he was

187

ashamed of ever having written such drivel, he invited a group of these actors to his summer home at Locust Point in New Jersey. This time, Moskvin, Knipper-Chekhova, and the Loushskies were joined by Feodor Chaliapin.

During the whole evening the actors entertained their host with improvised performances, and when at two in the morning everyone was ready to leave, Chaliapin became indignant at the very idea. "Where are you going?" he pleaded. "I am just getting in the mood. Just wait a minute. Sergei and I are going to show you something." And with Rachmaninoff at the piano, Chaliapin began to sing. He sang a lot and for a long time; he sang arias from the operas, and he sang songs of the Russian peasants, Russian workers, the Gypsy songs, and finally, because Rachmaninoff asked him, he sang the *Ochi Chornye*.

Next morning, Elena Somov,[1] an old friend of the Rachmaninoff family who was their neighbor, was surprised to see the composer walking at such an early hour in his garden. Despite the sleepless night he looked much younger.

"Fedia made me very happy last night," he said to her. "Did you notice how he pronounced 'You have ruined me, *ochi chornye*'? This will stay in my memory for at least twenty years."

But these were rare occasions. Rachmaninoff longed for the evenings with his old friends who were now among the large colony of Russian *émigrés* in France. Furthermore, in 1923 Rachmaninoff succeeded in getting his in-laws, the Satins, out of Russia, and from then on he arranged his life in such a way that during the winter he concertized in the

[1] *In Memory of Rachmaninoff*, published by Sophia Satin (in Russian), New York, 1946.

United States, while in the spring he left for a vacation in Europe—in Germany or France.

When Rachmaninoff wrote to Marietta Shaginian that he was just an average man, he spoke the truth of himself as a man if not as a musician. Rachmaninoff's life during the first decade after he left Russia was uneventful. His was the life of a successful concert pianist who devoted every minute he was not at the piano to his family. It was the life of a man who was homesick but who was slowly adjusting himself to a new environment and who found happiness in his own family. Rachmaninoff's letters to his friends were rather repetitious accounts of his concert tours. However, I prefer my reader to learn about this period of his life from Rachmaninoff himself for two reasons: because his letters to Vladimir Vilshau,[2] his old friend in Moscow, tell more of his personal life than any other documents, and because these letters served as affidavits of his life in exile to the authorities in Soviet Russia when the time came to establish definitively his position in regard to his native country.

Dear Vladimir Robertovich—

I was very happy to receive your letter, which reached me on the eve of my departure from Germany to America. I will say only a few words about myself and my family.

I particularly dislike my occupation! In all this time I have not composed a single line. I only play the piano and give many concerts. For the last four years I have been working very hard. I am making progress, but, frankly speaking, the more I play the more I see my shortcomings. Probably I will never learn, or if I do, then perhaps only on the eve of my

[2] Vladimir R. Vilshau, (1872-   ), pianist, a friend of Rachmaninoff's from Conservatory days. Professor at the Moscow Conservatory.

death. Financially I am well provided for. I am a plutocrat! But my health is getting worse; how can one expect the contrary if one considers that during my whole life I have never known peace because of dissatisfaction with myself? Years ago when I was composing, I tormented myself because I composed badly, and now I torment myself because I play badly. Deep in my heart I have the firm belief that I can do both much better. I live with this belief!

My wife has changed very little. She is the same, except perhaps for the addition of a few gray hairs. The children are well. The eldest will graduate from the University[3] in two years. She is full of joy and spirit and loves America. The youngest will graduate from high school in three years. She is melancholic and hates America. The difference between the two does not end here; it is as though they were born of different parents!

Good-by, Vladimir Robertovich. I am not going to write you for a long time. Don't be angry with me, but during the concert season I have no time. After the winter season I have accepted some concerts in Australia. But if you will write me, I will be very grateful. The best from my heart. Give my greetings to everyone I love.

S. Rachmaninoff

New York
September 9, 1922

My dear Vladimir Robertovich—

I have received your letter with the numerous signatures as well as the cantata.[4]

---

[3] Vassar College.
[4] Greetings were sent to Rachmaninoff on the anniversary of his fiftieth birthday, April 2, 1923. The words to the cantata were written by V. R. Vilshau, the music composed by Reinhold Gliere.

I was very much touched by the words as well as by the sound. Thank you all. . . .

I am not going to say any more. I have finished my season and my hands are numb. My best wishes and greetings to everybody.

Yours,

S. R.

New York
May 1, 1923

My dear Vladimir Robertovich—

I am dictating this letter. I am playing the piano while Tanya is writing this letter. First of all, I want to thank you for the dear, warm and interesting letters you write me so regularly, and with which you spoil me. I am also impressed by your kindness and your tact in never mentioning my answers to you.

I want to write you a few lines about myself and the family. We are still sitting in Germany. This happened suddenly. My eldest daughter Irina decided to get married (to Peter Volkonsky). We have changed all our plans and will remain here until the wedding, which will be on September 24th. On September 25th I am going to England, where, starting October 2nd, I have concerts for three consecutive weeks. My wife and the one who is writing you these lines will join me in London and then we all—that is, the three of us that are left (Irina and her husband will spend the winter in Munich)—will depart on October 22nd to America. I begin my season there on November 14th and will finish it on May 1st.

I wish you and your family the best from my heart.

Yours,

S. R.

August 21, 1924

My dear friend Vladimir Robertovich—

Last night I received your letter (dated June 1st and addressed to New York), which was forwarded to me. We all—that is, the whole family, including the Volkonskys—left New York on May 23rd. About a week before our departure we sent you a letter with my Dresden address, and asked you to write me there. Apparently this letter was lost. (This is terrible, if my letters which are so rare do not reach you.)

When we reached Europe we separated. Natasha went to Paris with the Volkonskys and I to Dresden with Tanya, where we arrived on June 3rd and where without seeing friends or relatives we went straight to the sanatorium from which I am writing you now. I came to take a cure and Tanechka is playing chaperone to me! Tomorrow it will be a whole month since we came here. (I am writing very badly: my hands are shaking. Old age is no joke!) I feel a little better, but only a little. These sanatoriums have changed since the war, as has the whole world. Tomorrow I am going to move to a hotel, where I will live in freedom for a few days, and then we will go to Paris, where Natasha has found us a place for the summer. We will stay there until October 15th.

Here is the address: Monsieur S. Rachm.

Le Château de Sorbeville à Orsai

Seine et Oise

France

My vacation will end with my departure from here. In France I will again sit at the piano and do the exercises for the fourth and fifth fingers. Once, about five years ago, Hofmann[5] told me that "our second fingers are lazy." I began to watch it and "pull it" along! Then I noticed that the third finger has the same weakness. And now, the longer I live, the more I be-

[5] Josef Hofmann, the pianist.

come convinced that both the fourth and fifth fingers do not work conscientiously. Therefore only the first finger is left and that one probably only temporarily! So, now I began to watch it askance.

Thus I have three months for the preparation of my program, after which I will depart with Natasha to America on October 15th. This time I accepted only twenty to twenty-five concerts, which will last from November 2nd until December 5th. Afterward I have two weeks to make the records for gramophone and mechanical pianos and I will be free for Christmas. Then where I will be or where I will go I do not know. The Volkonskys and Tanya will remain in Paris for the winter. Here you have our plans for the near future. I hope to receive a letter from you in Paris. I am glad that your family is in the country and I hope that your boy is getting over his whooping cough.

Greetings to everybody. I embrace you.

Yours,

Dresden   S. R.
July 2, 1925

My dear Vladimir Robertovich—

It is a great happiness for me to receive your letters and I assure you if it were not for this accursed life here, which together with my work takes up my whole day and with the continuous hurry to do what is necessary for my work and a lot that is not necessary and rather senseless such as all sorts of visits, making appointments, people bothering me, propositions, etc.—if it were not for all this, I would write you more often.

I have got accustomed to and love this country. But there is one thing missing here and that is peace. On the other hand, it has now become hard to find this in Europe. Or perhaps I do not know how to arrange it for myself, or perhaps there is none anywhere.

And thus I am always in a hurry, always worried that I will be too late! Right now, just before our departure for Europe, it seems worse than ever. We intended to leave and even had the tickets for the day after tomorrow. But we could not do it; we did not get ready. Now we have changed the date to April 30th, and I hope with God's help we will manage it this time. We are going to see our children in Paris, whom I miss terribly. Just as before they are the "light in the window"! They are dear indeed, and it is touching how they behave toward me, I who am old now. Therefore I consider that apparently in my life I must have succeeded in one good deed for which God sends me this happiness. I also have had a son-in-law. He was good to me, just like my children! But he did not remain alive. And besides, I must say, he was "not from this world"! You probably know that I have a granddaughter.[6] This little one we saw the last time when she was one month old. Now she is eight months. Already a grown-up human being! Her picture when she was six months old hangs over my bed. She is lying naked on a piece of fur and is smiling! And I, whenever I look at her, smile too! Well, it is to her that we are going!

We expect to stay in Paris until June 1st, not later than the 15th. Then we will go to Germany, where we have a place on Weisser Hirsch. We will live all together. Only Irina will go for a month to the Volkonskys. We will spend three months in Germany. And then return to Paris. . . . We have the tickets for a boat to America on November 3rd. Here are the addresses and I hope you will write me. Irina Volkonsky, 27 Rue Cardi-

[6] Sophia Volkonsky.

net, Paris XVII, or Waldemar von Satin, Arnstadstrasse 22, Dresden.

I am sending you under separate cover a few of my arrangements for piano. I hope they will reach you.

Greetings to your wife and children. I embrace you.

Yours,

S. R.

New York
April 19, 1926

More than ten years passed during which Rachmaninoff did not start anything new, and during which he arranged for piano a few charming pieces by Fritz Kreisler (*Liebesfreude* and *Liebesleid*), the Menuet from Bizet's *Suite Arlésienne*, and Mendelssohn's Scherzo from *A Midsummer Night's Dream*.

On August 29, 1928, Rachmaninoff invited a few friends to his summer place in Viller-sur-Mer, in Normandy, to hear his new composition—his fourth piano concerto in C minor, which he had started in the first months of the Revolution in Russia. Nicolay Medtner, also a refugee from Russia, was living in Paris, and Rachmaninoff dedicated this work to him, while Medtner in turn dedicated his second piano concerto to Rachmaninoff. Rachmaninoff's fourth concerto[7] is a rather weak composition and certainly cannot stand comparison with his second or third. Even though he began it at a very gloomy period in his life, this composition is written in a rather light vein. Only once is the somber call of death announced, but it fades away as though not noticed.

Perhaps Rachmaninoff realized that in this first attempt to return to composing he failed to find himself again, for

[7] Rachmaninoff played the concerto for the first time in Berlin on December 8, 1931, with Bruno Walter conducting the Berlin Philharmonic.

his following compositions were all written on ready-made themes.

After spending several summers in different parts of Germany and France, the Rachmaninoffs at last found what seemed to be an ideal place for the composer's vacations.

The three summers of 1929, 1930, and 1931, spent at Clairefontaine near Rambouillet in France, were probably the happiest since the family had left Ivanovka. The place itself was very much like a Russian country estate—Le Pavillon, the manor house, with its spacious rooms and broad lawn enclosed by old chestnut and lime trees; its long avenues, which led into the park with a tennis court and further on to the woods where, according to Russian tradition, "one goes to gather mushrooms in the early fall"; and finally its ponds, from which the nostalgic sound of croaking frogs broke the silence of the summer nights.

"I would not exchange this concert for the most beautiful chorus of nightingales," said Rachmaninoff.

The village of Clairefontaine was only an hour's drive from Paris and, as Rachmaninoff said to Feodor Chaliapin (the son of the singer): "I cannot live without Russians." The Rachmaninoff home was always filled with visitors from the city. There was Feodor Chaliapin, the singer; the Medtners, with whom Rachmaninoff had become very close since they both left Russia; the stage director Mikhail Chekhov, the nephew of the author, who amused Rachmaninoff with his theatrical anecdotes; Katherine and Alfred Swan; and all the young friends of Sergei Rachmaninoff's daughters.

When in the mornings the guests assembled at the large table on the veranda for a Russian breakfast of tea with cheese, ham, sausage, hardboiled eggs, butter, and honey, just as they would at Ivanovka, Rachmaninoff was playing the last chords of his morning practicing, for he was an early riser.

Then the gay crowd would move to the tennis court, where Rachmaninoff would take his place as a referee, and, lighting his cigarette, would watch the game and join them in their disputes over the rules. Little Sophinka, his granddaughter, age four or five, would appear carrying a tennis racket as big as herself, looking for a partner. Rachmaninoff would stop his conversation and, beaming, follow her every move with his eyes and listen with tenderness and pride to everything she said.

In this happy atmosphere Rachmaninoff was not any more the "buttoned-up," the fierce-looking great artist. A good listener, he loved stories and jokes, and in turn he entertained his friends with his own stories. He grew very much attached to the young Chaliapin, whom he called simply Fedia, just as he had his father. And he told stories about the famous singer.

Rachmaninoff remembered how Chaliapin had criticized his way of bowing to his public, how he had told him that one should greet his audience with a happy smile and not look, à la Rachmaninoff, like an undertaker, and how he even had offered to teach him this art, though nothing came of it.

"But Fedia knew how," added Rachmaninoff. "Though Fedia was a bass, he bowed like a tenor."

Rachmaninoff loved to talk with his young friends about the beauty of the Russian landscape, the birch trees, the dark woods, the ponds at the end of the village, the broken-down huts and barns, and the steady drizzling of the autumn rain.

"I love our short gray days," he said as he squinted his eyes and looked through the smoke of his cigarette. Feodor Chaliapin would come and the two would take long walks, Rachmaninoff urging his friend to tell him stories. Then they would return to the house and Rachmaninoff would go to the piano. "No, I do not feel like singing. I am not in voice today,"

Chaliapin would protest, "and I am not going to sing today," and then Chaliapin would sing for hours.

Or the Medtners would come for a visit and the composer would try to discuss music seriously with Rachmaninoff. But he never succeeded.

"I have known Rachmaninoff from my early years," complained Medtner to Alfred Swan,[8] "all my life has passed parallel to his, but with no one have I talked so little about music as with him. Once I even told him how I wanted to discuss with him the subject of harmony. Immediately his face became very distant and he said: 'Yes, yes, we must sometime,' but he never broached the subject again. A creator must be a ne'er-do-well, to a certain extent. If Rachmaninoff could only become such a ne'er-do-well, if only for a short time, then he would again begin to compose. But he is tied hand and foot by his obligations; everything with him is measured by the hour."

"The most curious things about these words was," said Alfred Swan, "that Rachmaninoff expressed himself in almost identical terms about Medtner. 'Medtner's whole mode of life in Montmorency[9] is so monotonous. An artist cannot give everything from within. There must be outward impressions. I told him once: 'You should go and spend the night in some den, get thoroughly drunk. An artist cannot be a moralist.' "

"In the evenings a game of poker was usually arranged, at which Medtner was always the loser, or suddenly the girls would exclaim: 'Father, play us *Boublichki!*' It was then a popular Russian song about a sad man who was longing for the hard doughnuts (Russian style) of the old times. And Rachmaninoff accompanied while the whole party sang *Bou-*

[8] *Musical Quarterly*, v. 30, January-April, 1944.
[9] A suburb of Paris.

blichki. But Rachmaninoff did not like to dwell on this. It cost him too much. So he said," relates Alfred Swan.

Rachmaninoff's inner world was closed tight within him and only on occasion would he communicate it in his own words.

"The older we get, the more we lose that divine self-confidence which is the treasure of youth," he said in an interview in England,[10] "and the fewer are those moments when we believe that what we have done is good. We get lucrative contracts—more, in fact, than we can accept—but we are still longing for that inner satisfaction which is independent of outside success, and which we felt at the beginning of our career at the time of our troubles when success seemed far away.

"Nowdays it very rarely happens to me to feel sincerely satisfied with myself, to feel that what I do is really a success. Such occasions stick in my memory for a long time—for nearly the rest of my life. I recollect the city where I felt this thrill of satisfaction last, and I remember all the details. I remember the Concert Hall, where everything seemed to me to be perfect that night—the lighting, the piano, the audience. Only on such nights do I feel happy and satisfied. The last time I had this happy feeling was in Vienna.

"There is, however, a burden which age perhaps is laying on my shoulders. Heavier than any other, it was unknown to me in my youth. It is that I have no country. I had to leave the land where I was born, where I passed my youth, where I struggled and suffered all the sorrows of the young, and where I finally achieved success.

"The whole world is open to me, and success awaits me everywhere. Only one place is closed to me, and that is my own country—Russia."

[10] "Some Critical Moments in My Career," by S. Rachmaninoff (an interview). *Musical Times*, June, 1930.

. XV .

Boycott of Rachmaninoff's Music in Soviet Russia

AT THE END OF 1930 and through the first months of 1931, the Soviet Government was conducting one of its periodical purges in the characteristic way which is now so well known: denouncements, confessions, and sentences to death and exile. This caused a wave of resentment to sweep across the Western world just at the time when Rabindranath Tagore, the Hindu poet-philosopher, was being feted in New York City.

Rachmaninoff was not associated with any political organization of the Russian *émigrés*. Nevertheless, with two other Russians—Iwan I. Ostromislensky, a professor of chemistry, and Count Ilya L. Tolstoy, the son of the author—he signed the following letter, which was published in the New York *Times* on January 15, 1931.

TAGORE ON RUSSIA
The "Circle of Russian Culture"
challenges some of his statements.

To the Editors of the New York *Times*.

"The Circle of Russian Culture," the aim of which is to foster intellectual intercourse among the Russian immigrants in New York, feels compelled to comment on a recent interview given by Rabindranath Tagore.

He visited Russia, and many of his statements concerning that country have appeared in different periodicals, both in this country and elsewhere. Much to our surprise, he has given praise to the activities of the Bolsheviki and seemed rather delighted with their achievements in the field of public education. Strangely, not a word did he utter on the horrors perpetrated by the Soviet Government and the OGPU in particular.

Time and again statements similar to his have been given out to the press by persons who, officially or otherwise, have been kept on the payroll of the Communist oppressors of Russia. The value of such utterances is well known to every thinking man or woman. Nor is it possible to answer every one of these misstatements individually.

Tagore's case is different: he is considered among the great living men of our age. His voice is heard and listened to all over the world.

By eulogizing the dubious pedagogical achievements of the Soviets, and by carefully omitting every reference to the indescribable torture to which the Soviets have been subjecting the Russian people for a period of over thirteen years, he has created a false impression that no outrages actually exist under the blessing of the Soviet regime.

In view of the misunderstanding which may thus arise, we wish to ask whether he is aware of the fact that all Russia is groaning under the terrible yoke of a numerically negligible but well-organized gang of Communists, who are forcibly, by means of Red Terror, imposing their misrule upon the Russian people?

Does he know that, according to statistical data disseminated by the Bolsheviki themselves, between 1923 and 1928 more than three million persons, mostly workers and peasants, were held in prisons and concentration camps which are nothing but torture houses?

He cannot be ignorant of the fact that the Communist rulers of

Russia, in order to squeeze the maximum quantity of food out of the peasants, and also with the intent of reducing them to a state of abject misery, are, and have been, penalizing dissenters by exiling them to the extreme north, where those who by a miracle are able to survive the severe climate are compelled by force to perform certain work which cannot be compared even with the abomination of the galleys of olden times. There unfortunate sufferers are being daily and systematically subjected to indescribable privations, humiliations, suffering, and torture.

At the very time of his visit in Russia, forty-six Russian professors and engineers were executed by the OGPU without any pretense of trial, on the alleged ground that they dared to interfere with, or doubt the wisdom of, the notorious Five-Year Plan.

At no time in no country has there ever existed a Government responsible for so many cruelties, wholesale murders, and common-law crimes in general as those perpetrated by the Bolsheviki.

Is it really possible that, with all his love for humanity, wisdom, and philosophy, he could not find words of sympathy and pity for the Russian Nation?

By his evasive attitude toward the Communist gravediggers of Russia, by the quasi-cordial stand which he has taken toward them, he has lent strong and unjust support to a group of professional murderers. By concealing from the world the truth about Russia he has inflicted, perhaps unwittingly, great harm upon the whole population of Russia, and possibly the world at large.

Iwan I. Ostromislensky
Sergei Rachmaninoff
Count Ilya L. Tolstoy

New York
January 12, 1931

Here is what had actually happened.

Three months before this letter was written, on October 9, 1930, Rabindranath Tagore came to this country, as he said, "to see old friends, make new ones, and to lecture," under the auspices of the American Friends Society of Philadelphia. While the liner *Bremen*, on which he arrived in New York, lay in quarantine, Rabindranath Tagore, sitting over an unfinished breakfast in his cabin, recounted to reporters of the *Telegram* and the *Times* his ideals and the dreams he held for the people of India.

In reference to Russia, Tagore said that there he found "many things which he believed might well do for India, such as the educational programs for the masses."

He said that "ten years ago Russia and India were similarly situated, so far as the peasant classes were concerned, while today Russian peasants are bright and answer questions quickly." "That is not so in India," he said, "and education is what must be given to her people before she can stand upon her own feet."

He said that he "yearned for the political peace for India which learning seems to have brought Russia," and that he noticed that "conflicts between divergent racial groups in Russia no longer seem to exist."

"That should be a lesson to India," he declared. "I went to Russia with prejudices, but found that the situation had changed miraculously. It is a mistaken idea that Russia is turning out only factory hands. The theaters and operas are beginning to grow again and for the first time the lower classes are able to enhance their lives with these things."

On November 8, 1930, Tagore spoke over station WABC in New York and was interrogated on the subject "Youth Rebuilding the World" by Chester S. Williams, executive secretary of the National Student Federation of America.

"Is there a genuine sense of social responsibility growing up in Russia which is of future world significance?"

"On this subject Tagore's opinions and viewpoint are those of a student of education, and not those of a politician," reported the *Telegram*. "He has consistently refused to commit himself on the national and international questions involved in the Soviet experiment, declaring after his visit to Russia this year that he is interested in education, which he regards as the only means to secure liberty."

Thus Tagore spoke of India and of his own people, referring to Russia only in comparison to his own country.

Anyone can see that the letter which Rachmaninoff signed had no direct bearing upon what Tagore said, that the two other authors of the letter just used Tagore's name for their own protest on a subject which had nothing to do with Tagore's interviews and which was written in an undignified manner certainly not characteristic of Rachmaninoff.

I am sure that Rachmaninoff lent his name out of friendship to the other two co-signers and not out of a conviction as to the justness of the content of the letter. Referring to this incident one prominent Russian musician who lives in France said to me: "Rachmaninoff lived in a Russian ghetto." By this phrase he meant the impoverished nobility and the exiled intellectuals whose emotions blinded them to any rational analyses.

The Soviet newspapers did not react to Rachmaninoff's letter immediately, probably because their attention and space were entirely devoted to the speeches at the purge trials. However, two months later, March 9th, the Moscow *Evening* carried an indignant report of a concert at the Moscow Conservatory, at which Rachmaninoff's *Bells* was performed.

The sound of bells, a liturgy, the devil knows what, the fear of an elemental upheaval, in fact everything that was in perfect harmony with that regime which had rotted away long before the October Revolution, filled the concert hall.

The music is composed by Rachmaninoff, an *émigré*, a violent enemy of Soviet Russia, while the words are written by another *émigré*, the mystic Balmont. The performance was conducted by

Albert Coates, who also left Russia in 1917 and has now returned at the invitation issued because of his foreign passport.

To complete this strange picture one has only to describe the audience: some kind of ancient figures in long frock coats, decrepit women dressed in old-fashioned silks smelling of moth balls, bald scalps, trembling cheeks, washed-out eyes, long gloves, lorgnettes. . . .

According to *Rachmaninoff's Recollections*, *Pravda* reserved for itself even more violent comments to show its wrath.

Who is the composer of this work? Sergei Rachmaninoff, the former bard of the Russian wholesale merchants and the bourgeoisie—a composer who was played out long ago and whose music is that of an insignificant imitator and reactionary: a former estate owner, who, as recently as 1918, burned with a hatred of Russia when the peasants took away his land—a sworn and active enemy of the Soviet Government.

And the author of the text (after Edgar Allan Poe) is the half-idiotic, decadent, and mystic Balmont, who has long ago identified himself with the "White" émigrés.

It was not so long ago that this very same Sergei Rachmaninoff, together with Ilya Tolstoy, published an official letter in the newspaper New York Times (of January 15, 1931) on the occasion of Rabindranath Tagore's imminent journey to the USSR, which is unprecedented in its impudence, and in which these two "soldiers of the White Guards" raised a volume of complaint against the tortures inflicted by the OGPU and the "slavery" in this country, and called the Soviet Government a government of murderers, criminals, and professional executioners.

In the short history of the Soviet Union clashes between Bolshevism and art had been frequent and more than one artist suffered the "people's wrath" because he thought he was still a "Free Artist." Feodor Chaliapin was deprived of the honorary title of "People's Artist" because of his "anti-Soviet conduct abroad," and now Rachmaninoff's music came for its *dies irae* in Soviet Russia.

Ten days later the collective representing the musicians of the Leningrad and Moscow Conservatories pronounced the death verdict for Rachmaninoff's works. Rachmaninoff was found guilty of writing "anti-Soviet articles in America." They were referring to the letter quoted above and to "another communication also published in January," which was an appeal to the State Department asking the American people to refrain from buying Soviet goods. It was signed by two hundred and ten prominent Russians here and abroad, including many scientists, statesmen, musicians, artists, clergymen, and industrialists.[1] Sergei Rachmaninoff's name was among those who signed this appeal. Therefore, the Soviet musicians suddenly decided that all of the music of the defendant must be a portrayal of "the decay of the petty bourgeois spirit particularly harmful to conditions in the acute struggle on the music front," and the collective unanimously adopted the resolution to boycott Sergei Rachmaninoff's works.

Overwhelmed by this logic of the St. Petersburg and Moscow colleagues, the Kharkov News, the official Ukrainian organ, published the announcement of a resolution taken by the United Ukrainian High Schools: ". . . an author of works which, in their emotional and mental effects, are bourgeois through and through, the composer of Liturgies, Vesper Masses, and The Bells, that manufacturer of fox trots, Rachmaninoff, was and is a servant and tool of the worst enemies of the Proletariat—the world-bourgeoisie and world-capitalism. We invite the Ukrainian proletariat youth and all Government institutions to boycott Rachmaninoff's work. Down with Rachmaninoff! Down with the whole Rachmaninoff worship!"

Though the New York Times[2] reported that on hearing the

[1] New York Herald Tribune, March 20, 1931.
[2] March 29, 1931.

news Rachmaninoff had said: "I am quite indifferent," and, according to some sources, he said that he was "proud of being the object of 'their' wrath," it was not so. He was hurt and felt it very deeply. For when twelve years later I spoke to him about it, the subject was still a sore spot which he did not want to discuss. He brushed it off by saying that the rumors of a "boycott" were not true, and as a proof of his conviction he pointed to the mounting stack of letters on his desk which he was receiving from Russian composers, his old friends in Soviet Russia.

From my conversation with him I gained the impression that Rachmaninoff had separated in his mind the Russian people from those who governed the country and he pretended he was "quite indifferent" to anything the latter said or did in connection with him or his work.

.XVI.

Rhapsody on a Theme of Paganini

IN THE FIRST YEARS of the nineteen-thirties, Rachmaninoff again felt an urge to compose. Whether because his summer place at Clairefontaine was too noisy and gay with all the visiting friends of the younger generation and because of its proximity to Paris, where the Russian colony was always mixing in political intrigues, Rachmaninoff bought himself a small place "without any neighbors," as he put it, on the lake of Firwaldstadt, near Lucerne. Here he supervised the building of his new home which he christened Senar—composed out of the two first letters of his own and his wife's first names, adding the last "R" from the family name.

Everyone in the family teased him for choosing this particular spot for, as Mrs. Rachmaninoff remarked, "even Baedeker says that it rains there more than anywhere else in the world." But the composer was happy in his seclusion, where he was usually joined by his children and grandchildren, and where he relaxed at his favorite sport, motor-boating on the lake.

. . . Now I have finished all my concerts (until October 3rd in America) and I feel, as one would expect, like a squeezed lemon, tired and nervous, and I am generally unpleasant for

those around me. This exhaustion is progressing with every year, though at the same time every year I cut down the number of my concerts [Rachmaninoff wrote Vladimir Vilshau from Paris].

In three days I am going to Switzerland. There on the lake of Lucerne I have a small place where I expect to spend the whole summer. I love to live there. My occupation there is gardening and taking care of flowers. This time the beginning of my stay there will be marred by a small operation which I have to have as soon as I arrive. Don't be frightened! I am told it is not a serious operation. Perhaps on the 1st of May they will let me out of the hospital. But unfortunately I will be late for planting the flowers and, of course, I will be temporarily weak. I am going there with my wife. By the way, now we always travel together to all my concerts and she is going to stay in an adjoining room in the hospital.

The children will come to Switzerland much later. At first, Sofinka[1] (Volkonskaya) will appear with her governess, about May 1st. Irinochka will arrive about May 15th. And toward June 1st Tanyusha will arrive with her son. Her husband works here and he will come toward the 1st of July. (Tanya's husband Boris Conus is the son of Jule.)[2]

I love my grandchildren very much, but I love my own daughters even more. They are very good. Not at all the modern kind! I continue to remain conservative in my tastes.

Sofinka is now eight years old. She is so pretty. She is very talented, just like her mother. She has been studying piano for the last two years. She has an excellent ear and wonderful hands. She is working here with Olga Nikolaevna Conus (the

[1] Rachmaninoff's granddaughter.
[2] One of the three Conus brothers.

wife of Lev).[3] The boy Sasha (Tanya's son) was one year old last March 8th. Well, there is not much one can say about that one. Perhaps just that he has a calming effect on me. We talk very little, and his little face is so funny and so gay that even looking at him I feel better. Thus we are occupied with a silent conversation together.

I want to give you my summer address; perhaps you will find time to write me. It will make me very happy.

Greetings to your wife and children. I embrace you.

Yours,

S. Rachmaninoff

Paris
April 6, 1934
Hertenstein b/Lucerne
Villa Senar

But instead of cutting down on the number of concerts (in the last three years he had refused to accept more than forty to forty-five concerts), Rachmaninoff let himself be talked into accepting sixty-five. "Will I be able to bear it?" he complained in his letter to Vilshau. "I am beginning to exhaust myself. Often it is too difficult for me to play. I have become old."

However, in the same letter he announced this happy news: "Two weeks ago I finished a new piece. It is called a Fantasy for piano and orchestra in a form of Variations on the theme of Paganini (the one on which Liszt and Brahms wrote their variations). It is a very long piece, about twenty to twenty-five minutes. That is the size of a piano concerto. I am not going to have it published before next spring. I am going to try it out in New York and London, so that I can make the

---

[3] Another of the three Conus brothers.

necessary corrections. The composition is very difficult and I should start practicing it, but with every year I become more and more lazy about this finger work. I try to shirk practicing by playing something old, something that already sits firmly in my fingers. . . ."

The Rhapsody on the theme of Paganini is undoubtedly one of the most important works of the composer written after he left Russia and will probably live as long as his second and third concertos. It belongs to the few compositions for piano and orchestra which, like Liszt's *Danse Macabre* and César Franck's *Symphonic Variations*, are written in a form of variations. For his theme Rachmaninoff chose Paganini's Caprice in A minor known better through the brilliant Liszt and Brahms variations in piano arrangement than in its original version.

The twenty-four variations of the Rhapsody are divided into three groups, for Rachmaninoff always used three movements as a basis for his symphonic works. The striking feature of this composition is that it shows a new style for Rachmaninoff. It has no songlike Russian themes. Laconic in its statements, with a scarcity of pedal and with rather dry, *martellato* coloring of short episodes, it sounds like a contemporary composition. The few variations written in the old Rachmaninoff style only emphasize further his new approach. There is no way to determine whether Rachmaninoff had a definite programmatic-choreographic plan while composing it, but three years later he wrote to Mikhail Fokine, the Russian choreographer:

Dear Mikhail Mikhailovich—
I just cannot catch you. I telephoned you in Lucerne on August 15th (you came to see us on 13th) and was told that "you had left yesterday." After receiving your letter yesterday

I called you at Montreux. The same answer—"had left yester-day." Where to? You are like a meteor or, to put it more po-etically, like a new moon. I will address this letter to London.

About my Rhapsody I want to say that I will be very happy if you will do something with it. Last night I was thinking about a possible subject, and here is what came into my head. I will give you only the main structure now; the details are still in a haze. Why not resurrect the legend about Paganini, who, for perfection in his art and for a woman, sold his soul to an evil spirit? All the variations which have the theme of Dies Irae represent the evil spirit. The variations from No. 11 to No. 18 are love episodes. Paganini himself appears in the "theme" (his first appearance) and again, for the last time, but conquered, in variation No. 23. The first twelve measures after all the variations to the end of the composition represent the triumph of the conquerors. The evil spirit appears for the first time in variation No. 7, where at the place marked 19 one can have the dialogue with Paganini about his own theme and the one of Dies Irae. Variations Nos. 8, 9, 10 are the develop-ment of the "evil spirit." Variation No. 11 is a turning point into the domain of love. Variation No. 12—the Menuet—portrays the first appearance of the woman. Variation No. 13 is the first conversation between the woman and Paganini. Variation No. 19—Paganini's triumph, his diabolic pizzicato.

It would be interesting to represent Paganini with his violin —not a real violin, of course, but something fantastic. Also, it seems to me that the other personages representing the evil spirit at the end of the piece should be drawn as caricatures in their fight for the woman and Paganini's art. Definitely as cari-catures resembling Paganini. They also should be with violins but even more fantastic and grotesque. You are not going to laugh at me, are you?

I want so much to see you in order to talk to you about it in more detail if, of course, my sketch and my thoughts are interesting and valuable to you. . . .[4]
Hertenstein b/Lucerne
Villa Senar
August 29, 1937

Two years later, on June 30, 1939, *Paganini*, a fantastic ballet in three scenes by S. Rachmaninoff and M. Fokine, was presented to the London public at Covent Garden. Far from "laughing" at Rachmaninoff's suggestions as they were outlined in his letter, Fokine agreed with the composer and based his story on the old legend about Paganini, "who sold his soul to an evil spirit in exchange for perfection in his art."

The ballet portrays Paganini's magnetism as mixed with the superstitious influence of the evil spirit. Evil is conquered in the end by the spirit of Divine Genius, which leads the great violinist to immortality. Rachmaninoff composed a new ending especially for the ballet, and this spectacle was acclaimed by the critics as one of the Fokine's finest works.

[4] From Rachmaninoff's family archive. *In Memory of Rachmaninoff*, New York, 1946.

.XVII.

A Touring Virtuoso

THERE IS VERY LITTLE that I can add to Rachmaninoff's own description of his life as given in his letters to Vladimir Vilshau. The life of a touring virtuoso varies little from year to year. It suffices to say that Rachmaninoff reached the peak of his popularity during the last ten years of his life and that his appearances were one continual triumph despite the terrible physical effort they cost him.

"My health is getting bad," he complained to Vilshau. "I am rapidly falling apart. When I had my health, then I was exceptionally lazy. Now that I am losing my health, I do nothing else but think about working. This is a proof that I do not belong to the truly talented men, for I consider that a real talent should also possess a gift for working from the first day he becomes conscious of his talent. But in my youth I did everything to kill it. One can hardly expect a resurrection in old age. Thus it is very difficult to augment my capacity now. It only shows that during my life I did not do all that I could have done and the knowledge of this will not make my remaining days very happy. I am putting a period here. I am apologizing for the minor mode."

When in the spring of 1936 Rachmaninoff returned to Senar, he gave this full account in a letter to Vilshau.

My dear friend Vladimir Robertovich—

Last night I arrived in Senar and today I received your letter of April 10th. You ask so many questions. . . . I will try to answer them. If I fail to answer them all, it will be only because you have too many.

On April 2nd I finished my season. I started on October 19th. I gave sixty-one concerts—thirty-five in America, fourteen in England, three in Switzerland, three in Paris, two in Warsaw, and one in each of the other countries, Vienna, Budapest, etc. My next season is already planned. I will start on October 16th and finish it on April 6th.

Toward the end of each season I have to go "under the whip"—that is, I become so tired that in the intermissions I have to drink port wine. I must confess it does not help much. It is all just imagination. It is very strange how our lives are arranged: When one is young and strong, all one does is await engagements. But they do not come. But when one is old, then one has so many engagements one does not know where to hide from them. I cannot accept even one half.

During the last ten years Natasha has traveled with me everywhere. She at least helps me with taking care of my things, because often we arrive in a town only a few hours before the concert and then I have to leave immediately afterward.

The programs of my concerts generally consist of the works of other composers. I do not like to play my own compositions. I usually put just two or three little things of my own on the program "just for looks." What do I play? I have played a great many programs. My favorite program is a concert with two parts: in the first Chopin and in the second Liszt. To such

programs I do not need to add myself. But these are special
programs, and one cannot play them often. Usually my programs are well-known Bach, Beethoven, Schubert, Chopin,
and at the end Liszt. I do not play the works of modern composers.

The best violinist is Kreisler. Next to him or along with him
goes Jascha Heifetz. [Rachmaninoff was answering Vilshau's
questions.]

The best pianist, probably, after all is still Hofmann, but
only under one condition—when he is "in the mood." If not,
then you could not recognize the old Hofmann. Lately Horowitz has acquired a big name. He has colossal octaves! After
his marriage to Toscanini's daughter (the best conductor)
many hoped that his playing would gain a little musicality. . . .
So far this has not happened. Everyone is consoling himself
that he has not been married a very long time. The best orchestras are in America: in Philadelphia (with which I always
do my gramophone recordings) and the one in New York.
Those who have not heard them do not know what an orchestra is.

I have not published my memoirs. You have probably heard
about Riesemann's book, which is called "Rachmaninoff's Recollections Dictated to Riesemann." It was published in America and in England. Of course, it is in English. If you wish, I
will send it to you. The book is very boring. By the way, there
is a lot in it that is not true, which proves that I did not dictate
the book, but that Riesemann composed it out of his head.

Last March, while I was in England, I received a book and
was asked to give an authorization, but I have read only three
chapters out of the book. I did not have the patience to go any
further. For God's sake, do not think that I am posing. But
even in this kind of writing one must feel a talent. And there

was nothing noticeable! Neither in Riesemann's (Riesemann died last year and this is why I do not swear at him as much as I otherwise would), nor in the book of the Englishman.[1]

You ask me to send some criticisms . . . but I do not collect them. . . . I do not have any. I am sending you just this one, which I received from a friend, an Englishman. It was written by the famous London critic Ernest Newman. At the concert I played my own third concerto. If you cannot understand English, throw it away.

You also ask me about Natasha and my children. But about them one can say only one thing, that it would be difficult to find a better wife or better children. Here you have somebody about whom one should write a book!

Good-by. Greetings!

Yours,
S. R.

Villa Senar
April 15, 1936

Here is what Oskar von Riesemann wrote in the preface to *Rachmaninoff's Recollections Told to Oskar von Riesemann.*

[1] Rachmaninoff advised me not to read it, as it contained nothing not already in Riesemann's book. This is literally true. Watson Lyle's book does not even correct a few obvious errors in Riesemann's.

In all fairness to Oskar von Riesemann I quote the letter which Rachmaninoff wrote him, the photostat of which is published in Riesemann's book.

Villa Senar,
Hertenstein b/Lucerne

"My dear Mr. Riesemann—

I have read with interest the manuscript of your book and wish to thank you for the sympathetic understanding with which you have treated our intimate talks at Clairefontaine.

"If you have overemphasized the importance of some of my modest achievements, I am sure it is only because of our long and close friendship.

"Believe me,
Sincerely,
S. Rachmaninoff."

July 28, 1933

Never before have I felt such regret at my inability to write Russian shorthand: I am afraid there are moments when the necessary translation into English prevented me from doing justice to the plastic clarity and calm strength of expression shown by the narrator.

It is not often that a biographer is able to draw from such a truly living source. In this case the opportunity was accepted all the more gratefully because this living source proved the only possible one. The material usually at the disposal of biographers, such as letters, manuscripts, newspaper cuttings, etc., was not opened up. It remained in Soviet Russia and its use was withheld. It seems to me, however, that when one considers the absolute authenticity of personal communication, this can hardly be counted as a loss; nor is the fact that the choice of material was largely left to the central figure in this biography of any real importance. From the biography of a living person consideration for the feelings of others demands, as a matter of principle, that certain matter should be omitted. Of the proper exercise of this principle the subject is in general the best judge. The missing chapters in the story are most fitly to be considered only in historic retrospect and should be added by later writers. I hope that the following pages will, one day, be richly supplemented; they need no verification and may, therefore, constitute the foundation of every future Rachmaninoff biography.

Rachmaninoff also read this page in Riesemann's preface and apparently did not object. Yet he certainly was aware of the fact that at the time Riesemann's book was the sole volume of information about him and that the title of the book carried his name *Rachmaninoff's Recollections Told to Oskar von Riesemann.*

I have checked the Riesemann story with all the available sources. Rachmaninoff's remark that "a lot of it Riesemann composed out of his head" is unfair and could only have been based on a few unimportant errors in Riesemann's book and a certain slant which one feels is more Riesemann's than Rachmaninoff's but with which, I am sure, at the time of their conversations Rachmaninoff was in accord. When I spoke to Rachmaninoff about Riesemann's book, he told me that he did not like the book, but he explained to me that while he was telling his story to Riesemann, he thought he was only giving Riesemann material for a book, never suspecting that he would be quoted verbatim.

But Rachmaninoff never did send the book to Vilshau. In his letter he apologized for his "thoughtless promise," as he put it, saying that "because of certain conditions which were no fault of his he regretted, but could not send it." Rachmaninoff realized that the book contained too many of both Riesemann's and his own remarks which would not be welcomed in Soviet Russia.

A quarter of a century after Rachmaninoff had written his last symphonic work, *The Bells,* he composed his third symphony. Unlike his first two symphonies, this work consists of three instead of the four movements with a short scherzando episode introduced in the second movement, a device he had been using in his piano concertos. Like his Paganini Variations, this work is written in a new style, but its main picture is so thoroughly Russian that one might call the symphony "My Memories of Russia." If in his former orchestra works one could trace Tchaikovsky's influence, this time one feels the influence of Rimsky-Korsakov in its orchestration, and of Borodin in its epic breadth.

But in commenting on Rachmaninoff's works of this period, there is one hard fact to be faced, discouraging as it was for the composer who still felt in full possession of his creative ability. And that is that Rachmaninoff had already said what he had to say too many times. By saying it each time in a different way he added nothing new, and his picture of his native land was dated. His contemporary Igor Stravinsky and his juniors Prokofiev and Shostakovich have brought these pictures up to date and told their fantastic story far more convincingly and interestingly. It was sad, but nevertheless true, that while musicians all over the world were extremely interested in the character of the next composition of every other contemporary composer, there was no genuine interest shown in Rachmaninoff as a symphonic composer. The musicians dismissed him with: "He has written himself out."

But I doubt very much that Rachmaninoff was aware of this. Although he had sometimes vacillated, he had stood alone for many years supported only by his own conviction of the value of his orchestral works. And it must have been hard for him to realize that the old problem of what he wanted to be— a composer, conductor, or pianist—had finally been solved by none other than his own public.

"I marvel at men like Richard Strauss," Rachmaninoff said to me. "As a conductor he must constantly study old as well as new scores. His head is full of the music of other composers, and yet he writes his own at the same time. This is very difficult to do."

Perhaps this was one of the reasons why Rachmaninoff declined the invitations of the orchestras when he first came to this country; he may have wanted to save himself for his own work. Or was it because he shrank from open competition, that he preferred a field where he knew he stood above any comparison? He would have had to match his powers with many conductors, including his old acquaintance Serge Koussevitzky, who in a short time had gained the highest position in this field. Needless to say the prospect of a repetition of the Moscow days was hardly attractive to him. And while his career as a symphonic composer made little progress for the simple reason that conductors who championed Russian music seldom played his works, the demand for him as a pianist grew from year to year.

How strangely our life is arranged [Rachmaninoff wrote to Vilshau]. "When I was young and strong and was striving to get engagements for any kind of a concert, then either I had only a few or none at all. Now, when I am old, sick, and tired, there is no end to them. I have a manager,[2] an impresario with whom I have been working in America for the last nineteen years. We have become friends. Now our job consists of choosing certain concerts out of all the engagements offered. I have also turned over to him the general representation of my concerts in Europe. Thus the season for next year looks this way: thirty-two concerts in America, from October 17th to December 20th. I shall rest in January. In February, twelve concerts in the Scandinavian countries, four concerts in Holland, and one in Vienna, Budapest, Paris, and somewhere else. In March, twelve concerts in England, and finally, on April 10th, the last concert in Vienna, where, after twenty years, I shall again conduct. The program will be my third symphony and The Bells.

Besides all these trips I shall have two extra trips which coincide with my vacation. On September 5th I am going to record my third symphony in London. For this they will give me the London Philharmonic orchestra and three rehearsals on September 2nd, 3rd, and 4th. But as the sale of such important works is usually very poor, the orchestra very expensive, and the company loses money, they want a "bribe"— that is, they want me also to record my first piano concerto. As I am worried about my hands (I have lost the habit of

[2] Charles Foley.

conducting), I cannot "throw in," as they ask me, the recording of my concerto. Therefore I have decided first to go home and then return to London on September 21st or 22nd. And on October 1st my boat sails for America.

Let me say a few words about my new symphony. It was played in New York, Philadelphia, Chicago, etc. I was at the first two performances. It was played wonderfully (the Philadelphia orchestra about which I have written you, Stokowski conducting). The reception by the public and critics was . . . sour. . . . I personally am firmly convinced that the composition is good. But . . . sometimes authors are mistaken! However, I am still of my opinion. The symphony (the score and the orchestral parts) was published two weeks ago.

Today I began to practice my first concerto. Fortunately, it is not very difficult. Because the recordings of this concerto will be on sale this winter, I have promised to play it at my second concert in London on April 2nd, which I shall give with the orchestra. Here is the program: my first concerto, Beethoven's first concerto (what heavenly music!) and my Rhapsody.

Well, enough about myself. I have written too much. Forgive me. My Natasha also begins to get a little sick. But out of our whole family she is probably the strongest, or perhaps the one who has the most patience. She is our support and consolation. Without her we would be lost. I pray God may give her health.

Good-by. I embrace you.

Yours,
S.R.

Villa Senar
June 7, 1937

I have been reading the book Little Golden America, by I. Ilf and Petrov. If you want to learn something about America, do

*not miss it. There is a lot in it that is interesting! There are
also a few funny lines about me. But this is the only part which
is not true!*

The following is an excerpt from the *Little Golden America*
—the "few funny lines" to which Rachmaninoff referred in
his letter.

The Best Musicians in the World

. . . Rich America has taken possession of the best musicians in
the world. In New York, in Carnegie Hall, we heard Rachmaninoff
and Stokowski.

Rachmaninoff, according to what a composer told us, before
coming out on the stage sits in his dressing room and tells anecdotes. But as soon as the bell rings, he rises from his seat and,
assuming the expression of a Russian exile's great sorrow, goes forth
to the stage.

The night we went to hear him he appeared tall, bent, and thin,
with a long sad face, his hair closely clipped; he sat down at the
piano, separated the folds of his old-fashioned black swallow-tail,
adjusted one of his cuffs with his large hand, and turned to the
public. His expression seemed to say: "Yes, I am an unfortunate
exile and am obliged to play before you for your contemptible
dollars, and for all this humiliation I ask very little—silence."

There was such dead silence, as if the thousand auditors in the
gallery lay dead, poisoned by some new, hitherto unknown musical
gas. Rachmaninoff finished. We expected an explosion. But in the
orchestra only normal applause resounded. We did not trust our
ears. We sensed cold indifference—as if the public had come not
to hear remarkable music remarkably played but rather to discharge
a dull duty. Only from the gallery did we hear several enthusiastic
exclamations.[3]

But what Rachmaninoff thought of American audiences
has been already recorded in his *Recollections*, which were

[3] *Little Golden America: Two famous Soviet humorists survey the United
States*, by Ilya Ilf and Eugene Petrov (first published in the USSR, 1936).

published two years before the Russian humorists heard Rachmaninoff in Carnegie Hall.

"In the course of my last eleven years of concert experience in America, separated from my first visit by an absence of ten years, I have had ample opportunity of convincing myself of the great progress made by American audiences both in their power of assimilation and in their musical taste. Their artistic demands have grown to an astonishing extent. The man who exposes his art to public opinion notices this immediately. This opinion is not mine alone, but is shared by all other artists who have given concerts in the U.S.A., and with whom I have discussed the subject. From this one may conclude that the remarkable efforts of American, and especially New York society, to raise the standard of musical life have not been in vain. They have used every means in their power and have not spared any money in their effort to surpass Europe in this respect. They have succeeded. No man will dare to dispute the fact."

With every passing year Rachmaninoff felt more and more the weight of his "compulsory concert service," as he called it in his letters to Vilshau, and yet this work was the only happiness he had outside of his personal life. "Now the time has come," he wrote, "when one does not walk by oneself, but when one is led by the arm. Looking from the outside, this might appear to be respect, but on the other hand one is being helped so that one will not fall into small pieces. However, last season I gave fifty-nine concerts. Probably I shall give the same number during the coming season. Well, for how many such seasons can I hold out? That I do not know. But I do know that while I am working, I feel innerly somehow stronger than when I do not work. Therefore I pray to God that I can work up to my last days. . . ."

.XVIII.

Last Years

As if sensing the approach of World War II, Rachmaninoff returned to the United States in 1939, earlier than usual, and spent the rest of the summer on Long Island. The war separated him from his Senar in Switzerland, which he considered at long last his home, and from his youngest daughter Tatiana, who remained with her husband and her little boy in France.

"I am very much worried about them," Rachmaninoff said to me as he looked up from his desk at the picture of his daughter, which hung on the wall in his study. "I have bought them a small place near Paris, but now they are in German-occupied France."

If Rachmaninoff was upset and worried at the beginning of the war, he became doubly depressed when the German armies marched into Russia. He shuddered at the thought of the destruction of the relics and old Russian cities which the Germans laid waste on their way to Moscow. And when Rachmaninoff started his winter season, he donated the entire proceeds from many of his concerts to the Red Army.

For years Rachmaninoff had been known in Russian circles both here and abroad for his support of those who were in need, though he preferred to be anonymous or to "disappear" as soon as he had made his generous gesture.

But with the medical supplies which Rachmaninoff sent to Russia a note was attached. It read:

From one of the Russians to the Russian people in their fight against their foe. I want to believe, I do believe in complete victory.

Sergei Rachmaninoff

March 25, 1942.

"Rachmaninoff is Red," whispered the Russian émigrés, for they hoped with a Nazi victory to see at last the destruction of Bolshevism in Russia. But to Rachmaninoff war meant catastrophe and suffering for Russia and the Russian people, whose proud son he was before anything else in the world. His action in behalf of the Red Army did not mean that he had made peace with those who were in power in Russia.

I remember how upset he was because Serge Koussevitzky, after a concert at the Berkshire Festival where he conducted Shostakovich's seventh symphony, entertained Ambassador Litvinoff. Rachmaninoff insisted on asking me for all the details: "Where did Litvinoff stay while in the Berkshires? Was it possible that he was Koussevitzky's guest?" And was I sure that I saw Litvinoff in a box at the concert, or perhaps I was mistaken?

Finally, not able to control his emotions, he rose to his six feet and three inches and, throwing down on his desk a small silver paper-knife he had been gesticulating with, he walked out of the room. Later he returned, apologizing and muttering something about how disgusted he was.

Rachmaninoff, even after living in this country almost twenty-five years, had very few American friends. He stayed in his "lair," as he said to me, and the only friends with whom he occasionally liked to spend an evening chatting or playing his favorite card game, whist, were Russians. Serge Koussevitzky was not among them. Rachmaninoff apparently never forgave Koussevitzky the Moscow days. One would think that these two outstanding Russian musicians could have forgotten their grievances and combined their talents to give the world a unique opportunity in art. This would have benefited them both and who can tell what artistic heights they could have scaled if they had joined their names and talents in musical enterprises.

But Rachmaninoff avoided Koussevitzky and even chose to ally himself with Leopold Stokowski and the Philadelphia Orchestra for the first performances of his works. During all these years he played with Koussevitzky only two or three times and only because their concert managers arranged these appearances.

With the strong propaganda during the war for Soviet music, Rachmaninoff's name was relegated to the background. And he felt this keenly. But Rachmaninoff was also interested in the new music which was coming from his native land. But not as a politician. He listened to Shostakovich's symphonies, and he spoke to me about him.

Rachmaninoff thought that Shostakovich was very talented, but he hoped that sooner or later Shostakovich would leave Russia so that his creative ability would be free to develop and not remain attached to the tail of ever changing political lines. However, as he spoke of Dmitri Shostakovich, I felt Rachmaninoff's great pride that the music to which millions were listening at the moment came from a Slav like himself.

In the years of 1940-41, Rachmaninoff composed the Three Symphonic Dances to which at first he wanted to give the program titles of "Morning," "Noon," and "Evening," the three stages in human life. There is a suggestion that they could be interpreted as a *Danse Macabre*, for the choral of the *Dies Irae*, which had haunted the composer since his youth, is present again. The freedom of the rhythm prevents one from imagining any definite choreographic plan and a vague jazz influence makes one wonder if the composer was not experimenting further in his new style.

But as a whole this composition did not measure up to the other symphonic works of the composer and Rachmaninoff must have been hurt when his favored Philadelphia Orchestra, to whom he always gave his compositions for recording, failed to use it.

After each strenuous winter season, Rachmaninoff longed for a peaceful vacation, which was not complete unless he had a few Russians around him. In California he made friends with the Russian actors and theatrical and film producers, and because of their company and the climate Rachmaninoff bought himself a house in Beverly Hills.

"I am going to die in this house," Rachmaninoff said, but he did not know how prophetic his words were.

The season of 1942-43 was the last Rachmaninoff played. It marked fifty years of his concert career as a pianist and he was nearing his seventieth birthday. After the close of his tour he planned to retire to his new home in California. His friends urged him to rest and to devote himself to composing, but he said: "The bad part of it is that it is hard for me to give concerts. And what life will I have without them, without music? . . . And I am too tired to compose. Where am I to get the necessary strength, the necessary fire? . . ."

"And how about your Symphonic Dances? How did you compose them?" persisted an old friend and admirer.

Rachmaninoff loved this last composition, perhaps because it was his latest creation.

"I don't know how it happened," Rachmaninoff said. "It must have been my last spark. . . ."

I saw Rachmaninoff a few hours before he started on the last stretch of his tour. Among other things, we spoke about American composers and the future of American music. Rachmaninoff looked grave and shook his head. He thought that the young American composers were on the wrong track.

"The trouble is that there are no proper teachers for beginners. The well-known modern and ultra-modern composers are not the right ones for an American student to go to. The young musician must first learn the rules and gain a fundamental knowledge of the language he is going to write in, as did Beethoven and Chopin; he must know these rules thoroughly before he can afford to tear them down and begin to write any way he pleases—calling it 'modern.'

"I have had young men come to me with their compositions, and when I point out to them what is obviously a wrong note, they tell me that I do not understand—that this is the modern way of composing. It does not take me long to discover that they do not know the simplest, the most elementary rules of harmony that the students of my time in the Moscow Conservatory had mastered by their second year of study.

"If they persist the way they are going now, there is no hope for them."

And then, after a long pause, he added:

"The seed of the future music of America lies in a true

Negro music. What character there is in a Negro's face alone! This is what they should work from. . . ."

Knowing how meticulous Rachmaninoff was about anyone quoting him, and how particularly correct he wanted to be toward the musicians in the United States—for he felt he had no right to be harsh in his criticism because he was not yet an American citizen—I sent a copy of my article to catch him en route on his tour. Here is what he wrote me, apparently on the day that he stopped playing.

Pushkin once said: "There is no truth on earth, or even above it." It seems to me that there is truth on earth, only it is hidden and it is not customary[1] to speak of it.

My words on page eight,[2] in reference to the American composers, are the holy truth. I do not want to substitute a lie for the truth. But as the truth is unbearable, I prefer to say nothing at all. Therefore, please omit the four lines.[3] Please do this for me. Everything else is acceptable.

I am ailing all the time. And I play fewer concerts than the number I cancel. Right now, I have canceled three concerts, so that I can go "direkt"[4] to California to "summer quarters."[5]

See you soon!
S. Rachmaninoff

February 22, 1943

By the time he reached Chicago, Rachmaninoff was not feeling well. The Russian doctor whom Rachmaninoff consulted told him that he had a light case of pleurisy but that he

---

[1] Underlined by S. Rachmaninoff.
[2] In the manuscript of my article for Vogue.—V.S.
[3] In my article I omitted the four lines which were uncomplimentary to the American composers.—V.S.
[4] Rachmaninoff wrote this word in German.
[5] Rachmaninoff quoted from Pushkin's poem *Borodino*.

would lose his cough as soon as it would get warmer. However, in New Orleans the composer felt worse. His cough bothered him and he had such a pain in his back that he was afraid that soon he would not be able to get up.

This is when he decided to cancel his three concerts in Texas and go *direkt* to California. After sixty hours on the train the Rachmaninoffs arrived in Los Angeles, where an ambulance was waiting for him. He was transported to the hospital, but after the doctors diagnosed his illness as cancer, Mrs. Rachmaninoff took him home to 610 Elm Street, Beverly Hills.

"How good it is to be at home," Rachmaninoff said to his nurse, Olga Mordovskaya. Rachmaninoff insisted on having a Russian nurse.

His daughter Irina and his sister-in-law Sophia Satin came from New York, and the young Feodor Chaliapin came every day to the house either to help the family or to distract the composer. He even gave Rachmaninoff a short haircut, "like a convict," as his father used to call it.

"They say I am getting better . . . but I am losing my strength. . . . Don't the doctors notice this?" Rachmaninoff said. His sole concern in those long quiet days was Tatiana, his daughter.

"I am afraid I will not see her again," he said. And then he wanted to know the latest news from the Russian front. When he heard that the Russians had retaken several towns, he would say: "Thank God! May God give them strength."

And when a radio was installed in his room, he wanted to hear music broadcast from Moscow.

In the last week of March his health took a rapid change for the worse. He could not eat anything and the smell and the sight of the food were revolting to him. He suffered from the pain in his arms and sides, and it was difficult for him to breathe.

"I don't know which way to lie in my bed. I think the doctors do not know what is the matter with me. I cannot eat and I am losing my strength," he kept saying.

When Mrs. Rachmaninoff suggested helping him to turn on the other side, he said: "I don't know what to say. I am suffering so. You yourself decide for me."

"This was the first time," his nurse said later, "that he expressed surrender. He did not ask to be read to any more, talked less, and often groaned with pain."

Sometimes he would call to Mrs. Rachmaninoff and ask her who was playing music. The house was silent, but Rachmaninoff heard music. "A . . ah, then it is in my head," he would murmur.

Feodor Chaliapin remembered that he had once asked Rachmaninoff how he composed, where he got the sounds. "I hear it in my head," Rachmaninoff had told him. "And when I write it down then it stops."

On March 26th, Rachmaninoff lost consciousness. His temperature went up, his pulse became irregular, his cheeks were burning, and he occasionally groaned with pain.

A cable arrived signed by the Moscow composers wishing him a happy birthday. But it was not read to him. It had come too late.

On March 28th, four days before his seventieth birthday, Sergei Rachmaninoff was no more.

. XIX .

Reinstatement of Rachmaninoff's Music in Soviet Russia

A FTER TWENTY-FIVE YEARS of exile from his native land, and five weeks before he died, Rachmaninoff became an American citizen. If it took him so long to make this final decision, it was not because he could not accept the United States as his new home, but because he could not bring himself to cut the last link with his own country—Russia.

For more than three-quarters of his life he was a man separated from his native land, but in the history of music a place has been reserved for him for the last fifty years. Sergei Rachmaninoff was indisputably one of the greatest pianists of our time; and while he was not a teacher and left no pupils to carry on in a "Rachmaninoff" tradition, his way of playing the piano influenced scores of pianists, including Vladimir Horowitz and Emile Gilels, Soviet Russia's most remarkable virtuoso. It is in the basic approach to the treatment of the instrument that one recognizes Rachmaninoff's influence, which differed from the old Romantic school of the past generations of pianists. If these young musicians do not play as Rachmaninoff did, it is because they lack his type of personality, which was the dominating factor in his performances.

As an orchestra conductor Rachmaninoff will be remembered only in Russia, for outside of his native land he did not conduct often enough to leave much impression.

But as a composer "the Rachmaninoff chapter" belongs to the Russian branch of the history of music. With the ever-changing tastes and convictions of our time, which have been particularly influenced by the political situation, Rachmaninoff's music has not yet been definitively classified. However, he, who had been boycotted by the Soviet musicians only less than two decades ago, since the end of the last war has been reinstated into the family of Russian composers and is even hailed as an "example" to the younger generation as the epitome of all things truly Russian.

Rachmaninoff did not live long enough to see Dmitri Shostakovich and Sergei Prokofiev bow to the Soviet Government's criticism of their compositions or to hear about his own complete rehabilitation in his native country. Already during the last war, when Rachmaninoff had shown his sincere interest in the victory of the Russian people, the attitude of the Soviet Government toward the exiled composer became conciliatory. But after his death Rachmaninoff was acclaimed as a true Russian composer, and both the Soviet musicologists and those who wrote articles and commentaries about him took a new position toward him. The main theme in these articles was: Sergei Rachmaninoff made a fatal mistake in leaving Russia; and though he always remained a true son of his fatherland, he paid dearly for his mistake, for he became a victim of the American way of life. This assumption is based on Rachmaninoff's own letters to his friends in Russia and on the "Materials,"[1] which was sent by S. A. Satin to Moscow.

[1] Material for a biography of S. Rachmaninoff which Miss Satin had sent to Moscow. Society of the Cultural Link with Foreign Countries, Moscow.

Since the repatriation of an *émigré* is done by the Soviet authorities according to a sort of political dossier, with the reason for one's departure from Russia as a starting point, the articles written about Rachmaninoff had first "to clear him through." Professor K. A. Kouznetsov, in his article, "The Creative Life of S. V. Rachmaninoff,"[2] says that "The 'Materials' of S. A. Satin with reference to her conversations with the composer point to the fundamental reason for Rachmaninoff's departure from Russia. Rachmaninoff assumed that with the changing conditions in Soviet Russia there would be no place for his artistic activity. But, already during the last war," continues Professor Kouznetsov, "Rachmaninoff found with us a common language and common emotions, and he was happy in the conviction that there always was and will be a place for his art in our musical culture." Referring to Rachmaninoff's long silence as a composer after he had left Russia and to his "resurrection" with his last symphony, Kouznetsov says in the same article that "A sad picture is painted to us in the 'Materials' of S. A. Satin. We see Rachmaninoff somewhere at a railroad station guarded by his constant traveling companion, Nataly Alexandrovna (Mrs. Rachmaninoff). Both of them are trying to get rid of intrusive photographers. One of the photographers succeeded in taking a picture of Sergei Vasilievich covering his face with his hands. Next day in the local paper his picture was published with the caption 'The hands which are worth one million.' Where then," asks Kouznetsov, "did he find the strength and the source for his creative resurrection? In 'Materials' S. Satin speaks clearly about it. She describes the composer as a man who never lost interest in anything that was going on in his native land, faraway Soviet Russia. Rachmaninoff made the utmost effort never to

[2] *Sovietskaya Musyka*, Vol. IV. Moscow, 1945.

lose close contact with his own Russian culture. Whether in America or during his travels on the European continent, Rachmaninoff, an avid reader, collected the latest publications in our Russian literature. Rachmaninoff became more and more convinced that the Revolution meant the creation of a great new culture by the Russian people. And through this thought his own creative ability returned to him," concludes Kouznetsov.

Another Soviet writer, G. Kogan, in his commentaries on the recently published letters of Rachmaninoff to V. Vilshau, which are offered to the Russian public as the fundamental material on Rachmaninoff's life after he left Russia, said the following:

Material security and world fame did not give Rachmaninoff satisfaction. Worried over the future of his family, he was forced to concertize and "make recordings" without interruption and in such vast numbers that it went beyond his wishes and human possibilities and turned into a "compulsory concert service." In his old age, sick and tired, Rachmaninoff had to travel all the time from one city to another, from concert hall to train, and from train to concert hall, sustaining his ebbing forces by artificial means, without having a minute's time to write a letter, with hands so tired that he could not hold a pen. And for his beloved occupation —composing—there was practically no time and no strength left. During the last twenty-five years of living abroad he has written only a few compositions and those mostly are arrangements of other composers' works and themes.

What a great contrast to this [exclaims G. Kogan in the same article] present the conditions in which the Soviet composers and performers are living. The "Talents" in Soviet music know neither the difficulties of "receiving an engagement" during their youth, nor that exploitation in old age about which Rachmaninoff complained in his letters. At any age the Soviet composers have a wide opportunity to use their talents and are free from the yoke of working beyond one's strength. Rachmaninoff, according to his own words, "got used to America"; he even assures us that he loves that country. But his letters are full of bitter complaints about the "accursed life there," about "the sweating system of work," about "the continual hurry to do what is necessary and a lot that is not necessary and rather senseless," about the impossibility of quiet creative work. For a true description of America he suggests the book of the Soviet writers Ilf and Petrov.

No, Rachmaninoff did not succeed in Americanizing himself! He feels old-fashioned, "conservative," surrounded by a feverish business and cultural decadence. He cannot make peace with the "postwar world" (of the twenties and thirties), its art and customs. He is happy that his daughters are not "contemporary," and he is sarcastic about the modern composers for whom, he says, he is not yet mature enough and about the virtuoso temporarily in vogue whose marriage even to the daughter of a famous conductor did not gain him any musicality. Everywhere, in America and in Western Europe, Rachmaninoff was seeking that quiet—so dear to his heart, so necessary for his art—which he had lost with his departure from his native land, but nowhere in a world of degenerate capitalistic civilization could he find this quiet.

As I pointed out earlier, Marietta Shaginian (whose publication of Rachmaninoff's letters is considered by Professor Kouznetsov as the most valuable addition to the "Materials" for future biographers) took it upon herself to ascribe to Rachmaninoff a dissatisfaction with the political state of affairs in Russia prior to the Revolution. And, as for the musicologists, Daniel Zhitomirsky maneuvers Rachmaninoff the composer along a rather devious path back into the family of Russian composers.

"In the course of many years music critics have stubbornly discounted Rachmaninoff as a contemporary composer. . . . But his style is far from being as conservative as they describe it. . . . To be sure, Rachmaninoff did not belong to the category of revolutionary innovators, but he preserved to the end a live and sharp sense of contemporaneity. . . ."

And, discussing Rachmaninoff's Rhapsody on the theme of Paganini, Daniel Zhitomirsky points to the heritage link: Rachmaninoff-Prokofiev, in the fourteenth variation. It is well known that Sergei Prokofiev, who has returned to Russia, has been accepted into the family of Russian composers, even if at times not wholeheartedly.

An extensive and most thorough research has been made to collect all the unpublished works of Sergei Rachmaninoff, as well as letters and other documents concerning his person. Practically all the unpublished works are in the process of publication. I have heard of a plan for a Rachmaninoff museum in Moscow where the archives will be kept.

The history of Russian music is very short. It is only a little over one hundred years since Mikhail Glinka's *A Life for the Tsar* (the first truly Russian opera) was presented, and less than one hundred years since the nationalists, the so-called "Mighty Five," declared a holy war against the Western influence in Russian music and set out to create their own "national" music. "Soviet music," written according to the demands of the State, is still in its infancy. Strictly speaking, Rachmaninoff's music is closer to the Glinka-Dargomyzhski period than to the latter two. Not a member of any of these three groups, Rachmaninoff was one of the last Romanticists of an era which negated Romanticism.

Rachmaninoff's muse was capricious and he composed spasmodically. Gloomy by nature, he was "the bard of intimate moods," as Gregory Prokofiev, the Moscow critic, called him. His peaceful, *meditatio* music spoke always of one and the same theme: of the sad fate of man in this harsh world of ours. He was no innovator, and no fighter.

Once uprooted from his own country, he was faced with the European postwar "modern" music, which by-passed his contemporaries in style if not in years. Rachmaninoff appeared like a ghost from the past—perhaps a pleasant past, but a past, nevertheless.

Rachmaninoff, away from Russia, lost his native soil, his people, his sounding board. For years his muse was silent, and when he did compose again during the last years of his life, it was only a nostalgic echo of what he had said before. Rachmaninoff's tragedy was that "his" Russia was no more and he could not live without a Russia. Not long before he died he listened to recordings of Russian folk songs made in Soviet Russia. He controlled his emotions for some time, and then burst into bitter sobs.

Rachmaninoff's wish was to have his remains transported to Russia and laid at rest in the cemetery of Novo-Devichy Monastery.[3] The monastery was built in 1524 by Duke Vassily III, the father of Ivan the Terrible. Boris Godunov came here for protection, and it was here that he plotted for and usurped the kingdom. Peter the Great incarcerated his rebellious sister Sophia in this monastery. In 1812 the building was almost razed by Napoleon and only the bravery of the nuns saved it. In the cloister of this cemetery rest many eminent Russians, among them Alexander Scriabin and Anton Chekhov of whose remark, "Young man, I see a brilliant future written on your face," Sergei Rachmaninoff said: "I will remember this to my dying hour."

But, in Kensico Cemetery near the Kensico dam in New York State, there is a simple grave on the top of a hill. A green hedge encloses the plot and the two low benches on either

[3] Professor K. A. Kouznetsov's article "The Creative Life of S. V. Rachmaninoff," *Sovietskaya Musyka*, Vol. IV. Moscow, 1945.

side of the grave. A great artist with a proud heart is buried here. At the head of the grave stands a white cross on which is inscribed:

SERGEI RACHMANINOFF

April 2, 1873—March 28, 1943

LIST OF RACHMANINOFF'S COMPOSITIONS

OPERAS

WITHOUT OPUS—*Aleko:* Opera in one act. Libretto by V. I. Nemirovich-Danchenko after A. Pushkin's poem "Gypsies." Composed: April, 1892. Published: A. Gutheil, 1892. First performance: Moscow, April 27, 1893—Bolshoi Theater.

OPUS 24—*The Miser Knight:* Opera in three scenes. Text by Alexander Pushkin. Composed: February, 1904. Published: A. Gutheil, 1905. First performance: Moscow, January 11, 1906—Bolshoi Theater.

OPUS 25—*Francesca da Rimini:* Opera in two scenes with a Prologue and an Epilogue. Libretto by Modest Tchaikovsky. Composed: 1904. Published: A. Gutheil, 1904. First performance: Moscow, January 11, 1906—Bolshoi Theater.

VOCAL AND VOCAL-SYMPHONIC MUSIC

CHORUS AND ORCHESTRA

OPUS 20—*The Spring:* Cantata for baritone solo, mixed chorus, and orchestra. Text after N. A. Nekrassov's poem. Composed: January-March, 1902. Dedicated to Nikita S. Morozov. Published: A. Gutheil. First performance: Moscow, March 11, 1902.

OPUS 35—*The Bells:* Choral symphony for orchestra chorus, and solo soprano, tenor, and baritone. Text after Edgar Allan Poe's poem, translated by Constantin Balmont. Composed: January-April, 1913. Dedicated to "my friend Wilhelm Mengelberg and his orchestra in Amsterdam." Published: A. Gutheil, 1920. First performance: St. Petersburg, November 30, 1913.

OPUS 41—*Three Russian Folk Songs* for chorus and orchestra. Composed: 1928. Dedicated to Leopold Stokowski. Published by edition "Tair" in Paris.

CHORUS WITH PIANO

OPUS 15—*Six Songs* for female or boys' voices with piano accompaniment. Composed: 1895. Published: P. Yurgenson, 1896: 1. "Be praised!" (words by N. Nekrassov).
2. "The Night" (words by V. Ladishensky).
3. "The Spruce Tree" (words by M. Lermontov).
4. "Dreaming Waves" (words by K. P.).
5. "Captivity" (words by N. Zyganov).
6. "The Angel" (words by M. Lermontov).

CHOIR WITHOUT ACCOMPANIMENT

WITHOUT OPUS—*Pantelei the Consoler* for mixed choir a capella. Text by A. Tolstoy. Composed: June-July, 1900. Unpublished.

OPUS 31—*Liturgy of St. John Chrysostomus:* for mixed choir. Composed: in summer, 1910. Published: A. Gutheil. First performance: Moscow, November 25, 1910.

OPUS 37—*Vesper Mass* for boys' and men's voices, "In Memory of Stepan Smolensky." Composed: January-February, 1915. Published: Grandes Editions Russes. First performance: Moscow, March 10, 1915.

VOICE WITH PIANO

WITHOUT OPUS—*Songs:* Composed: 1887-1893. Unpublished. 1. "At the gate of the holy place" (words by M. Lermontov; composed in 1890).

2. "The song of a disappointed man" (words by D. Rathaus; composed in 1893).
3. "The faded flower" (composed in 1893).
4. "In the silence of the mysterious night" (words by A. Foet).
5. "A sad night" (words by I. Bounin).
6. "I will say nothing to you" (words by A. Foet).
7. "Boatmen's song" edited by Ivan Shishov; published by Musgiz, 1944.

OPUS 4—*Six Songs:* Composed: 1889-1893. Published: A. Gutheil.
1. "Oh, stay, my love, forsake me not!" (words by D. Merezhkovsky, English version by Edward Agate); for soprano or baritone. Composed: 1891.
2. "Morning" ["I love thee well!"] (words by M. L. Yanov, English version by Edward Agate). Composed: 1891. Dedicated to Y. S. Sakhnovsky.
3. "When silent night doth hold me" (words by A. Foet, English version by Edward Agate); for soprano or baritone. Composed: 1889. Dedicated to V. D. Scalon.
4. "Oh, never sing to me" (words by A. Pushkin, English version by Edward Agate); for soprano or tenor. Composed: in summer, 1893. Dedicated to N. A. Satin.
5. "The harvest of sorrow" (words by A. Tolstoy, English version by Rosa Newmarch); for soprano or tenor. Composed: in summer, 1893. Dedicated to E. N. Lyssikova.
6. "So many hours, so many fancies" (words by Count Golenistchev-Koutousov, English version by Edward Agate); for soprano or tenor. Composed: in summer, 1893. Dedicated to Countess O. A. Golenistchev-Koutousov.

OPUS 8—*Six songs:* Composed: October, 1893. Published: A. Gutheil, 1894. 1. "The Water Lily" ["From reeds on the river"] (words by H. Heine-A. Plechtcheyev, English version by Edward Agate); for mezzo-soprano. Dedicated to A. A. Yaroshevsky.

2. "Like blossom dew-freshen'd to gladness" (words by H. Heine-A. Plechtcheyev, English version by Edward Agate); for mezzo-soprano or baritone. Dedicated to M. A. Slonov.

3. "Brooding" ["The days in turn pass all too soon"] (words by V. Shevchenko-A. Plechtcheyev, English version by Edward Agate); for mezzo-soprano or baritone. Dedicated to L. G. Yakovlev.

4. "The soldier's wife" ["For a life of pain I have giv'n my love"] (words by V. Shevchenko-A. Plechtcheyev, English version by Edward Agate); for mezzo-soprano. Dedicated to M. V. Olferyeva.

5. "A dream" ["My native land I once enjoyed"] (words by H. Heine-A. Plechtcheyev, English version by Edward Agate); for soprano or tenor. Dedicated to N. D. Scalon.

6. "A prayer" ["Oh, Lord of grace! I stand before Thee self-confessed"] (words by Goethe-A. Plechtcheyev, English version by Edward Agate). Dedicated to M. A. Deisha-Sionitzkaya.

OPUS 14—*Twelve songs:* Composed: 1896. Published: A. Gutheil, 1896. 1. "I wait for thee!" (words by M. Davidova, English version by Edward Agate); for soprano. Dedicated to N. D. Scalon.

2. "The little island" (words by Shelley-C. Balmont, English version by Edward Agate); for soprano or tenor. Dedicated to N. A. Satin.

3. "How few the joys" (words by A. Foet, English version by Edward Agate); for contralto or basso. Dedicated to Z. A. Pribytkova.

4. "I came to her" (words by A. Kolzov, English version by Edward Agate); for mezzo-soprano or baritone. Dedicated to Y. S. Sakhnovsky.

5. "Midsummer nights" (words by D. Rathaus, English version by Edward Agate); for soprano or tenor. Dedicated to M. I. Gutheil.

6. "The world would see thee smile" (words by A. Tolstoy, English version by Edward Agate); for mezzo-soprano or baritone. Dedicated to A. N. Ivanovsky.

7. "Believe it not" (words by A. Tolstoy, English version by Edward Agate); for soprano or tenor. Dedicated to A. G. Klokatcheva.

8. "Oh, do not grieve" (words by A. Apouchtine, English version by Rosa Newmarch); for mezzo-soprano or baritone. Dedicated to N. A. Alexandrova.

9. "As fair as day in blaze of noon" (words by N. Minsky, English version by Edward Agate); for mezzo-soprano or baritone. Dedicated to E. A. Lavrovskaya.

10. "Love's flame" (words by N. Minsky, English version by Edward Agate); for contralto or basso. Dedicated to E. A. Lavrovskaya.

11. "Spring Waters" (words by F. Tyoutchev, English version by Rosa Newmarch); for soprano or tenor. Dedicated to A. D. Onazkaya.

12. "This Time" (words by S. Nadson, English version by Edward Agate); for contralto or basso.

OPUS 21—*Twelve songs:* Composed #1: March, 1900; the rest in April, 1900. Published: A. Gutheil, 1900. 1. "Fate" (after Beethoven's Fifth Symphony; words by A. Apouchtine, English version by Rosa Newmarch); for baritone or mezzo-soprano. Dedicated to F. I. Chaliapin.

2. "By the grave" ["In gloom of night I stand alone"] (words by S. Nadson, English version by Rosa Newmarch); for contralto.

3. "Twilight" ["Alone and lost in dreams"] (words by M. Guyot-I. Tchorshevsky; English version by Edward Agate); for soprano or tenor. Dedicated to N. I. Vrubel.

4. "The Answer" ["They wonder'd a while"] (words by V. Hugo-L. Mey; English version by Edward Agate); for soprano or tenor. Dedicated to E. Y. Kreuzer.

5. "The Lilacs" ["At the red of the dawn"] (words by E. Beketova; English version by Rosa Newmarch); for soprano.

6. "Loneliness" ["Oh, heart of mine"] (words by Alfred de Musset-A. Apouchtine; English version by Edward Agate); for soprano. Dedicated to Princess A. A. Lieven.

7. "How fair this spot" (words by G. Galina; English version by Rosa Newmarch); for soprano.

8. "On the death of a linnet" (words by V. Zhukovsky; English version by Edward Agate); for mezzo-soprano or baritone. Dedicated to O. A. Troubnikova.

9. "Melodie" ["On slumber-laden wings"] (words by S. Nadson); for soprano or tenor. Dedicated to N. Lanting.

10. "Before the image" (words by Count A. Golenistchev-Koutousov; English version by Edward Agate); for mezzo-soprano. Dedicated to M. A. Ivanova.

11. "No prophet I" (words by A. Krouglova; English version by Edward Agate); for soprano.

12. "Sorrow in springtime" (words by G. Galina; English version by Rosa Newmarch); for soprano. Dedicated to V. A. Satin.

WITHOUT OPUS—*The Night:* Words by D. Rathaus; Published: in "Collection of composition by the contemporary Russian composers" V. 2., pages 53-7. Publishing house: Yurgenson, 1904.

OPUS 26—*Fifteen Songs:* Composed: in summer, 1906. Dedicated to M. S. and A. M. Kersin. Published: A. Gutheil. 1. "The heart's secret" (words by A. Tolstoy; English version by Edward Agate); for mezzo-soprano. Composed: August 14.

2. "All once I gladly owned" (words by F. Tyoutchev; English version by Edward Agate); for mezzo-soprano. Composed: August 15.

3. "Come, let us rest" (words by A. Chekhov from "Uncle Vanya"; English version by Edward Agate); for contralto or basso. Composed: August 14.

4. "Two partings" (a dialogue; words by A. Kolzov; English version by Edward Agate); for baritone and soprano. Composed: August 22.

5. "Beloved, let us fly" (words by Count A. Golenistchev-Koutousov; English version by Edward Agate); for tenor. Composed: August 22.

6. "Christ is risen" (words by D. Merezhkovsky; English version by Rosa Newmarch); for mezzo-soprano. Composed: August 23.

7. "To the children" (words by A. Chomyakov; English version by Rosa Newmarch); for mezzo-soprano. Composed: September 9.

8. "The pity I implore!" (words by D. Merezhkovsky; English version by Edward Agate); for tenor. Composed: August 25. .

9. "Let me rest here alone" (words by Shevchenko-I. Bounin; English version by Edward Agate); for tenor. Composed: September 4.

10. "Before my window" (words by G. Galina; English version by Rosa Newmarch); for soprano. Composed: September 17.

11. "The Fountains" (words by F. Tyoutchev; English version by Edward Agate); for tenor. Composed: September 6.

12. "Night is mournful" (words by I. Bounin; English version by Rosa Newmarch); for tenor. Composed: September 3.

13. "When yesterday we met" (words by J. Polonsky; English version by Rosa Newmarch); for mezzo-soprano. Composed: September 3.

14. "The Ring" ["Here the tapers I hold"] (words by A. Kolzov; English version by Edward Agate); for mezzo-soprano. Composed: September 10.

15. "All things depart" (words by D. Rathaus; English version by Edward Agate); for basso. Composed: September 5.

Letter to C. S. Stanislavsky: to the Ten Years' Jubilee of the Moscow Art Theater; for voice and piano. Composed: autumn, 1908. Published: A Gutheil.

OPUS 34—*Fourteen Songs*: Published: A. Gutheil, 1913-15. 1. "The Muse" ["From childhood's early days"] (words by A. Pushkin; English version by Edward Agate); for soprano and tenor. Composed: June 6, 1912. Dedicated: to "Re."

2. "The Soul's Concealment" (words by A. Korinfsky; English version by Edward Agate); for contralto or basso. Composed: July 5, 1912. Dedicated: to F. I. Chaliapin.

3. "The Storm" ["I saw the maid on rocky strand"] (words by A. Pushkin; English version by Edward Agate); for tenor or soprano. Composed: July 7, 1912. Dedicated to L. V. Sobinov.

4. "Day to Night comparing went the Wind her way" (words by C. Balmont; English version by Edward Agate); for tenor or soprano. Composed: July 9, 1912. Dedicated to L. V. Sobinov.
5. "Arion" ["Full many souls the vessels held"] (words by A. Pushkin; English version by Edward Agate); for tenor or soprano. Composed: June 8, 1912. Dedicated to L. V. Sobinov.
6. "The raising of Lazarus" ["Oh, Lord of heaven!"] (words by A. Chomyakov; English version by Edward Agate); for basso or contralto. Composed: June 4, 1912. Dedicated to F. I. Chaliapin.
7. "So dread a fate I'll never believe" (words by A. Maykov; English version by Edward Agate); for mezzo-soprano. Composed: March 7, 1910; revised June 13, 1912. Dedicated to V. F. Komisarjev-skaya "in memory."
8. "Music" ["How it flows, how it grows!"] (words by Y. Polonsky; English version by Edward Agate); for mezzo-soprano. Composed: June 12, 1912. Dedicated to "P. Tch."
9. "The Poet" ["You know him well"] (words by F. Tyoutchev; English version by Edward Agate); for baritone or mezzo-soprano. Composed: June 12, 1912. Dedicated to F. I. Chaliapin.
10. "The hour I mind me" (words by F. Tyoutchev; English version by Edward Agate); for tenor or soprano. Dedicated to L. V. Sobinov.
11. "With holy banner firmly held . . ." (words by A. Foeth; English version by Edward Agate); for basso or contralto. Composed: June 11, 1912. Dedicated to F. I. Chaliapin.
12. "What wealth of rapture!" (words by A. Foeth; English version by Edward Agate); for tenor or soprano. Composed: June 19, 1912. Dedicated to L. V. Sobinov.
13. "Discord" ["What if fate should decree that apart we remain"] (words by Y. Polonsky; English version by Edward Agate); for soprano. Composed: June 17, 1912. Dedicated to F. Litvinne.
14. "Vocalise"; for soprano or tenor. Dedicated to A. V. Neshdanova. Without date.

OPUS 38—Six Songs: For soprano. Composed: 1916. Dedicated to N. P. Koshetz. Published: Grandes Editions Russes, 1916. 1. "In my garden at night" (words by A. Bloch from "Isaakian"; English version by Kurt Schindler). Composed: September 12, 1916.
2. "To her" ["Grasses dew-pearl'd so tearfully"] (words by A. Byelyi; English version by Edward Agate). Composed: September 12, 1916.
3. "Daisies" ["Behold, my friend, the daisies sweet and tender"] (words by I. Severyanin; English version by Kurt Schindler).
4. "The Pied Piper" (words by V. Bryousov; English version by Kurt Schindler). Composed: September 12, 1916.

5. "Dreams" ["Say, oh, whither art bound?"] (words by F. Sologoub; English version by Edward Agate).
6. "A-ou" ["Was it a dream?"] (words by C. Balmont; English version by Kurt Schindler).

COMPOSITIONS FOR SYMPHONIC ORCHESTRA

WITHOUT OPUS—*Scherzo:* Allegro. F major. Composed: February 5-21, 1887. Being published.

WITHOUT OPUS—*Prince Rostislav:* Symphonic poem for large orchestra. On a poem of Rostislav by A. Tolstoy. Being published.

WITHOUT OPUS—*Youthful Symphony:* Composed: September 28, 1891. Being published.

WITHOUT OPUS—*Intermezzo for orchestra:* First performance Moscow, Moscow Conservatory, October 31, 1892. Unpublished.

OPUS 7—*The Rock:* Fantasia for orchestra after M. Lermontov's poem. Composed: summer, 1893. First performance: Moscow, March 20, 1896. Published: Yurgenson.

OPUS 12—*Capriccio on Gypsy themes:* for large orchestra. Composed: summer, 1894. Dedicated to P. Ladyshensky. Published: A. Gutheil.

OPUS 13—*First Symphony D minor:* Composed: January-August, 1895. Dedicated to "A. L." First performance: St. Petersburg, March 15, 1897.

OPUS 27—*Second Symphony E minor:* Composed: October, 1906-April, 1907. Dedicated to S. I. Tancyev. First performance: St. Petersburg, January 26, 1908.

OPUS 29—*The Island of Death:* symphonic poem for large orchestra. Composed: spring, 1909. Dedicated to N. Struve. First performance: Moscow, April 18, 1909.

OPUS 44—*Third Symphony A minor:* Composed: 1935-36. First performance: Philadelphia, November 6, 1936. Published: Edition "Tair."

OPUS 45—*Symphonic Dances:* Composed: 1940-41. Dedicated to E. Ormandy. First performance: January 3, 1941.

COMPOSITIONS FOR STRING ORCHESTRA

WITHOUT OPUS—*Andante and Scherzo:* First performance: Moscow, Moscow Conservatory, February 24, 1891. Being published.

COMPOSITIONS FOR PIANO AND ORCHESTRA

OPUS 1—*First Piano Concerto F-sharp minor:* Composed: 1890-91. Dedicated to A. Siloti. Published: A. Gutheil. Revised: November, 1917. Published: Grandes Éditions Russes.

Opus 18—*Second Piano Concerto C minor:* Composed: April, 1901. Dedicated to Dr. N. Dahl. First performance: Moscow, October 27, 1901.

Opus 30—*Third Piano Concerto D minor:* Composed: summer, 1909. Dedicated to Josef Hofmann. First performance: New York City.

Opus 40—*Fourth Piano Concerto G minor:* Composed: 1917-27. Dedicated to N. Medtner. First performance: Berlin. Published: Edition "Tair," Paris.

Opus 43—*Rhapsody on a Theme of Paganini:* Composed: 1934. First performance: Baltimore. Published: Edition "Tair," Paris.

COMPOSITIONS FOR PIANO (TWO HANDS)

Without opus—*Romance. Prelude. Melodie. Gavotte.* Composed: 1897. Being published.

Opus 3—*Five pieces for piano:* Composed: autumn, 1892. Dedicated to A. Arensky. Published: A Gutheil. 1. Elegie (E-flat minor)
2. Prelude (C-sharp minor)
3. Melodie (E major)
4. Polichinelle (F-sharp minor)
5. Serenade (B-flat minor)

Opus 10—*Seven pieces for piano:* Composed: November, 1893-January, 1894. Dedicated to P. Pabst. 1. Nocturne (A minor)
2. Waltz (A minor)
3. Barcarolle (G minor)
4. Melodie (E minor)
5. Humoreske (G major)
6. Romance (F minor)
7. Mazurka (D-flat major)

Opus 16—*Six Moments Musicaux:* Composed: October-December, 1896. Dedicated to A. Zatavevich. Published: P. Yurgenson. 1. Andantino (B-flat minor)
2. Allegretto (E-flat minor)
3. Andante cantabile (B minor)
4. Presto (E minor)
5. Adagio sostenuto (D-flat major)
6. Maestoso (C major)

Opus 22—*Variations on a Theme of Chopin:* Composed: August, 1902-February, 1903. Dedicated to I. Leshetizky. Published: A. Gutheil.

Opus 23—*Ten Preludes:* Composed: 1903. Dedicated to A. Siloti. Published: A. Gutheil. 1. Largo (F-sharp minor)
2. Maestoso (B-flat major)
3. Tempo di minuetto (D minor)
4. Andante cantabile (D major)
5. A la Marcia (G minor)

6. Andante (E-flat major)
7. Allegro (C minor)
8. Allegro vivace (A-flat major)
9. Presto (E-flat minor)
10. Largo (G-flat major)

OPUS 28—*First Sonata (D minor)*: Composed: January, February-May 14, 1907. Published: A. Gutheil.

OPUS 32—*Thirteen Preludes*: 1. Allegretto vivace (C major), August 30, 1910.

  2. Allegretto (B-flat major), September 2, 1910
  3. Allegro vivace (E major), September 3, 1910
  4. Allegro con fuoco (E minor), August 28, 1910
  5. Moderato (G major), August 23, 1910
  6. Moderato (F minor), August 24, 1910
  7. Moderato (F major).
  8. Vivo (A minor), August 24, 1910
  9. Allegro moderato (A major), August 26, 1910
  10. Lento (B minor), September 6, 1910
  11. Allegretto (B minor), August 23, 1910
  12. Allegro (G-sharp minor), August 23, 1910
  13. Grave (D-flat major), September 10, 1910

WITHOUT OPUS—*Polka by V. R.*: (on the theme of V. Rachmaninoff, composer's father). Composed: March, 1911. Dedicated to L. Godowski. Published: Grandes Editions Russes.

OPUS 33—*Six Etudes-Tableaux*: Published: A. Gutheil. 1. Allegro non troppo (F minor), August 11, 1911

  2. Allegro (C major), August 16, 1911
  3. Non allegro, presto (E-flat minor), August 23, 1911
  4. Allegro con fuoco (E-flat major), August 17, 1911
  5. Moderato (C minor), August 15, 1911
  6. Grave (C-sharp minor), August 13, 1911

OPUS 36—*Second Piano Sonata (B-flat minor)*: Composed: January-September 13, 1913. Dedicated to M. Pressman. Published: A. Gutheil. Second edition; revised: Edition "Tair," Paris, summer, 1931.

OPUS 39—*Nine Etudes-Tableaux*: Published: Grandes Editions Russes. 1. Allegro agitato (C minor), October 8, 1916

  2. Lento assai (A minor)
  3. Allegro molto (F-sharp minor), September 14, 1916
  4. Allegro assai (B minor), September 14, 1916
  5. Appassionato (E-flat minor), February 17, 1917
  6. Allegro (A minor), September 8, 1911; revised: September 27, 1916
  7. Lento lugubre (C minor)
  8. Allegro moderato (D minor)

9. Tempo di Marcia (D major), February 2, 1917

OPUS 42—*Variations on a Theme of Corelli:* Composed: summer, 1932. Published: Edition "Tair," Paris.

WITHOUT OPUS—*Polka Italienne:* for piano duet

WITHOUT OPUS—*Oriental Sketch.* Published: Charles Foley, New York.

COMPOSITIONS FOR PIANO (FOUR HANDS)

WITHOUT OPUS—*Polka Italienne:* Dedicated to S. Siloti. Published: P. Yurgenson.

OPUS 11—*Six piano duets:* Composed: 1894. Published: A. Gutheil.
1. Barcarolle (G minor)
2. Scherzo (D major)
3. Russian Song (B minor)
4. Waltz (A major)
5. Romance (C minor)
6. "Slava" (C major)

COMPOSITIONS FOR TWO PIANOS (FOUR HANDS)

WITHOUT OPUS—*Rhapsody on Russian themes:* Composed: January 12-14, 1891. First performance: Moscow, Moscow Conservatory. Being published.

OPUS 5—FANTASIA (*First suite*): Composed Summer, 1893. Dedicated to P. Tchaikovsky. 1. Barcarolle
2. "Oh night, oh love"
3. Tears
4. Easter

OPUS 17—*Second Suite:* Composed: December, 1900-April, 1901. Dedicated to A. Goldenweiser. Published: A. Gutheil. 1. Introduction
2. Waltz
3. Romance
4. Tarantella

COMPOSITIONS FOR VIOLIN AND PIANO

OPUS 6—*Two pieces for violin and piano:* Composed: 1893. Dedicated to J. Conus. Published: A. Gutheil. 1. Romance (D minor)
2. Dance Hongroise

COMPOSITIONS FOR CELLO AND PIANO

OPUS 2—*Two pieces for cello and piano:* Composed: 1892. Dedicated to A. Brandoukov. Published: A. Gutheil. 1. Prelude (F major)
2. Dance Orientale

OPUS 19—*Sonata (C minor)*: Composed: December 12, 1901. Dedicated to A. Brandoukov. Published: A. Gutheil.

WITHOUT OPUS—*Trio elegiaque* for piano, violin, and cello: Published: Musgiz, 1947.

OPUS 9—*Trio elegiaque* for piano, violin, and cello (D minor): "In Memory of Peter Tchaikovsky." Composed: October 25-December 15, 1893.

TRANSCRIPTIONS FOR PIANO

J. S. BACH: *"Prelude, Gavotte, and Gigue"* from Violin Partita in E major.
  "Prelude" from Cello Sonata in E major. Published by edition "Tair" in Paris.

G. BIZET: *"Menuetto"* from the "Arlésienne Suite."

F. KREISLER: *"Liebesfreude"*
  "Liebesleid"

F. MENDELSSOHN: *"Scherzo"* from "Midsummer Night's Dream." Published by edition "Tair" in Paris.

M. MOUSSORGSKY: *"Gopak"*

N. RIMSKY-KORSAKOV: *"Bumble-Bee."* Published: Carl Fischer, Inc. New York.

P. TCHAIKOVSKY: *"Lullaby"*

F. SCHUBERT: *"The Brook."* Published by edition "Tair" in Paris.

S. RACHMANINOFF: *"Lilacs"* (Song, Opus 21, No. 5)
  "Daisies" (Song, Opus 38, No. 3)

BIBLIOGRAPHY

[In this bibliography the transliteration of Russian names is not always consistent with the text of the biography, or even with itself. For the convenience of other researchers, the names here are spelled as they are given in the library files and English language publications consulted.]

I. GENERAL WORKS

ASAFIEV, B. V.: Russian Music from the Beginning of XIX Century; Academia, 1930.

BELAYEV, VICTOR: "Sergei Rachmaninoff," *Musical Quarterly*; July, 1927, No. 3.

BOELZA, IGOR: "Sergei Rachmaninoff," *Soviet Literature*; Musgiz, 1946, No. 1.

BROWER, H.: " 'Beware of the indifferent piano teacher,' warns Rachmaninoff," *Musician*, v. 30; February, 1925.

CHVOSCHINSKAYA, ELENA: "Memoirs," *Russkaya Starina*; 1897.

GLEBOV, IGOR: "Sergei Taneyev," *VOKS*; 1945, No. 7.

HENDERSON, A. M.: "Personal Memories of Rachmaninoff," *Musical Opinion*; May, 1943, No. 788.

HULL, A. EAGLEFIELD: "A Great Russian Tone-Poet, Scriabin," Kegan Paul, Trench, Trubner & Co., Ltd.; London, 1916.

HULL, ROBIN: "Rachmaninoff's Third Symphony," *Monthly Mus. Record*; November, 1937, No. 791.

KOLODIN, IRVING: "Sergei Rachmaninoff," *The International Cyclopedia of Music and Musicians*, edited by O. Thompson; New York, 1944.

KOUZNETSOV, CONSTANTIN: "Sergei Rachmaninoff's Musical Life," *VOKS Bulletin*; 1945, No. 6.

LAKOND, VLADIMIR: *The Diaries of Tchaikovsky*, W. W. Norton & Co.; New York, 1945.

LYLE, WATSON: *Rachmaninoff, a biography*; London, 1939.

MARTENS, F. H.: "Rachmaninoff," *Little Biographies*, v. 2 "Pamphlet"; New York, 1922.

MONTAGU-NATHAN, M.: *Contemporary Russian Composers*; London, 1917.

NESTYEV, ISRAEL: *Sergei Prokofiev*, Alfred A. Knopf; New York, 1946.

PRESSMAN, MIKHAIL: *Twenty-five Years Since Scriabin's Death*; Gosizd, 1940.

PROKOFIEV, GREGORY: "The Bard of Intimate Moods" (Sergei Rachmaninoff), *Russkaya Musykalnaya Gazeta*; 1909, Nos. 48, 49, 50, 51, 52; 1910, Nos. 2, 6, 7, 26, 27, 28, 29, 30, 31, 37, 38, 40.

RACHMANINOFF, SERGEI: "Some Critical Moments in My Career," *Musical Times*; June, 1930.

"My Prelude in C-sharp Minor," *Delineator*, v. 75; February, 1910.

"National and Radical Impressions in the Music of Today and Yesterday," *Etude*, v. 37; October, 1919.

"Sergei I. Taneev," (Obituary), *Russkie Vedomosty*; June 16, 1915.

"Letters to Re" (Marietta Shaginian), *Novy Mir*, 1943; No. 4, Moscow.

"Letters to M. A. Slonov and A. V. Zataevich," *Sovietskaya Musyka*; 1945, No. 4.

"Letters to N. S. Morozov," *Rachmaninoff*, collection of articles and material; Musgiz; Moscow, 1947.

"Letters to V. R. Vilshau," *Sovietskaya Musyka*; 1948.

"Rachmaninoff about Himself," *Ogonek*; 1943, Nos. 12, 13.

S. V. Rachmaninoff and Russian Opera, collection of articles; VTO, 1947.

RIESEMANN, OSKAR VON: *Rachmaninoff's Recollections Told to Oskar von Riesemann*, The Macmillan Company; New York, 1934.

RIMSKY-KORSAKOV, NICOLAS: *My Musical Life*, Alfred A. Knopf; New York, 1923.

SABANEEFF, LEONID: *Modern Russian Composers*, International Publishers; New York, 1927.

S. I. Taneyev, Tair; Paris, 1930.

The History of Russian Music; Russian Art.

My Recollections of Scriabin; Gosizd, 1925.

SATIN, SOPHIA A.: *In Memory of Rachmaninoff*, private publication, New York, 1946.

SHAGINIAN, MARIETTA: "S. V. Rachmaninoff" (Musical-psychological study), *Trudy i Dni*, vol. 4-5; July-October, 1912.

"Supplement to Letters," *Novy Mir*, 1943; No. 4, Moscow.

SMITH, MOSES: *Koussevitzky*, Allen, Town & Heath, Inc.; New York, 1947.

SOLOVZOV, ALEXANDER: *S. V. Rachmaninoff*; Musgiz, 1947

SWAN, ALFRED: "The Present State of Russian Music," *Musical Quarterly*; January, 1940, No. 1.

SWAN, ALFRED AND KATHERINE: "Rachmaninoff" (Personal reminiscences), *Musical Quarterly*; April, 1944, No. 2.

TELYAKOVSKY, VLADIMIR A.: *Imperial Theatres and 1905*, Academia; Leningrad, 1926.

TROUBNIKOVA, ANNA: "Sergei Rachmaninoff" (Recollections of composer's cousin), *Ogonek*; 1946, No. 4.

WOLFING: *Modernism and Music*, Musaget; Moscow, 1912.

ROSENFELD, PAUL: *Musical Portraits*, Harcourt, Brace; New York, 1920.

II. ARTICLES ON SPECIAL ASPECTS OF RACHMANINOFF'S
CAREER AND COMPOSITIONS

A–Operas

"ALEKO"

N. KASHKIN: "Aleko," *Moskovskie Vedomosty*; April 29, 1893, No. 116.
N. KASHKIN: "Aleko," *Russkie Vedomosty*; May 5, 1893, No. 121.
S. KROUGLIKOV: "Aleko," *Dnevnik Artista*; 1893, No. 6; pp. 22-6.
M. IVANOV: "Pushkin i musika" ["Pushkin and music"]; St. Petersburg, 1899; pp. 109-11.
"Obozrenie deyatelnosti Imperatorskich scen" [Survey of Imperial Theaters]; Season 1892-3; Moscow Opera.
First performance of "Aleko" at Bolshoi Theater: *Eshegodnik Imperatorskich Teatrov*; 1892-3; pp. 329-30.
"Po povodu ispolneniya operi v Mosc. Novom Teatre" [" 'Aleko' at Moscow New Theater"]; *Eshegodnik Imperatorskich Teatrov*; 1903-4; pp. 153-4.
Y. SAKHNOVSKY: " 'Aleko' v Novom Teatre" [" 'Aleko' at the New Theater"]; *Curier*; Sept. 23, 1903, No. 204.
N. KASHKIN: "Novi Teatr" ["New Theater"]; *Moscovskie Vedomosty*; Sept. 23, 1903, No. 260.
K. D. "Novinki opernavo repertuara" ["Novelties in the opera repertory"]; *Russkoe Slovo*; Sept. 24, 1903, No. 261.
Y. ENGEL: "Tri novinki Novavo Teatra" ["Three novelties of the new theater"]; *Russkie Vedomosty*; Sept. 25, 1903, No. 263.
S. KROUGLIKOV: "Tri operi" ["Three operas"]; *Novosty Dnya.*; Sept. 27, 1903, No. 7293.
N. SHEBUYEV: "Moscovskie Arabesky" ["Moscow Arabesques"]; *Teatr i Iskusstvo*; 1903, No. 40; p. 733.
N. SAVVIN: "Musika v Provinzii" ["Music in province"]; *Russkaya Musikalnaya Gazeta*; 1904, Nos. 17-8; pp. 475-6.
N. KOUROV: " 'Aleko' v Narodnom Dome" [" 'Aleko' at Narodni Dom"]; *Rance Utro.*; Sept. 22, 1912, No. 218.
N. KOUROV: "Aleko," *Teatr*; 1912, No. 1124.
A. KOPTYAEV: "V obschestve zygan" ["With the Gypsies"]; *Birshevie Vedomosty*; Nov. 30, 1914, No. 14527.
S. ROSOVSKY: "Marinsky Teatr 'Aleko' " [" 'Aleko' at Marinsky Theater"]; *Den*; Nov. 30, 1914, No. 326.
CHERNOGORSKY: "Marinsky Teatr" ["Marinsky Theater"]; *Teatr i Iskusstvo.*; 1914, No. 49; p. 933.
BERTRAM: "Marinsky Teatr" ["Marinsky Theater"]; *Russkaya Musikalnaya Gazeta*; 1914, No. 49.

N. STRELNIKOV: " 'Aleko' i Chaliapin" [" 'Aleko' and Chaliapin"]; *Ghisn Isskustva*; 1921, Nos. 724-6.

G. TYMOFEYEV: "Marinsky Teatr" ["Marinsky Theater"]; *Rech*, St. Petersburg; Nov. 30, 1914, No. 324.

N. BERNSTEIN: "V chest S. V. Rachmaninova" ["In S. V. Rachmaninoff's honor"]; *Musika i Teatr.*; 1923, No. 19.

DEM.: "Rachmaninovsky vecher" ["Rachmaninoff's evening"]; *Eshenedelnik Petrogradskich Gosud. Academ. teatrov*; 1923, No. 36; p. 13.

N. YANTAREV: " 'Aleko' i 'Yolanta' " [" 'Aleko' and 'Yolanta' "]; *Musika i Teatr*; 1924, No. 9; pp. 3-4.

Es: " 'Aleko' i 'Yolanta' " [" 'Aleko' and 'Yolanta' "]; *Ghisn Isskustva*; 1924, No. 11; pp. 3-4.

S. BOUGOSLAVSKY: "Pushkinsky spectacle Musikalnoy studii im. V. I. Nemirovich-Danchenko" ["Performance of Pushkin's work at the Musical Studio of Nemirovich Danchenko"]; *Musika i Revoluziya*; 1926, No. 11; p. 32.

K. MARIAN: " 'Aleko' v Mosc. Gos. Conservatorii" [" 'Aleko' at the Moscow Conservatory"]; *Pravda*; 1929, No. 3; p. 35.

B. VOLGIN: "Aleko," *Trud*; May 18, 1940, No. 113.

E. ISTOMINA: " 'Aleko' v concertnom ispolnenii" [" 'Aleko' in concert version"]; *Vechernyaya Moscva*; June 4, 1945, No. 129.

"THE MISER KNIGHT" AND "FRANCESCA DA RIMINI"

N. KASHKIN: "Novie operi na scene Bolshovo teatra" ["New operas at Bolshoi Theater"]; *Moscovskie Vedomosty*; Jan. 10, 1906, No. 7.

N. KASHKIN: "Ispolnenie oper S. V. Rachmaninova na scene Bolshovo teatra" ["Performance of S. V. Rachmaninoff's operas at Bolshoi Theater"]; *Moscovskie Vedomosty*; Jan. 15, 1906, No. 12.

S. KROUGLIKOV: "Rachmaninovsky spectacle" ["Rachmaninoff's evening"]; *Russkoe Slovo*; Jan. 11, 1906, No. 10.

S. KROUGLIKOV: " 'Skoupoy Rizar' i 'Francesca da Rimini' " [" 'The Miser Knight' and 'Francesca da Rimini' "]; *Russkoe Slovo*; Jan. 15, 1906, No. 14.

Y. ENGEL: "Dve novinki Bolshovo Teatra" ["Two novelties at Bolshoi Theater"]; *Russkie Vedomosty*; Jan. 14, 1906, No. 13.

E. ROSENOV: "Novie operi Rachmaninova" ["Rachmaninoff's new operas"]; *Novosty Dnya*; Jan. 16, 1906, No. 8098.

WOLFING: " 'Skoupoy Rizar' i 'Francesca da Rimini' " [" 'The Miser Knight' and 'Francesca da Rimini' "]; *Zolotoe Runo*; 1906, No. 1.

A. LIVIN: "Novie opery Rachmaninova na scene Mosc. Bolshovo Teatra" ["Rachmaninoff's new operas at Bolshoi Theater"]; *Russkaya Musikalnaya Gazeta*; 1906, Nos. 4-5; pp. 123-6.

G. Prokofiev: " 'Skoupoy Rizar' i 'Francesca da Rimini' " [" 'The Miser Knight' and 'Francesca da Rimini' "]; *Russkaya Musikalnaya Gazeta*; 1907, No. 4; pp. 123-30.

E. Gunst: " 'Francesca da Rimini' i 'Skoupoy Rizar' " [" 'Francesca da Rimini' and 'The Miser Knight' "]; *Maska*; 1912, No. 1.

B. Karagichev: "Skoupoy Rizar" ["The Miser Knight"]; *Musika*; 1912, No. 96; pp. 796-800.

Y. Sakhnovsky: "Vozobnovlenie 'Francesci' i 'Skoupovo Rizarya' " ["Revival of 'The Miser Knight' "]; *Russkoe Slovo*; Nov. 28, 1912, No. 223.

N. Kourov: " 'Francesca da Rimini' i 'Skoupoy Rizar' " [" 'Francesca da Rimini' and 'The Miser Knight' "]; *Ranee Utro.*; Oct. 2, 1912, No. 225

Y. Engel: " 'Skoupoy Rizar' i 'Francesca da Rimini' " [" 'The Miser Knight' and 'Francesca da Rimini' "]; *Russkie Vedomosty*; Oct. 2, 1912, No. 226.

Y. Sakhnovsky: " 'Francesca da Rimini' i 'Skoupoy Rizar' " [" 'Francesca da Rimini' and 'The Miser Knight' "]; *Russkoe Slovo*; Oct. 3, 1912, No. 227.

M. Yuryev: "Zametki ob opere" ["Notes about opera"]; *Rampa i Shisn*; 1912, No. 41; pp. 12-3.

G. Tymofeyev: "Narodny Dom. G. A. Baklanov 'Skoupoy Rizar' " ["Narodny Dom. G. A. Baklanov in 'The Miser Knight' "]; *Rech*; Oct. 4, 1913, No. 271.

P.: "Musikalnie nabroski" ["Musical sketches"]; *Novoe Vremya*; Oct. 15, 1912, No. 13145.

N. Kourov: "V Bolshom Teatre" ["At the Bolshoi Theater"]; *Teatr*; 1912, No. 1130; pp. 4-5; No. 1132; pp. 4-5.

G. Nossov: "Skoupoy Rizar" ["The Miser Knight"]; *Shisn Iskusstva*; 1921, No. 818.

M. Pekelis: "Francesca da Rimini," *Sovetskoe Iskusstvo*; Dec. 29, 1940, No. 65.

E. Kann: "Francesca da Rimini," *Teatralnaya Nedelya*; 1940, No. 163; p. 18.

M. Kiselev: "Francesca da Rimini," *Sovetskaya Musika*; 1941, No. 2; pp. 74-6.

M. Sokolsky: "Repertuar i Masterstvo" ["Repertory and Mastery"]; *Sovietskoe Iskusstvo*; Dec. 5, 1944, No. 5.

I. Martynov: "Francesca da Rimini," *Vechernyaya Moscva*; Dec. 6, 1944.

B–Symphonic and Vocal-Symphonic Music

N. Kashkin: "VIII Symphonicheskoe Sobranie" ["VIII Symphonic Concert"]; *Russkie Vedomosty*; Feb. 21, 1893, No. 50; Ob ispolnenii v concerte Feb. 19, 1893 zyganskich tanzev iz operi "Aleko" [About concert performance of Gypsy dances from opera "Aleko"].

M.: "IX Symphonicheskoe Sobranie" ["IX Symphonic Concert"]; "Symph. Fantasia Utcs" ["Symph. Fantasy Rock"]; *Novosty Dnya;* March 22, 1894, No. 3867.

KORESCHENKO: "IX Symphonicheskoe Sobranie" ["IX Symphonic Concert"]; "Symph. Fantasia Utcs" ["Symph. Fantasy Rock"]; *Moscovskie Vedomosty;* March 22, 1894, No. 80.

C. CUI: "III *Russki Symphonicheski Concert"* ["III Symphonic Concert"]; "Pervaya Symphonia" ["First Symphony"]; *Novosty;* March 17, 1897, No. 75.

N. FINDEISEN: "III i IV Russkie Symphonicheskie Concerti" ["III and IV Symphonic Concerts"]; "Pervaya Symphonia" ["First Symphony"]; *Russkaya Musikalnaya Gazeta;* 1897, No. 4.

N. KASHKIN: "Blagotvoritelni Concert Siloti, Rachmaninova i Chaliapina" ["Benefit performance of Siloti, Rachmaninoff and Chaliapin"]; "Vtoroi f-p concert" ["Second piano concerto"]; *Moscovskie Vedomosty;* Dec. 4, 1900, No. 335.

SAMAROV: "Concert Siloti, Rachmaninova i Chaliapina," *Novosty Dnya;* Dec. 4, 1900, No. 6301.

I. LIPAYEV: "Iz Moscvi" ["From Moscow"]; "Vtoroi f-p concert v ispolnenii avtora" ["Second piano concerto performed by the composer"]; *Russkaya Musikalnaya Gazeta;* 1901, No. 45; p. 133.

N. KASHKIN: "Musika v Peterburge" ["Music in St. Petersburg"]; *Moscovskie Vedomosty;* Feb. 12, 1903, No. 43.

Y. ENGEL: "V Philarmonicheski concert" ["V Philharmonic Concert"]; "Vtoraya Symphonia i Vtoroi f-p Concert" ["Second Symphony and Second Piano Concerto"]; *Russkie Vedomosty;* Feb. 6, 1908, No. 30.

Y. ENGEL: "VI Philharmonic Concert" ["VI Philharmonic Concert"]; "Vtoraya Symphonia i 'Ostrov Mertvich' " ["Second Symphony and The Island of Death' "]; *Russkie Vedomosty;* April 21, 1909, No. 90.

NOT SIGNED: "Zagranichnaya pechat o Russkoi musike" ["Foreign Press about Russian Music"]; *Russkaya Musikalnaya Gazeta;* 1909, No. 9; pp. 253-4.

G. PROKOFIEV: "Symphonicheskoe sobranie Philarmonicheskavo Obschestva" ["Philharmonic Concert"]; "Treti f-p concert" ["Third piano concerto"]; *Russkie Vedomosty;* April 7, 1910, No. 79.

G. PROKOFIEV: "Moscovskie concerti" ["Moscow concerts"]; "Vtoraya symphonia i treti f-p concert" ["Second symphony and third piano concerto"]; *Russkaya Musikalnaya Gazeta;* 1910, Nos. 16-7; pp. 445-6.

N. KASHKIN: "Liturgia S. V. Rachmaninova" ["S. V. Rachmaninoff's Liturgy"]; *Russkoe Slovo;* Nov. 26, 1910, No. 276.

BIBLIOGRAPHY

Y. ENGEL: "Taneyev, Rachmaninov, Scriabin," *Russkie Vedomosty;* Nov. 30, 1910, No. 276.

"Ostrov mertvich" ["The Island of Death"]; *Russkaya Musikalnaya Gazeta;* 1911, Nos. 8-9; pp. 239-41.

"St. Peterburgskie concerti" ["St. Petersburg Concerts"]; *Russkaya Musikalnaya Gazeta;* 1911, No. 14; pp. 366-8.

B. TYOUNEEV: "Kolokola" ["The Bells"]; *Russkaya Musikalnaya Gazeta;* 1913, No. 49; pp. 1140-51.

V. KARATYGIN: "I obschedostupni concert Siloti" ["Siloti's first popular concert"]; "Vtoraya symphonia" ["Second Symphony"]; *Rech;* 1913, No. 274.

G. PROKOFIEV: "V symphonicheski concert Koussevitzkavo" ["Koussevitzky's fifth concert"]; "3 f-p concert v ispolnenii avtora" ["Third piano concerto performed by the composer"]; *Russkie Vedomosty;* Dec. 20, 1913, No. 293.

G. PROKOFIEV: "VI Symphonicheskoe sobranie philarmonicheskavo obschestva" ["VI Philharmonic concert"]; "Kolokola" ["The Bells"]; *Russkie Vedomosty;* Feb. 9, 1914, No. 33.

Y. SAKHNOVSKY: "Kolokola" ["The Bells"]; *Russkoe Slovo;* Feb. 9, 1914, No. 33.

N. KOUROV: "Kolokola" ["The Bells"]; *Rance Utro;* Feb. 9, 1914, No. 33.

FLORESTAN [V. DERGANOVSKY]: "Kolokola" ["The Bells"]; *Utro Rossii;* March 11, 1914, No. 34.

Y. SAKHNOVSKY: "Vsenoshnoe bdenie" ["Vesper Mass"]; *Russkoe Slovo;* March 11, 1915, No. 57.

N. KOUROV: "Vsenoshnoe bdenie" ["Vesper Mass"]; *Russkoe Slovo;* March 11, 1915, No. 57.

G. PROKOFIEV: "Vsenoshnoe bdenie" ["Vesper Mass"]; *Russkie Vedomosty;* March 14, 1915, No. 60.

V. KARATYGIN: "IV concert Siloti" ["Siloti's fourth concert"]; "Vtoroi f-p concert" ["Second piano concerto"]; *Rech;* Nov. 23, 1915, No. 323.

Y. SAKHNOVSKY: "Rachmaninovsky concert" ["Rachmaninoff's concert"]; " 'Vesna,' 'Kolokola,' 3 f-p concert" [" 'The Spring,' 'The Bells,' Third piano concerto"]; *Russkoe Slovo;* Dec. 1, 1915, No. 275.

G. PROKOFIEV: "III symphonichesky concert Koussevitzkavo" ["Koussevitzky's third symphonic concert"]; *Russkie Vedomosty;* Dec. 3, 1915, No. 277.

E. BRAUDO: "Musika v Petrograde" ["Music in Petrograd"]; "Kolokola" ["The Bells"]; *Apollon;* 1916, No. 1; p. 43.

Y. SAKHNOVSKY: "V concert Koussevitzkavo" ["Koussevitzky's fifth concert"]; "3 f-p v ispolnenii avtora" ["Third piano concerto performed by the composer"]; *Russkoe Slovo;* 1916.

V. KARATYGIN: "VIII concert Siloti" ["Siloti's eighth concert"]; *Rech;* 1916, No. 31.

E. Braudo: "Concerti Siloti" ["Siloti's concerts"]; "3 f-p concert" ["Third concerto"]; *Apollon;* 1916, No. 2; pp. 46-7.

I. Glebov: "Concert Siloti" ["Siloti's concert"]; "3 f-p concert" ["Third piano concerto"]; *Musikalni Sovremenik;* Oct. 31, 1916, Nos. 5-6.

"Concert Siloti" ["Siloti's Concert"]; "2 f-p concert" ["Second piano concerto"]; *Musikalni Sovremenik;* Nov. 13, 1916, Nos. 5-6.

"Concerti Siloti" ["Siloti's concerts"]; "Ostrov Mertvich" ["The Island of Death"]; *Musikalni Sovremenik;* Dec. 9, 1916, Nos. 9-10.

A. Alshvang: " 'Kolokola' Rachmaninova" ["Rachmaninoff's 'Bells' "]; *Izd. Mosc. Gos. Philarmonii;* 1940.

I. Belza: "3 Symphonia Rachmaninova" ["Rachmaninoff's third symphony"]; *Izvestia;* June 12, 1943.

N. Golovanov: "3 Symphonia Rachmaninova" ["Rachmaninoff's third symphony"]; *Vechernyaya Moscva;* June 14, 1943.

I. Glebov: "3 Symphonia Rachmaninova" ["Rachmaninoff's third symphony"]; *Literatura i Iskusstvo;* June 19, 1943.

G. Khubov: "3 Symphonia Rachmaninova" ["Rachmaninoff's third symphony"]; *Pravda;* July 26, 1943.

A. Goldenweiser: "3 Symphonia Rachmaninova" ["Rachmaninoff's third symphony"]; *Ogonek;* 1943, No. 33; p. 14.

I. Martynov: "Na premiere 'Symphonicheskich tanzev' " ["First performance of 'Symphonic dances' "]; *Vechernyaya Moscva;* Nov. 27, 1943.

S. Korev: "Symphonicheskie tanzi" ["Symphonic dances"]; *Mosc. Bolshevik;* Nov. 30, 1943.

I. Balza: "Dve symphonii" ["Two symphonies"]; *Sovetskoe Iskusstvo;* Nov. 21, 1944, No. 3.

Y. Shaporin: "Concerti Rachmaninova" ["Rachmaninoff's concerts"]; *Literatura i Iskusstvo;* Oct. 7, 1944, No. 41.

G. Khubov: "Concert iz proizvedeni Rachmaninova" ["Concert devoted to works of Rachmaninoff"]; *Pravda;* Oct. 13, 1945.

V. Gorodnitzky: "Pervy concert" ["First concert"]; *Sovietskoe Iskusstvo;* Oct. 19, 1945, No. 42.

Sloushatel ["A listener"]: "Musikalni Dnevnik" ["Musical diary"]; *Sovietskoe Iskusstvo;* Oct. 26, 1945, No. 43.

C–Chamber and Instrumental Music

I. Lipaev: "Musikalnaya Shisn" ["Musical Life"]; *Russkaya Musikalnaya Gazeta;* 1897, No. 12; p. 1805.

N. Kashkin: "Novaya Sonata" ["New sonata"]; "Sonata dlya f-p i violonchelli" ["Sonata for piano and cello"]; *Moscovskie Vedomosty;* Nov. 30, 1902, No. 269.

R. Genika: "Correspondenzia iz Kharkova" ["Letter from Kharkov"]; Trio op. 9; *Russkaya Musikalnaya Gazeta;* 1906, Nos. 51-2.

NOT SIGNED: "Opera i concerti" ["Opera and concerts"]; Trio op. 9; *Russkaya Musikalnaya Gazeta*; 1908, No. 5.

G. PROKOFIEV: "Moscovskie concerti" ["Moscow Concerts"]; "f-p sonata op. 28 v ispolnenii Igumnova" ["Piano sonata op. 28 performed by Igumnov"]; *Russkaya Musikalnaya Gazeta*; 1908, No. 44; pp. 983-5.

G. CONUS: "Clavier—Abend" S. V. Rachmaninova; *Utro Rossii*; Dec. 15, 1911, No. 288.

Y. SAKHNOVSKY: "Clavier—Abend" S. V. Rachmaninova; *Russkoe Slovo*; Dec. 15, 1911, No. 288.

Y. ENGEL: "Rachmaninovsky concert" ["Rachmaninoff's concert"]; *Russkie Vedomosty*; Dec. 15, 1911, No. 288.

G. PROKOFIEV: "Concert Rachmaninova" ["Rachmaninoff's concert"]; *Russkaya Musikalnaya Gazeta*; 1919, No. 1; pp. 33-4.

R. GENIKA: "Correspondenzia iz Kharkova" ["Letter from Kharkov"]; [Sonata "Faust"]; *Russkaya Musikalnaya Gazeta*; 1912, No. 2; pp. 69-70.

V. KARATYGIN: "Concerti" ["Concerts"]; "2 f-p sonata" ["Second piano sonata"]; *Apollon*; 1913, No. 10; p. 77.

Y. ENGEL: "Concert Rachmaninova" ["Rachmaninoff's concert"]; "2 sonata, 'Etudi-kartini' Op. 39" ["Second sonata, 'Etudes-Tableaux,' Op. 39"]; *Russkie Vedomosty*; Dec. 7, 1915, No. 282.

D. GITOMIRSKI: "Fortepianoe tvorchestvo Rachmaninova" ["Rachmaninoff as composer for piano"]; *Sovietskaya Musika*; 1945, No. 4; pp. 80-103.

D–Vocal Music

C. CUI: "Russki Romance" ["Russian Song"]; St. Petersburg; 1896; pp. 197-8.

B. TYOUNEEV: "Romanci S. Rachmaninova" ["Rachmaninoff's songs"]; *Russkaya Musikalnaya Gazeta*: 1914, Nos. 42-3; pp. 761-7.

Y. SAKHNOVSKY: "Vecher romansov S. Rachmaninova" ["An evening of Rachmaninoff's songs"]; *Russkoe Slovo*; Oct. 25, 1916, No. 246.

Y. ENGEL: "Concerti Rachmaninova i N. Koshetz" ["Rachmaninoff's concerts with N. Koshetz"]; *Russkie Vedomosty*; Oct. 25, 1916, No. 246.

I. GLEBOV: "Vecher romansov S. Rachmaninova" ["An evening of Rachmaninoff's songs"]; *Musikalni Sovremenik*; Dec. 9, 1916, Nos. 9-10; pp. 14-5.

E–Rachmaninoff as Pianist

G. PROKOFIEV: "VI Symphonicheskoe sobranie Philarmonicheskovo obschestva" ["VI Philharmonic concert"]; "Ispolnenie Rachmaninovim pervavo f-p concerta Tchaikovskavo" ["Tchaikovsky's first piano concerto played by Rachmaninoff"]; *Russkie Vedomosty;* Dec. 20, 1911, No. 292.

Y. SAKHNOVSKY: "VI Symphonicheski concert Philarmonicheskavo obschestva" ["VI Philharmonic concert"]; *Russkoe Slovo;* Dec. 20, 1911, No. 292.

Y. ENGEL: "Scriabinsky zikl" ["Scriabin's cycle"]; "f-p concert Scriabina v ispolnenii Rachmaninova" ["Scriabin's piano concerto played by Rachmaninoff"]; *Russkie Vedomosty;* Oct. 13, 1915, No. 234.

Y. SAKHNOVSKY: "Zikl concertov pamyati A. N. Scriabina" ["Concerts in memory of Scriabin"]; *Russkoe Slovo;* Oct. 13, 1915, No. 234.

G. PROKOFIEV: "Concerti iz proizvedeni Scriabina" ["Concerts devoted to Scriabin's works"]; *Russkie Vedomosty;* Nov. 19, 1915, No. 266.

N. KOUROV: "Concert S. V. Rachmaninova" ["Rachmaninoff's recital"]; *Rance Utro;* Nov. 19, 1915, No. 267.

V. DERGANOVSKY: "Vechera Rachmaninova" ["Rachmaninoff's evening"]; *Utro Rossii;* Nov. 19, 1915, No. 918.

V. KARATYGIN: "Concert Rachmaninova" ["Rachmaninoff's recital"]; *Musikalni Sovremenik;* Nov. 29, 1915, No. 9.

G. PROKOFIEV: "O concertach Rachmaninova iz svoich proizvedeni i Scriabina" ["Rachmaninoff's concerts of his own and Scriabin's compositions"]; *Russkaya Musikalnaya Gazeta;* 1915, No. 49; pp. 801-2.

F–Rachmaninoff as Conductor

a) Rachmaninoff as opera conductor

Y.: "Samson i Dalila" ["Samson and Dalila"]; "O debute S. V. Rachmaninova kak dirigera v chastnoi opere S. I. Mamontova" ["S. Rachmaninoff's debut as conductor at S. Mamontov's opera house"]; *Novosti Sesona;* Oct. 14, 1897, No. 351.

A. G.: "Samson i Dalila" ["Samson and Dalila"]; *Russkoe Slovo;* Oct. 14, 1897, No. 275.

N. KASHKIN: "Teatr i Musika" ["Theater and Music"]; *Russkie Vedomosty;* Oct. 17, 1897, No. 287.

WITHOUT SIGNATURE: "Carmen," *Muskovskie Vedomosty;* Nov. 30, 1897, No. 330.

I. LYPAYEV: "Musikalnaya shisn Moscvi" ["Musical life in Moscow"]; *Russkaya Musikalnaya Gazeta;* 1898, No. 2; p. 202.

N. KASHKIN: "S. V. Rachmaninov"; "O debute Rachmaninova—dirigera v Bolshom Teatre" ["S. V. Rachmaninoff's debut at the Bolshoi Theater"]; *Moscovskie Vedomosty;* Sept. 5, 1904, No. 245.

N. KASHKIN: "Bolshoi Teatr" ["Bolshoi Theater"]; "O spectacle 'Evgeni Onegin'" ["About the performance of 'Eugene Onegin'"]; *Moscovski Vedomosty;* Sept. 12, 1902, No. 252.

S. KROUGLIKOV: "Evgeni Onegin" ["Eugene Onegin"); Novosty Dnya; Sept. 13, 1904, No. 7643.

N. KASHKIN: "Bolshoi Teatr" ["Bolshoi Theater"]; "O spectacle 'Knyaz Igor' " ["About the performance of 'Prince Igor' "]; Moscovskie Vedomosty; Sept. 20, 1904, No. 260.

Y. ENGEL: "Shisn za Tsarya" ["A Life for the Tsar"]; Russkie Vedomosty; Sept. 25, 1904, No. 267.

S. KROUGLIKOV: "A Life for the Tsar," Novosty Dnya; Sept. 24, 1904, No. 7655.

N. KASHKIN: "Bolshoi Teatr" ["Bolshoi Theater"]; O spectacle 'Pikovaya Dama' " ["About the performance of 'The Queen of Spades' "]; Moscovskie Vedomosty; Oct. 28, 1904, No. 298.

S. KROUGLIKOV: "Pikovaya Dama" ["The Queen of Spades"]; Novosty Dnya; Oct. 30, 1904, No. 7690.

N. KASHKIN: " 'Pan-Voevoda' opera Rimskavo-Korsakova" [Rimsky-Korsakov's opera 'Pan-Voevoda' "]; Moscovskie Vedomosty; Oct. 5, 1905, No. 264.

G–Rachmaninoff as Conductor

b) Rachmaninoff as symphony-orchestra conductor

N. KASHKIN: "S. V. Rachmaninoff, 'Don Juan' R. Straussa pod upr. S. V. Rachmaninova" ["R. Strauss's 'Don Juan' conducted by S. V. Rachmaninoff"]; Russkoe Slovo; Jan. 9, 1909, No. 6.

Y. SAKHNOVSKY: "V concert Philarmonicheskavo Obschestva" ["V Philharmonic Concert"]; Russkoe Slovo; Dec. 13, 1911, No. 286.

G. PROKOFIEV: "V Sobranie Philarmonicheskavo Obschestva" ["V Philharmonic Concert"]; Russkaya Musikalnaya Gazeta; 1912, No. 1.

WOLFING: "Iz Musikalnavo dnevnika" ["From musical diary"]; Trudi i Dni; 1912, Nos. 4-5.

G. PROKOFIEV: "Pervoe symphonicheskoe sobranie Philarmonicheskavo Obschestva" ["First Philharmonic Concert"]; "Fantasticheskaya symphonia Berlioza, 'Baletnaya suita' Glazunova" ["Berlioz's 'Fantastic Symphony,' Glazunov's 'Ballet Suite' "]; Russkie Vedomosty; Oct. 24, 1912, No. 245.

G. PROKOFIEV: "Vtoroe Symphonicheskoc Obschestvo Philarmonicheskavo Obschestva" ["Second Philharmonic Concert"]; "Symphonia g-moll Mozarta, ouvertura 'Oberon' Vebcra i dr. pod upr. Rachmaninova" ["Mozart's G-minor Symphony, Weber's overture 'Oberon' and other works conducted by Rachmaninoff"]; Russkie Vedomosty; Oct. 24, 1912, No. 232.

Y. ENGEL: "Symphonichesky Concert" ["Symphonic Concert"]; "Proizvedenia Griga pod upr. Rachmaninova" ["Grieg's works conducted by Rachmaninoff"]; Russkie Vedomosty; Oct. 24, 1912, No. 245.

G. Prokofiev: "Tretie symphonicheskoe sobranie Philarmonichcskavo Obschestva" ["Third Philharmonic Concert"]; " 'Shotlandskaya Symphonya' Mendelsona, 'Lyricheskaya Suita' Griga" ["Mendelssohn's 'Scotch Symphony,' Grieg's 'Suite Lyrique' "]; *Russkie Vedomosty*; Oct. 30, 1912, No. 250.

Y. Sakhnovsky: "Pyati Concert Philarmonii" ["V Philharmonic Concert"]; *Russkoe Slovo*; Dec. 3, 1912, No. 278.

INDEX

ABOUT THE AUTHOR

IT WOULD be difficult to imagine a man better equipped to tell the story of Rachmaninoff's life than Victor Seroff. Born in Batoum, Russia, Mr. Seroff was for many years a concert pianist and knows many of the composer's scores with the intimacy of one who has often performed them on the concert stage. In addition, he knew Rachmaninoff and interviewed him personally several times shortly before his death.

Mr. Seroff first studied law at the Universities of Tiflis and Vienna. While at Tiflis he began his musical studies at the conservatory, continuing them later at Salzburg, as well as studying privately under Moritz Rosenthal and Theodore Szanto. He has traveled extensively throughout Europe and the United States and has been a prolific contributor to a number of American magazines, including Collier's, Vogue, Harper's Bazaar, Town and Country, The Saturday Review of Literature, The Étude, This Week, and the New Republic.

An experienced biographer, Mr. Seroff has had two previous biographical books on Russian music published in recent years—The Mighty Five and Shostakovich. Although most of his time is devoted to teaching music and writing, he has recently made a free adaptation in English of Prokofieff's The Love for Three Oranges, produced with great success by the New York City Center Opera Company.

$$F = 9/5 + 32$$

$$F = 9/5(210) + 32$$

$$F = \frac{1880}{5} + 32$$

68   36
     37
     ────
      6